JUDGE THY NEIGHBOR

THE MIDDLE RANGE

THE MIDDLE RANGE

EDITED BY PETER S. BEARMAN AND SHAMUS R. KHAN

The Middle Range, coined and represented by Columbia sociologist Robert Merton, is a style of work that treats theory and observation as a single endeavor. This approach has yielded the most significant advances in the social sciences over the last half century; it is a defining feature of Columbia's department. This book series seeks to capitalize on the impact of approaches of the middle range and to solidify the association between Columbia University and its Press.

JUDGE THY NEIGHBOR

DENUNCIATIONS IN THE SPANISH INQUISITION, ROMANOV RUSSIA, AND NAZI GERMANY

PATRICK BERGEMANN

Columbia University Press   *New York*

Columbia University Press
Publishers Since 1893
New York   Chichester, West Sussex
cup.columbia.edu

Library of Congress Cataloging-in-Publication Data

Names: Bergemann, Patrick, author.
Title: Judge thy neighbor : denunciations in the Spanish Inquisition,
Romanov Russia, and Nazi Germany / Patrick Bergemann.
Description: New York : Columbia University Press, 2019. | Series: The Middle
Range | Includes bibliographical references and index.
Identifiers: LCCN 2018030838 | ISBN 9780231180160 (cloth : alk. paper) |
ISBN 9780231542388 (e-book)
Subjects: LCSH: Denunciation (Criminal law)—Europe—History. |
Malicious accusation—Europe—History. | Inquisition—Spain—History. |
Romanov, House of—History. | National socialism—Germany—History.
Classification: LCC KJC9520 .B47 2019 | DDC 363.25/2—dc23
LC record available at https://lccn.loc.gov/2018030838

Columbia University Press books are printed on permanent
and durable acid-free paper.
Printed in the United States of America

Cover design: Elliott Strunk

You shall not bear false witness against your neighbor.

—The Ninth Commandment (Exodus 20:16)

We are living at present in a sea of denunciations and human meanness.

—Adolf Hitler, 1933

CONTENTS

ACKNOWLEDGMENTS

Acknowledgments are, in a sense, positive denunciations: instead of identifying individuals for punishment, they recognize people for acclaim. It is my pleasure to "positively denounce" those who have been instrumental throughout the course of this project. Without their suggestions, comments, and advice, this book would not be what it is today.

First and foremost, I would like to thank Paolo Parigi, who made the offhand remark many years ago that the Spanish Inquisition would be an interesting topic for a dissertation. I do not think either of us expected me to take his comment quite so seriously. Since that first conversation, Paolo helped advance this project in countless ways, being a continual source of feedback and encouragement. Mark Granovetter, my dissertation advisor, also provided critical support along the way, constantly pushing me to refine and improve my thinking. His ability to point out theoretical inconsistencies and conceptual vagueness, as well as his exhortations to always read more broadly, improved the argument and expanded the breadth of this book.

A number of other people have touched this project at one time or another. Peter Bearman encouraged my progress in the latter stages of the work and provided incisive comments on various versions of the manuscript, helping not just with the argument but also with readability. Emily Erikson, Warner Henson II, Elizabeth Pontikes, and Johan Chu all aided me by reading chapters and providing feedback. Three anonymous reviewers at the *American Sociological Review* helped me reorient my thinking through their comments on a paper closely related to this work. Similarly, two book reviewers provided valuable feedback.

Various workshops and conferences improved parts of the book, especially those at Stanford University, Columbia University, and the University of Chicago. Because the topic of denunciation touches on several different fields and many people's lives, countless individuals provided me with references or mentioned instances of denunciation of which I was previously unaware. Many of the ideas generated by those conversations are captured in the book's final chapter.

I have been especially fortunate to have worked with two capable editors: Isabella Furth and Katherine Harper. Their careful editing of the manuscript has helped smooth out any rough edges. Everyone that I have interacted with at Columbia University Press has been easy to work with and they have taken a care with my manuscript that I deeply appreciate.

Finally, this book would not have been possible without my parents and their tireless support. I am grateful for their constant encouragement, both throughout the course of writing the book and before. I am also thankful to my brother Eric, who read every chapter and provided valuable feedback. When I was struggling to choose a title for the book, it was he who suggested *Judge Thy Neighbor*. As the title of a work serves as its first impression, I trust that his insight will lead to many more people opening the book to its very first page.

JUDGE THY NEIGHBOR

1

A THEORY OF DENUNCIATION

It was 1933 and Adolf Hitler was upset. He had just taken complete control of Germany by suspending civil liberties, obtaining the right to enact laws without the consent of the legislature, criminalizing any public disagreement with Nazi ideology, forming special courts to prosecute ideological offenses, and creating the Gestapo to ensure compliance. He had gone from an imprisoned revolutionary ten years before to the current chancellor of Germany. He had complete control of the judicial system, the political system, and the police.

Yet the common people were not behaving as anticipated. Hitler expected them to help enact his agenda, root out treason, and report any malfeasance to the appropriate authorities, even if that meant denouncing their neighbors. What he found instead was that citizens were *over*zealous in this activity. Denunciations came pouring in to the Gestapo in massive numbers from all corners of Germany. Yet these did not strike Hitler as the reports of good, loyal Germans dedicated to the Nazi cause. Instead, they were overwhelmingly petty and often spiteful, containing little in the way of real information about treasonous activity. "We are living at present in a sea of denunciations and human meanness," he complained to his advisors.[1]

The purpose of this book is to understand this behavior that disappointed Hitler: the act of denouncing. Why did all of those people come forward and whom did they accuse? Why did they denounce if not out of loyalty to the regime? How was their behavior affected and shaped by the institutional environment and community factors?

These questions are not relevant solely to Nazi Germany; they apply to denunciations in general. Denunciation on a similarly massive scale is common across countries and continents and throughout history. Most European countries have experienced such regimes at one time or another, as have many in the Americas, Africa, and Asia. Denunciations are known to have been common as far back as ancient Rome, where those who made them were known as *delatores*, and they took place in both the Republic and the Empire.[2] It was supposedly there that the most famous denouncer in history—Judas Iscariot—was central to the birth of one of the world's largest religions.[3]

In the early modern period, denunciation was prevalent in Spain during the Inquisition, in Russia under the Romanov dynasty, and in France during the Revolution. In the Republic of Venice, a "Lion's Mouth" postbox was set at the front of the Doge's Palace; whenever someone wished to denounce, he or she would insert an anonymous letter between the lion's jaws. In the twentieth century, settings for denunciations included Germany, Italy, Romania, Guatemala, the Dominican Republic, Argentina, and Libya. In the Soviet Union, it was often carried out by letter, particularly to local newspapers. In China during the Cultural Revolution, denunciations were often written publicly on walls. Reports from North Korea described weekly gatherings where citizens denounced their neighbors for at least two faults.[4]

Widespread denunciation is not limited to totalitarian or authoritarian regimes. The Catholic Church promoted denunciation in 1918 and again in 1935 when it codified every Christian's duty to denounce people, acts, or utterances representing danger to the faith or crimes against the Church.[5] And in the 1940s and 1950s, the United States was swept up in a flood of denunciations known as the McCarthy Era or Red Scare, in which more than ten thousand people lost their jobs after being accused of having communist sympathies.[6] Government agencies, universities, and the entertainment industry were especially caught up in the frenzy.

Yet denunciations do not occur only during certain time periods or in certain societies. They exist in every society. They go by various names with different connotations—ratting, tattling, squealing, whistle-blowing, snitching, etc.—but the essential act is the same.[7]

In modern America, citizens are encouraged to contact a local police station when they have knowledge of suspicious behavior. An ongoing campaign of the Department of Homeland Security urges people, "If you see something, say something." Figure 1.1 shows a bus station poster sponsored by the New York City Police Foundation that encourages citizens to report any crimes they know about to the authorities.

Such solicitations can be found in any number of public spaces, including subway stations, airports, and bus terminals, and their presence has only increased in the twenty-first century as fear of terrorism has grown. Additionally, ethnographic research of poor urban neighborhoods shows that denunciation is a common form of interaction with the police.[8] This is similarly the case among inmates reporting each other to guards in prisons.[9] Denunciation is a routine method of identifying and reporting wrongdoing, and therefore merits focused study to understand its dynamics.

Yet the phenomenon of denunciation has rarely received attention as a topic in its own right. The little study that has been

FIGURE 1.1 Poster at a bus stop at West 115th Street and Amsterdam Avenue, New York City. Photo by author.

done has been predominantly by historians investigating particular contexts. The editors of a volume on historical denunciations published in 1997 noted, "This is a topic that has not previously been systematically investigated or analyzed by scholars, and we are conscious that the present work is just scratching the surface."[10] In the more than twenty years since, researchers have continued to focus on individual cases rather than denunciation in general.

Judge Thy Neighbor takes a broader approach to the topic. By comparing disparate settings, I develop a general theory of the dynamics of denunciation, including how it functions and why people participate. The book argues that we can only truly understand denunciation by taking into account behavior at both the individual and institutional levels. Only then can we clarify broader systems of social control and the relationship between individual actors and the political and legal environment.

In addition to this multilevel orientation, the perspective taken in this work is sociological. Denunciations are not purely legal acts performed by concerned citizens. A denunciation is fundamentally a social act, both at the dyadic level between the denouncer and the person denounced and as a behavior embedded within a larger community and network of relationships. Studying it as such reveals much about the interplay between institutional structure and social dynamics.

In particular, this book focuses on repressive settings in which denunciation was widespread. "Repression" generally refers to the use of state power in ways that curtail freedoms of speech, association, and protest; that deny due process through biased policing based on political beliefs; and that infringe on rights of personal integrity such as freedom from torture and extrajudicial execution.[11] Denunciations are particularly prevalent in these settings—a puzzling fact, as denouncing others in such environments helps the authorities to enact repression and subjugate the populace. Nevertheless, individuals participate in mass numbers, facilitating an outcome that would seem to be undesirable to many.

Furthermore, conventional accounts of repression often focus on the actions of the authorities and the police, not those of ordinary citizens.[12] Only more recently have scholars begun to acknowledge the role of everyday individuals in the functioning of such regimes. This book helps to model that role in relation to particular institutional forms. Understanding these dynamics both reveals the functioning of denunciation in repressive regimes and provides insight into social control in other types of societies.

The settings evaluated in this book are Spain during the Inquisition, Russia during the Romanov dynasty, and Germany under the Nazis. Together, these three settings have been given prominent status in modern society as representations of terror and injustice. The Inquisition put hundreds of thousands of individuals on trial for crimes against the Church; Romanov Russia, like Russia throughout much of its history, practiced severe forms of repression; and the Gestapo in Nazi Germany brutally disrupted millions of lives. Across all three cases, many of those brought to trial or punished were not discovered by the police or by intelligence operatives, but instead were identified by neighbors with whom they had lived side by side, sometimes for decades.

DENUNCIATION DEFINED

What exactly is a denunciation? The concept is most easily understood through an example. Below is a short denunciation from the early years of the Spanish Inquisition, recorded by a notary in the village of Soria on July 19, 1491:

> This day appeared Juanes del Vallejo, chaplain, resident of Soria, and said that six months ago he was playing a ball game with Juan de Veteta, cleric, resident of Soria, and the witness saw how, in anger at the game, he said, "I reject our Saint Mary."[13]

As can be seen in this example, a denunciation is a notification to the authorities by a person or persons about deviant behavior by another person or persons. In this case, the denouncer—Juanes del Vallejo—reported that Juan de Veteta had made a statement that demonstrated a lack of respect for Christianity. Note that the deviant behavior does not have to be strictly illegal. Denunciations report behaviors that the authorities are interested in investigating and punishing, regardless of their formal codification in law.[14] Sometimes denunciations report behavior that appears suspicious, regardless of whether or not a crime has occurred.

Depending on the setting, denunciations may be made orally (as in this case) or in writing. They may be made on the record (as in this case, in which the denouncer is identified by name) or anonymously. Despite this variation, denunciations generally result in formal legal records that can lead to investigations, arrests, and prosecutions.

An important feature of denunciations is that they are *not* reports of crimes recounted by the victims. In the example above, Juan de Veteta is accused of saying something blasphemous, demonstrating his disregard for Christian values. That crime was not directed at Juanes del Vallejo; he merely bore witness to it. Thus, denunciations are often for victimless crimes.[15]

Consistent with this, denunciations are generally statements or actions that indicate some degree of disagreement or noncompliance with political or religious orthodoxy. In other words, the crimes tend to be political rather than personal. Because of this disassociation between the denouncer and the alleged offense, denunciations generally appear impersonal and disinterested. At the same time, they contain an implicit—and sometimes explicit—call for punishment.

Denunciations are often spontaneous: individuals present themselves to the authorities on their own accord to accuse others. In the above example, Juanes del Vallejo decided to come forward personally and report his accusation on that particular day in 1491. In other cases, denunciations are elicited more directly. For example, an individual may denounce others while being tortured or interrogated by the authorities.

Denouncing is closely related to, but nevertheless distinct from informing. Informants are recruited by the authorities and meet regularly with them to provide information. They are not usually employees of the state, but unlike denouncers, they develop ongoing relationships with police agents. They are also often directed to observe and report on particular groups or individuals, whereas denouncers generally choose their own targets.[16]

DENUNCIATION AS SOCIAL CONTROL

Denunciations do not happen in a vacuum; they take place within a broader context of social control. Social control is generally considered to be an organized reaction to deviant behavior.[17] This book is particularly concerned with *formal* social control, the way in which authorities ensure compliance among a population through the use of the legal system.[18] Formal social control includes the law, the police, and the courts, and is the means of both deterring deviant behavior and punishing it.[19]

Controlling a population, however, requires more than just the law, the police, and the courts. It also requires information.[20] Without information about who is breaking the law, deviant individuals will not be investigated by the police and they will not be prosecuted by the courts. If authorities lack that knowledge of whom to investigate and prosecute, wrongdoing goes unpunished, and others are not deterred from misbehaving.[21]

In order to be effective, therefore, a centralized authority that controls a broad territory with dispersed communities needs some means of determining who is disobeying the laws and who is a potential threat to the regime. Social control is largely limited by the quality and quantity of information available about transgressive behavior. This limitation is exacerbated in repressive regimes, which tend to regulate behavior, especially private behavior, more extensively. Authorities must therefore find some means of accessing knowledge of deviant behavior within local communities. One of the primary means of accomplishing this is by encouraging people to denounce others and facilitating those denunciations. This allows the authorities to gain desired information through the cooperation of local residents.

Consider the different actors involved in the denunciation from the Spanish Inquisition presented earlier. In addition to a willing denouncer, there was an inquisitor whose presence signaled his availability and interest in receiving denunciations. There was also a notary who dutifully recorded the complaint. Whereas the denouncer was acting independently, the other two parties served as representatives of the regime. They were the social control agents of early modern Spain, traveling from village to village and collecting information.

This leads to two questions. How do authorities structure institutions of social control in order to elicit widespread denunciations? And why do individuals participate when this inevitably helps to bring about their own repression? Answering both questions requires a consideration of how institutions of social control interact with individual action.

In order for widespread denunciation to occur, two components are required. First, the authorities must construct institutions of social control that elicit, facilitate, and process denunciations. In other words, they must create procedures and responsibilities among officials who organize the collection of and response to denunciations. Second, there must be individuals willing to provide information to the authorities about the deviant behavior of others. Only when authorities and citizens are aligned and cooperative will widespread denunciation occur.

The following section proposes two models of this interaction: the *coercion model* and the *volunteer model*. These models should be considered ideal types; they are simplified, analytical constructs that do not perfectly reflect the complexities of any particular setting.[22] Ideal types provide a basic method of comparative study, allowing researchers to generate generalized abstractions against which concrete cases can be assessed.[23] The hypotheses derived from these models can then be tested empirically, as will be done in the following chapters.

It is important to note that the coercion and volunteer models do not exhaust all possible motivations for denunciation. Other plausible rationales—ideology, security, and intergroup conflict—will be addressed. However, this book argues that the coercion and volunteer models reflect the dynamics of denunciation accurately across a variety of real-world contexts.

The Coercion Model

In the coercion model, authorities encourage denunciations from the populace through the use of incentives. Although these can take many forms, those that are fundamental to the coercion model are authority-based and direct. In other words, denunciation is a quid pro quo arrangement: in return for reporting a denunciation, a denouncer expects to receive individualized protection or benefits directly from the authorities to whom the report was made.

In repressive regimes, incentives are usually negative and take the form of explicit or implicit threats. The most extreme form of explicit threat is torture, where individuals are subjected to physical or emotional pain in order to elicit information about the misbehavior of others. Torture, however, is necessarily targeted in nature; it requires the authorities to identify a person they believe has useful knowledge. Thus, many repressive regimes maintain diffuse or generalized incentives, such as laws that call for punishing those who witness deviant behavior and neglect to report it. This way, all citizens feel the pressure to denounce.

Threats can also be implicit, as when individuals believe that not providing information about others' behavior will result in negative repercussions, even if there are no explicit threats or laws penalizing noncompliance. Implicit threats can be targeted, where particular individuals or groups perceive this coercive pressure, or diffuse, where the population does so more generally. Implicit threats do not even have to be real; so long as people perceive an implicit threat to exist, it will affect their behavior.

The Soviet Union in the late 1930s provides an example of negative incentives that pressured people to denounce. As historian Wendy Goldman has explained, "whereas there were no penalties for writing a [denunciation] without evidence, not writing one at all could invite serious consequences. Failure to report the arrest of a relative or to go on record with suspicions about a coworker who was subsequently arrested, for example, was grounds for expulsion from the Party."[24] This was a threat with serious implications. In Soviet Russia, expulsion from the Communist Party commonly led to the loss of employment and housing, along with the possibility of arrest, a labor camp sentence, or execution. Even people who avoided the camps or execution were stigmatized and generally unable to find new employment. Not denouncing, therefore, was extremely dangerous.

In some settings, incentives can be positive: for example, the promise of monetary rewards or career advancement.[25] Negative and positive incentives can also be combined, as when the provision of information is rewarded and its withholding is punished. Regardless of whether the incentives are positive or negative, their presence leads potential denouncers to orient toward the authorities in their decision-making process. In other words, individuals decide whether to denounce based primarily on the strength of the authority-based incentives. In such an environment, individuals who denounce do so primarily to avoid negative consequences or to gain positive rewards. Denouncers seek to satisfy the authorities and benefit or protect themselves and their families. This is not to argue that everyone or even most people will necessarily denounce, but that those who do will be motivated primarily by the nature and strength of the authority-based incentive structure.

Another way to think about the coercion model—and denunciation more generally—is as a set of relationships involving three distinct sets of actors: the denouncers, the people denounced, and the authorities to whom denunciations are reported. Among these three parties, the relationship between the denouncer and the authorities is of primary importance. The denouncer's main objective is to benefit him- or herself by appeasing or satisfying the authorities. The identity of the person denounced is almost incidental; that individual serves as an offering made by the denouncer to the authorities in the hopes of gaining something in return.[26]

The Volunteer Model

In contrast to the coercion model, authorities in the volunteer model offer no incentives to potential denouncers. Instead, they encourage denunciations without compelling them. Although authorities operating under this model tend to be just as eager and receptive as those in the coercion model, their methods are more reactive. Such was largely the case in Nazi Germany, where the Gestapo provided a venue for German citizens to report information without making any specific threats or offering any particular benefits.[27]

The fact that the authorities are reactive does not mean that they are passive. In order to elicit voluntary denunciations, they tend to structure institutions of social control in particular ways. Specifically, they protect denouncers by making the process of denouncing as easy and as safe as possible. Although this can take different forms, it frequently involves allowing individuals to report without being subjected to harsh interrogations, cross-examinations, or background checks. The authorities also protect denouncers from retaliation, whether by the person denounced, members of that person's family, or the community at large. The most common protective mechanism is anonymity, where the authorities conceal the identity of the denouncer from others.

A second key institutional feature in this model is not intended as a means of eliciting denunciations, but is rather a consequence of the authorities' eagerness to punish. This is the lack of protections afforded to those denounced, a scenario that is common across repressive settings. Authorities' desire for punishment and obedience often outweighs their passion for justice and due process. Thus, those denounced tend to experience significant hardship throughout the investigatory process and a high likelihood of punishment, regardless of whether they are guilty of any particular crime.

This combination of protection for denouncers and lack of protection for those denounced leads individuals to consider the indirect benefits they may derive from denouncing others, not from the authorities but within their local communities. Every community has an underlying network of negative relationships, or negative ties. A negative tie is an "enduring, recurring set of negative judgments, feelings and behavioral intentions toward another person—a negative person schema."[28] Negative ties often arise out of social, economic, or political rivalries, and although they tend to occur less frequently than positive ties, they are a fundamental and universal aspect of social experience.[29] In other words, negative ties constitute the "dark side of intimacy."[30]

Ordinarily, people seek to avoid those with whom they have negative ties or they gossip behind their backs.[31] However, "[people] are relieved when another supralocal actor performs his violence against those with whom [they] have disputes."[32] Authorities' eager appetite for denunciations provides such an opportunity. By giving access to a supralocal actor, the volunteer model offers the opportunity for "less a transgression of social ties and more their full, though perverse, expression."[33] In such a context, denunciations provide the means by which individuals can harm people they dislike and gain relative to them: dispute resolution can be as simple as making a brief report to the secret police. I refer to this behavior as *social opportunism*, as opposed to the personal or private opportunism found in the coercion model. Whereas the latter is direct and self-absorbed, the former is indirect and relational in nature.

Social opportunism is important because people tend to assess their well-being relative to those around them.[34] It is not absolute prosperity or status that matters, but relative prosperity or status. Social status and economic competition are therefore primarily local in nature, as people tend to compare themselves to those nearby. Denouncing becomes a way of gaining relative benefits through the diminishment or removal of a local rival.[35]

The volunteer model therefore contrasts with the coercion model in that denouncers are oriented internally toward their local community rather than externally toward the authorities. Another way to represent this is to again consider the three sets of actors involved in denunciations. Whereas in the coercion model the key relationship is between the denouncer and the authorities, in the volunteer model the key relationship is between the denouncer and the person denounced. In this model, the authorities—despite their role in enabling such behavior—become merely a tool for the resolution of private disputes.

Not every person takes advantage of such an opportunity, but some assuredly do. Just as the mere presence of a weapon or similar stimuli can cause people to become more aggressive, having a new means of harming others makes harmful behavior more likely.[36] Being able to submit denunciations may have a similar effect, as creating easy or default channels of action often has an unexpectedly large impact on behavior.[37] Acting on negative ties becomes much more likely when there is a powerful and attentive outlet that will shield a denouncer from negative attention.[38]

Note that this type of denouncing tends to be an unintentional byproduct of the aims of the authorities. When authorities are overeager for information and overzealous about punishing deviance, they unwittingly create institutional conditions that facilitate the resolution of private disputes with little regard for the broader purposes of the state. The very institutional features meant to effectively identify and punish deviants ultimately facilitate denunciations motivated by social opportunism.

ALTERNATIVE EXPLANATIONS

The coercion model and the volunteer model identify specific denouncer motivations that are prevalent under different conditions.[39] It is important, however, to consider other possible explanations for widespread denunciation. These can be sorted into a few broad categories. Three of the most plausible are ideology, security, and intergroup conflict. I include these alternatives not to set up additional competing models, but rather to suggest why each is unlikely to have much explanatory power.

Ideology

If the populace is generally supportive of the people in power or in favor of their policies, then individuals may come forward to denounce for ideological reasons. By reporting deviant behavior, they are both helping to enact the authorities' political agenda and protecting the regime from subversive activity. Denunciations driven by ideology would not be self-interested, but would work toward a purpose greater than the advancement of the denouncer and his or her family. This loyalty to the state would reinforce social control, as citizens monitor each other for signs of subversiveness.

In repressive regimes, the key mechanisms by which ideological conformity is fostered and maintained include state control of the media and the widespread use of propaganda, which allow the authorities to limit outside influences while shaping the preferences and attitudes of the population.[40] Such control can be further expanded through the politicization of all aspects of society, so that the public is constantly exposed to ideologically infused activities. In fact, one type of repression—totalitarianism—has been described by many scholars as being akin to a religion.[41] Denunciation is thus one of the ways in which individuals can express this pervasive ideology and political fervor.[42]

However, there are several reasons to be skeptical of the suggestion that ideology is a widespread driver of denunciation. Even in regimes where propaganda is considered to be particularly sophisticated, historians often note a lack of ideological motivation in the reporting of deviance. In their survey across a wide range of settings in modern Europe, Sheila Fitzpatrick and Robert Gellately find "relatively few cases where denunciations seemed to be motivated by genuine ideological fervor, and only a minority of the denunciations . . . are even couched in the language of devotion to the national or party cause."[43] Even in highly repressive settings, individuals may interpret prohibitions and propaganda as indicators of elite inferiority and defensiveness, making these tools less effective in altering people's beliefs.[44] Individuals may also react negatively to attempts to constrain their freedom of belief.[45]

Further, several historians have noted the prevalence of false denunciations in repressive settings, as determined by investigations of the secular or religious authorities.[46] These were not the result of misinterpretations or misunderstandings, but tended to arise from the intentional fabrication of criminal behavior. This was the case in Romanov Russia and in Nazi Germany (as will be seen in chapters 3 and 4). Such false denunciations contradict the importance of ideology as a motivation. Although ideology may explain some proportion of denunciations, it is unlikely to provide a general account of why people make them in repressive settings.

Security

It is also possible that individuals denounce out of a desire for security, because they feel threatened by the unlawful or deviant behavior of others. According to this theory, by alerting the authorities, denouncers hope to reduce or remove a threat out of concern for personal safety.

Although this is a plausible explanation, fairly few of the denunciations in repressive regimes involve physical threats. As mentioned earlier, denunciations tend to be for victimless crimes, where individuals are accused of not acting in accordance with state or religious orthodoxy. Some individuals might indeed view these as matters of state security; however, this would be because they have internalized the state or religious ideology. As a result, such denunciations would more properly be described as ideological, as discussed above. As will be seen in the following chapters, denunciations for crimes that threaten to cause direct harm to others are practically nonexistent.[47] In repressive settings, individuals generally have more to fear from the authorities and from the opportunistic denunciations of their neighbors than from unsanctioned violence or threats.

Intergroup Conflict

People may also denounce others as a result of ethnic or intergroup conflict. Tensions of this type are fairly common in repressive settings, and in such environments individuals may denounce in order to harm members of another group. This is particularly likely if there is interethnic competition for resources, especially if one or more groups perceive resource allocations to be unfair.[48] This may give rise to resentment, which can in turn lead individuals to denounce members of the opposing group.[49]

This would likely be amplified in settings where authorities label certain groups as particularly suspect. The Nazis specifically targeted Jews, communists, and socialists, while initially the Spanish Inquisition focused on converts from Judaism to Catholicism known as *conversos*. In the Soviet Union and Communist China, denunciations were encouraged against vestiges of the old power structure. To the extent that individuals see opportunities to punish disliked groups, they may act on their own prejudices.

Ethnic or class conflict is unlikely as a primary motivation, however. Citizen participation in social control also occurs in settings where there is not a salient ethnic or intergroup dimension. For example, there was no particularly relevant intergroup conflict in Russia in the 1600s, as we will see in chapter 3. Even in contexts where there are important intergroup conflicts, a large percentage of denunciations are often intragroup.

Although intergroup conflict may give rise to some portion of denunciations, it cannot explain their occurrence more generally. Nor can it explain the specificity with which denouncers target particular others.[50] As we will see, even in settings where tensions exist between groups, denunciations are ultimately motivated by authority-based incentives or personal animosity, not based strictly on group membership.

FROM INDIVIDUAL DENUNCIATIONS TO GLOBAL REPRESSION

Although the applicability of the coercion and volunteer models remains to be demonstrated in the following chapters, it is worthwhile to introduce their broader implications. By detailing the relationship between institutional structure and denouncer motivation in the enactment of social control, it is possible to better understand repression as a macro phenomenon. Individual acts based on self-interest can aggregate to have unintended global consequences.

In the aggregate, denunciations on a massive scale can result under both the coercion and the volunteer model; in repressive regimes these enhance social control and help the authorities to consolidate power. Regardless of what motivates denouncers, widespread denunciations provide the authorities with information they can use to punish and deter deviance. They also benefit the authorities in other ways. When individuals cooperate with the regime, even for personal reasons, this is a tacit acknowledgment of the authorities' legitimacy to investigate and adjudicate complaints. Importantly, this legitimization can occur even when citizens oppose the regime privately; it is public opinion, not private, that undergirds political power.[51] Widespread denouncing may give the impression of popular support for the authorities and their agenda; even when that impression is false, it can lead to the diffusion of regime-supporting norms.[52] Furthermore, because actors know that any person can denounce them at any time, their social associations likely become constrained. Caution prevents individuals from giving others an excuse to denounce them. Yet while the collaboration of ordinary citizens with social control agents ruptures horizontal bonds, it strengthens hierarchical bonds. Ultimately, this can lead to an orientation of society away from cooperation and trust and toward hierarchy and obedience.

While the coercion and the volunteer models share these commonalities, in other respects their implications are different. There are three key differences between them: the presence of authority-based incentives in the coercion model and their absence in the volunteer model; the proactive nature of the authorities in the coercion model and their reactive nature in the volunteer model; and the orientation of denouncers toward the authorities in the coercion model and toward their local communities in the volunteer model.

Despite the potential of widespread denunciation under both models, we would expect the volunteer model to be a more efficient system of social control.[53] It is more expensive for a state to employ an active police force that maintains and enforces incentives than a more reactive one that waits for denunciations to be reported. This is evident in the contrast between Nazi Germany and the Soviet Union. In 1937 Nazi Germany maintained an estimated seven thousand Gestapo officers for their voluntary system of denunciation: on average, one for every ten thousand residents.[54] The Soviet Union, which implemented an incentivized system, had one secret police officer for every five hundred residents during the same time period.[55] Yet both systems are commonly thought to have been effective. In fact, despite its relatively small numbers, the Gestapo became so notorious that for decades historians referred to it as "omniscient, omnipotent and omnipresent."[56]

Whether denouncers are oriented toward authorities or their local communities also has implications for the effectiveness of social control. These orientations should have varying effects on three different groups in the aggregate: the general public, actual denouncers, and potential denouncers. When individuals observe widespread denunciation, they contemplate a different set of concerns than when they face the personal decision of whether to make denunciations themselves.

In the coercion model, the incentive structure is often widely known. This means that the general public is inclined to interpret citizen participation in denunciations as a response to those incentives. If observers are upset about the increased fear and uncertainty that widespread denunciations arouse, they are likely to direct some of this anger toward the authorities for implementing the incentive structure. However, under the volunteer model, the lack of authority-based incentives suggests that individuals will likely attribute widespread denouncing to personal choice. They may interpret it as being driven by the desire to harm others or they may perceive it as an indication of popular support for the regime. In either case, any blame or dissatisfaction with social control under the volunteer model may be deflected away from the authorities and toward the populace.

Denouncers operating under the coercion model may resent the authorities for particularly forceful tactics.[57] Those under the volunteer model, however, may be grateful to them for assisting in the resolution of private disputes. We can also expect a similar dynamic among those who consider denouncing but do not go through with it. In a coercive environment, people who resist pressure to denounce are in implicit conflict with the authorities; they are choosing to defy the system's incentives and suffer the consequences. Under the volunteer model, however, those who do not denounce are not in conflict with anyone. Their orientation was never toward the authorities, so not denouncing will have little impact on their perception of that relationship. Under this model, actual and potential denouncers will likely direct less anger and dissatisfaction at the authorities.

Together, these differences suggest that the authorities may be less at risk for collective action against the regime under the volunteer model than under the coercion model. The former may therefore lead to a more stable system of repression. Paradoxically, the model that provides individuals with greater freedom to direct the policing power of the state may be the more effective form of social control.

The coercion model can be extremely powerful in some respects. As a means of rapidly gaining participation and subjugating a populace—especially if the authorities are seen as illegitimate—strong negative incentives may be the most effective. However, extended use of the coercion model may ultimately weaken the regime that it is meant to support.

FROM MODELS TO EVIDENCE

Simply asserting that the coercion and volunteer models are generally descriptive of systems in which denunciations take place is, of course, insufficient. Such an assertion is valid only to the extent that it is supported empirically. However, determining whether denouncer motivation accords with one of the two models is challenging for two reasons. First, when individuals make denunciations to the authorities, they generally do not also provide their motivations for coming forward. They are there to make a legal report about someone else, not to give information about themselves. Second, even if denouncers do indicate their motivation, those acting out of self-interest have an incentive to disguise that fact. In both the coercion and the volunteer models, denouncers are better off if they can convince the authorities of their loyalty and sincerity. In the coercion model, the authorities are more likely to view denouncers as good citizens and reward them if they perceive their statements as selfless and loyal. In the volunteer model, the authorities are more likely to presume the guilt of the person denounced if they believe the denouncer has no ulterior motives.

However, given the theorized differences between the two models, it is possible to posit hypotheses about the ways in which observable patterns of denunciations should differ. Recall that in the coercion model, the denouncers' primary goal is to appease the authorities in order to avoid negative consequences or to gain positive rewards. By contrast, denouncers in the volunteer model are interested primarily in harming specific individuals within their communities. There are six dimensions along which we can expect to see contrasting patterns of denunciations if the models are accurate.[58] These are explained in greater detail below.

Number Denounced

Denouncers in the coercion model seek to satisfy the authorities, and they are more likely to accomplish this goal by providing more information rather than less. Therefore, denouncers in the coercion model may denounce multiple people in the hopes that this will prove their helpfulness and please the authorities.

In the volunteer model, the number of denunciations per denouncer is contingent on the prevalence of negative ties within a community. In general, studies of negative ties have shown them to be sparse.[59] Because people tend to have few negative ties, we can expect denunciations in the volunteer model to be more targeted in nature and denouncers to more often denounce only one or relatively few individuals.

Prototypicality

In many settings, the authorities are especially interested in information about deviant behavior committed by particular groups of people or about specific crimes. For example, during the Spanish Inquisition the authorities were particularly interested in converts to Christianity who were practicing Judaism in secret. Although they were open to information about other types of deviant behavior, in their eyes this was the most prototypical offense. Denouncers under the coercion model are therefore most likely to denounce such crimes, as this has a greater likelihood of appeasing the authorities.

Denouncers under the volunteer model should tend to be much more idiosyncratic in whom they target. Negative ties arise from highly personalized conflicts, misunderstandings, and rivalries.[60] We can expect these personal reasons to be somewhat independent of the authorities' views of the prototypical offender or the prototypical crime. Therefore, denouncers in the coercion model should be more likely to make prototypical denunciations than those in the volunteer model.

Geographic Proximity

Close geographic proximity can be expected to be a characteristic of denunciations in the volunteer model. Because denouncers in this model seek to harm others and gain relative to them, they should tend to denounce those who are spatially close to them—that is, people within their own communities. Otherwise, they would be less likely to be able to gain at others' expense. Similarly, negative affect and negative relationships decay with distance. Not being near an insufferable person allows that individual to gradually fade from the would-be denouncer's memory, reducing the benefit of denouncing him or her.[61]

By contrast, we would not expect geographic proximity to be a relevant criterion in the coercion model. Denouncers in this model are simply trying to provide information that will satisfy the authorities, regardless of how spatially proximate the people denounced are. Because of this, there should be closer geographic proximity between denouncers and the people they denounce under the volunteer model than under the coercion model.

Relationship Closeness

"Relationship closeness" refers to the strength of the relationship between a denouncer and a person denounced. Do they know each other well? Are they distant acquaintances? This is often referred to as tie strength, where a stronger tie indicates a closer relationship. Under the volunteer model, denouncers will likely have closer relationships to the people they denounce than will those in the coercion model. Because negative ties and rivalries often require regular contact to be sustained, denouncers in the volunteer model should tend to denounce people with whom they commonly interact. This does not mean that people will denounce those closest to them, but rather that they will not denounce distant acquaintances. They will denounce people they know well enough to dislike and envy.

In the coercion model, relationship closeness is less salient. Although individuals may avoid denouncing those closest to them in an attempt to protect them from harm, they likely will not distinguish between people they interact with regularly and distant acquaintances. On average, therefore, denouncers in the volunteer model should denounce people in closer relationships with them than will denouncers in the coercion model.

Status Homophily

"Status homophily" refers to how similar in status denouncers are to the people they denounce. In the volunteer model, this status will probably be quite similar. Social or economic competition implies that an individual might attain a rival's position if that rival is harmed. This requires rivals to be similar in social status; harm that befalls someone with significantly higher or significantly lower status is less likely to confer advantage. In addition, negative ties are most likely to develop between individuals of similar status. As sociologist Georg Simmel has contended, "An enmity must excite consciousness the more deeply and energetically the greater the similarity between the parties among whom it originates."[62] Conflict is more likely to occur in symmetrical relationships where there is ambiguity between actors concerning their relative social rank. Because this ambiguity exists, statements made by the actors can be interpreted and misinterpreted in various ways and thus conflict is more likely. In asymmetrical relationships where ranks are differentiated and distinct, this is less likely because roles are well-understood.[63] Because of this, we can expect that most denunciations in the volunteer model will be between individuals of similar status.

By contrast, under the coercion model we would not expect to see denouncers attuned toward people of similar status. Often this model does not lead to any particular orientation regarding status, so there should be fewer within-status denunciations than we see under the volunteer model. In some cases authorities in the coercion model do prefer denunciations against individuals from a particular status grouping. For example, the authorities in the Soviet Union and Maoist China were particularly interested in denunciations against vestiges of the old power structure, whose members tended to have higher status than the average denouncer. In such cases, individuals in a coercive environment can be expected to prefer denouncing those of higher status. Overall, the volunteer model can be expected to produce more denunciations between individuals of similar status than are seen under the coercion model.

False Denunciations

Although denouncers' motivations in the volunteer model and the coercion model are distinct, both are inherently self-interested. Because of this, there are likely to be a substantial number of false denunciations in both models. In the coercion model, this should occur when a denouncer wants to appease the authorities but either does not have any relevant information or wants to protect the individuals whom he or she could honestly denounce. In the volunteer model, false denunciations occur when an individual wants to harm a particular target but does not have information about any deviant behavior. The models do not have implications as to the relative numbers of false denunciations under each, simply that false denunciations will be prevalent in both cases.

The expectation that there will be false denunciations, therefore, is not meant to show a difference between the two models—as are the other five hypotheses—but to acknowledge false denunciations as another expected outcome. Importantly, this expectation is distinct from what we would predict if there were widespread ideological denouncing.[64]

EMPIRICAL STRATEGY

The main empirical strategy used in this book is to select repressive settings that contain manifestations of both coercive incentives and voluntary denunciations. Within such settings, certain groups may experience authority-based incentives while others do not; alternatively, the authorities may shift institutional conditions from highly coercive to voluntary over time. This internal variation within cases allows for a direct comparison of denunciations under different institutional forms while keeping the broader context constant, providing evidence about denouncer motivation.[65] In order to establish the institutional conditions under which denunciations were elicited, I draw on historical laws and proclamations from each setting, along with secondary source materials.

To determine whether denouncer motivation accords with the expectations of the two models, I examine patterns using information gleaned from denunciation texts. Even though these tend to be spare, legalistic documents, they provide a wealth of information that can be used to infer denouncer motivation. This includes information about denouncers, the people denounced, and the crimes themselves. For example, in the denunciation quoted earlier in which Juan de Veteta allegedly blasphemed, it is possible to extract each of the participants' occupations, their respective genders, the villages in which they lived, the crime that was allegedly committed, and the social context within which the crime took place. Each denunciation can be coded for a variety of different variables which are used to evaluate the six hypotheses outlined above.

Furthermore, I use other historical records to supplement the analysis. One rich source of information is investigatory case files. These contain documentation of the investigations conducted by authorities after receiving a denunciation. Case files often indicate what the authorities learned from their interviews and interrogations, their determination of whether the allegation was substantiated or deemed to be false, and occasional other hints regarding denouncer motivation. Contemporary accounts by writers who lived through these time periods further augment the findings, as does subsequent analysis by modern historians. Together, these various sources provide insight into the dynamics of denunciation across different historical settings.

STRUCTURE OF THE BOOK

This book proceeds through three case studies, which cover the early years of the Spanish Inquisition in the late 1400s and early 1500s, the first decades of the Romanov dynasty in Russia in the seventeenth century, and Nazi Germany in the 1930s and 1940s. By examining cases that span widely divergent places and times, I provide broad support for the two models, showing that they describe general relationships between the institutional environment and denouncer behavior.

Each chapter brings a different approach to the understanding of denunciations. The Spanish Inquisition, discussed in chapter 2, was a system of social control and denunciation that began in 1481 and persisted for 356 years.[66] It was an effort directed by the monarchy to identify heresy and punish anyone who did not strictly follow the tenets of Christian orthodoxy. The chapter focuses on the first several decades of the Inquisition's existence and evaluates an institutional change in its procedures. Whereas at first there were strong authority-based incentives to denounce for a particular subgroup of the population—the conversos—this coercive pressure was removed in 1500 and denouncing became much more voluntary. By examining denunciations before and after this change, it is possible to observe the direct effect that these two different environments had on behavior.

Chapter 3 presents Russia during the early decades of the Romanov dynasty, which began in 1613. Following a period of turmoil known as the Time of Troubles, the new tsar, Mikhail Fedorovich Romanov, encouraged all citizens to report each other for any statements or deeds that did not fully support his reign. This tactic, known as the Sovereign's Word and Deed, led to many Russians denouncing each other. Most people experienced this context as voluntary in nature, with denouncing largely at their own discretion. However, those who denounced from prison perceived authority-based incentives: they believed that their actions could help them obtain an early release. By comparing these two different populations within the same regime, it is again possible to evaluate the two models. Additionally, this setting extends each model in distinctive ways. Here, the coercion model was based on positive rather than negative incentives, and those incentives were only perceived, rather than actually being offered by the authorities. There was also greater hardship and less likelihood of benefit for denouncers operating under the volunteer model at this time than can be found in the other case studies, yet particular conditions—such as heightened emotions immediately after an argument or fight—nevertheless spurred individuals to denounce in hopes of harming a neighbor.

Chapter 4 focuses on Nazi Germany from Hitler's ascension in 1933 until the fall of the Third Reich twelve years later. After gaining power, Hitler passed a series of increasingly restrictive laws aimed at controlling the everyday lives of ordinary Germans and persecuting several subgroups of the population. Much of this was accomplished through the use of denunciations, which individuals made freely without the presence of authority-based incentives. This chapter explores how denouncers in Nazi Germany were no differently motivated than those making voluntary denunciations in previous centuries, despite the reputed sophistication of Nazi propaganda. It also focuses on the role of the authorities in implementing and maintaining this system. Many Nazi records reveal officials' awareness of the widespread "misuse" of their system of social control for petty and spiteful purposes. Despite complaining at length about this behavior, they recognized the benefits of widespread denunciation and their actions were consistently ambivalent. Examining their internal debates reveals the compromises that even the most repressive regimes may make in order to elicit information from the populace and enact social control.

The final chapter assesses the results of the case studies and examines the strong regularities in patterns of denunciation across history and geography. It explores the macro implications of the models of denunciation in detail, and expands the theory to consider the conditions under which we would expect the volunteer model, the coercion model, or the use of informants to occur. Furthermore, denunciation is not just a phenomenon of violent and repressive regimes; it is also widely used in modern democracies. It pervades American society in a wide variety of forms, including plea-bargaining, whistle-blowing, crime reporting, and counterterrorism efforts. The dynamics are often similar, both in institutional structure and denouncer motivation, to what we observe in authoritarian settings. The fact that individuals are just as likely to denounce out of self-interest in modern democracies as in Nazi Germany poses a challenge for administering an effective yet just form of social control.

Having already covered both the past and present of denunciations, the chapter finally addresses their future. As surveillance technologies become increasingly sophisticated, the need for information from local citizens may diminish substantially. Nevertheless, denunciations are unlikely to disappear. Denunciations are about more than the information they provide: they are systems of political and social engagement that bind authorities to their citizens and legitimize the authorities' right to investigate and adjudicate the populace. Many of their effects are not replaceable by automated software and surveillance. Denunciations form a fundamental relationship between citizen and state, and are a core component of social control, past, present, and future.

2

THE SPANISH INQUISITION

In 1478, Pope Sixtus IV gave his formal consent to Queen Isabella and King Ferdinand of Spain to appoint two to three priests over forty years of age as inquisitors. Two years later, the royal order was given to establish the first tribunal in Seville. In 1481, the tribunal began accepting confessions and denunciations, and later that year, the first heretics were brought to trial. With two inquisitors in a single city, the Spanish Inquisition had begun.

It is unlikely that any of the early participants could have predicted how long the Inquisition would last and how far it would spread. For 356 years it reigned as the ecumenical law of the land, combating all types of heresy and religious transgressions by Christians. Estimates of the number of trials that took place over this time period are in the hundreds of thousands,[1] and the number of individuals who were denounced but did not experience formal trials may have been substantially higher.[2] Ultimately the Spanish Inquisition extended far beyond Spain and was implemented in Spanish colonies throughout the world, including Colombia, Mexico, and Peru. Punishments for those convicted were brutal, with burning at the stake the sentence for the most serious crimes and public humiliation and impoverishment for more minor offenses.

This chapter focuses in particular on the early decades, for several reasons. First, the Inquisition was most active in this period, both in terms of inquisitor activity and the volume of denunciations. More than half of all trials occurred in the first thirty years.[3] Second, this was a period of widespread uncertainty and unrest, as the two largest kingdoms of Spain had recently undergone civil wars. One of the monarchs' primary concerns was consolidating power and achieving social control. Finally, the first decades encompass a major institutional change in Inquisitorial procedures. Prior to 1500, the Inquisition was highly coercive, placing enormous pressure on individuals to confess their transgressions and denounce others. In 1500, however, this pressure abated and denunciations became more voluntary. Within the first few decades of the Inquisition's existence, it is possible to observe instances of both the coercion and volunteer models within the same historical context.

HISTORICAL BACKGROUND

In 1469, Isabella of Castile and Ferdinand of Aragon married, setting the stage for the unification of the two largest kingdoms on the Iberian Peninsula, which ultimately formed the majority of modern Spain. This was no easy union, however. Although the marriage between the two monarchs was stable,[4] each one's initial hold on his or her kingdom was tenuous at best.[5]

When King Henry IV of Castile died in 1474, he had not declared his successor. Both Henry's half-sister Isabella and his daughter Joanna had legitimate claims to the throne. To resolve the situation, officials asked Isabella to wait until the judiciary could address the competing claims properly. Instead, she crowned herself Queen of Castile the very next day. In response, King Alfonso of Portugal invaded Castile with a promise to marry Joanna and take the throne. This war lasted until 1479, when Isabella emerged victorious and faced the difficult task of rebuilding her war-torn kingdom.

Also in 1479, King Juan II of Aragon passed away and his son Ferdinand ascended to the throne. Although Ferdinand's claim was uncontested, his kingdom was not far removed from a civil war of its own. In 1462, Catalonia had rebelled, and it had taken ten years to reach an uneasy peace. Despite this resolution, the three realms of Aragon—Valencia, Aragon, and Catalonia—maintained powerful elites who served as a check on Ferdinand's power. The geography of this time period can be seen in figure 2.1.

In addition to these political divisions, the monarchs oversaw a population with other internal tensions. Conflicts among

FIGURE 2.1 The Iberian Peninsula, 1492.

Adapted from Ramsey Muir, *Philips' New Historical Atlas for Students* (London: George Philip & Son, 1911), 18.

Christians, Jews, and Muslims occurred periodically, with the most devastating outbreak of Christian hostility against Jews taking place in 1391, with massacres in a number of Spanish cities. Thousands of Jews were forced to accept baptism. This gave rise to a sizable population of *conversos*: Jews who had converted to Christianity, and later their descendants. Over the succeeding decades, tensions arose between Old Christians—Christians with no Jewish or Muslim heritage—and conversos. Anti-converso riots broke out in several cities in 1449 and again in the 1470s. Some of this violence stemmed from resentment that conversos did not face the same occupational restrictions that Jews did; the former could freely hold all positions in Spanish society and accordingly many of them rose to higher status.

Within this environment of recent civil war and internal unrest, the monarchs worked to consolidate power and ensure stability within their kingdoms. They used a variety of mechanisms for this, including expelling the Jews in 1492, expelling the Muslims in 1502, and acting forcefully whenever localities refused to obey royal decrees.[6] One of their most effective methods was the Spanish Inquisition.

The Inquisition was dedicated to the enactment of social control over the religious lives of its subjects. In particular, the early Inquisition targeted conversos, seeking to identify those who were not fulfilling their duties as devout Christians and particularly those who were secretly following Jewish precepts.[7] In practice, however, it took an interest in a wide variety of transgressions, including blasphemous statements, indications of skepticism or doubt about Christianity or the Inquisition, and the following of Jewish traditions that were cultural rather than religious in nature. By identifying transgressors, the Inquisition punished heretics, removed their perceived negative influence from society, and deterred others from betraying the faith.

The Inquisition also served as a broader form of control that accomplished other political ends of the monarchy. This can be seen in the placement of the early tribunals. The Inquisition started in the frontier region bordering Granada, where the crown had the least political control and a strong interest in maintaining security. The monarchy then targeted other "trouble" areas, such as Ciudad Real, which had been at the center of a 1474 uprising.

These political goals are also evident in the Inquisition's expansion into Aragon in 1484. At the time, Aragon already had a functioning inquisition established by the pope, though it operated on a very small scale. Instead of expanding this, Ferdinand worked actively against those inquisitors until the pope conceded. In 1486, Pope Sixtus IV removed all papal inquisitors from Aragon, leaving the crown entirely in control of inquisitorial activities within its borders. The Spanish Inquisition was the only inquisition in history in which local monarchs successfully wrested inquisitorial power from the pope; this unified the Castilian and Aragonese tribunals and created the first legal and institutional link between the two kingdoms, thereby furthering the monarchs' goal of political consolidation.[8] Within a few years of its inception, the Inquisition was established throughout the majority of both kingdoms.

A map of the implementation of the tribunals can be seen in figure 2.2.

In addition to consolidating power and enacting social control over conversos, the Inquisition may have helped to appease other subpopulations, further bolstering the stability of the realm. The monarchs owed a debt to the Castilian oligarchs who had provided Isabella with troops and financial support during her war of succession and who may have resented the conversos's rise to prominent political and economic positions.[9]

FIGURE 2.2 Locations and foundings of Spanish Inquisition tribunals. This map does not include tribunals founded in Spanish colonies in the Americas. The Toledo tribunal started in Ciudad Real in 1483 before moving to Toledo in 1485.

Adapted from Homza (2006, xlv).

Middle- and lower-class Old Christians may have held a similar animus, as the former fought with conversos for jobs and the latter resented them as tax collectors.[10]

Regardless of which groups benefited from the Inquisition, the crown institutionalized a system for the consolidation of power and social control over a sizable minority, which was later expanded to the entire population in 1525. To put it mildly, "the State found in the Inquisition a convenient tool for the supervision of public life."[11]

INQUISITORIAL PROCEDURES

The Spanish Inquisition was a strict bureaucracy and inquisitors were expected to follow specific procedures when carrying out their duties. Although these were still being sorted out in the early years of the tribunals, they were based largely on the prevailing secular and ecclesiastical law of the period.

Tribunals were typically set up in a populous city and this was generally where the trials took place. Each tribunal was also responsible for all the surrounding villages in the region. Thus, inquisitors were itinerant and were expected to visit each village in turn. Although the actual amount of time they spent on visitations varied, they could spend up to ten months a year traveling from village to village.[12]

When inquisitors arrived at a new location, they gave a sermon to the entire village in the local church. They described different types of heresy and exhorted the populace to come forward to confess and denounce. As the original instructions published in 1484 state, inquisitors were also to

> explain their license, authority, and intention in such a way that the population becomes calm and edified. At the end of the sermon, all faithful Christians must be ordered to raise their hands; a cross and the Gospels should be put before them, so that they may swear to favor the Holy Inquisition and its ministers. . . . Moreover, at the end of the sermon, the inquisitors shall read and proclaim a clear warning, with censures, which speaks generally against those who are rebels and contrarians.[13]

During the first two decades of the Inquisition, the inquisitors then read the Edict of Grace. This guaranteed a grace period—customarily thirty days—during which any villagers who came forward and freely confessed everything they knew would not be taken to trial or be eligible for the Inquisition's worst punishments.[14] Instead, so long as the inquisitors believed a penitent had disclosed everything he knew—and had denounced others—that individual escaped with minor penalties or penances.[15] A confession that did not include a denunciation of others was considered incomplete. Conversos thus faced intense pressure to speak to the inquisitors during this thirty-day period, as not cooperating put them at risk. Any cooperation that occurred after the grace period afforded no protection.

The Edict of Grace created a highly coercive environment. Conversos had strong incentives from the authorities to cooperate and denounce; otherwise they risked extreme consequences. If someone denounced them and they were taken to trial, the likelihood of being found innocent was almost nonexistent. Avoiding a trial was highly desirable, as punishments for guilty verdicts could be quite severe. Those convicted could be forced to forfeit all of their property or face the worst punishment of all, burning at the stake.

In 1500, the Edict of Grace was replaced by the Edict of Faith.[16] The only change indicated by the new edict was that protection was no longer offered to those who came forward within the first thirty days. Although individuals were still encouraged to confess and denounce, they gained no benefits and mitigated no risks by doing so. The strong authority-based incentive to denounce was no longer in effect. With this change, the environment changed to correspond with the volunteer model described in chapter 1.[17]

What was the reason for this change? It turned out that the protection offered to those who confessed and denounced during the Edict of Grace was an empty promise. Inquisitors reserved the right to reopen an individual's case if any new information came to light or if they decided that a penitent had not shared everything that he knew. The original confession could then be used as evidence against that person at trial. The authorities exercised this right quite vigorously; in the Valencia tribunal, 88 percent of those who presented themselves during the Edict of Grace were later prosecuted.[18] By 1500, it was widely known that the Edict of Grace offered no genuine protection and the pretense was dropped. It was replaced by the Edict of Faith, which explicitly *did not* provide lesser punishments for those who confessed and denounced.

Regardless of which edict was in effect, the procedure for receiving testimony remained the same. When an individual provided information to the Inquisition, a notary recorded it. Confessions were written in the *Book of Confessions*, while denunciations were written in the *Book of Declarations*.

Inquisitorial procedure is best known for those who were taken to trial. However, not everyone denounced was tried, and it remains uncertain why some individuals were chosen instead of others. Small offenses could be punished by inquisitors on the spot, usually by a fine. Although it is likely that such an outcome occurred primarily with confessors, the specifics are not completely clear. Such lacunae prevent a complete understanding of the full range of consequences faced by those who found themselves under the scrutiny of the Inquisition. Fortunately, however, most of the procedures are known.

After a denunciation was made, a preliminary investigation followed. The prosecutor then made his first appearance before the court to ask for the arrest of the suspect, if he had not already been detained. The prosecutor also requested that an inventory of the defendant's property be drawn up. Each defendant was responsible for paying for his own incarceration, which usually lasted the duration of the trial. To this end, his possessions were auctioned off one by one. Even if he was found innocent, none of the funds used to pay for his incarceration were reimbursed.

During the initial appearance, the prosecutor announced his intention to accuse before the court and either read the written testimony from the *Book of Declarations* or presented a witness to recount the offense. After any witnesses left, the defendant was brought in. He was told neither who his accusers were nor the nature of the crime. Instead, the court warned him that if he did not confess, he would be guilty of concealing information. In three separate audiences he was pressured to confess before having any idea of what he was accused. Finally, he was informed of the charge, but in such a vague way as to make it impossible to pinpoint exactly who had denounced him, or when and where the alleged crime took place. If the defendant continued to deny having committed any crimes or provided an unsatisfactory confession, he could be tortured.[19] Standards of evidence required two eyewitnesses to convict; in the case where only one eyewitness was present, torture could be used to encourage the defendant to provide the other account.

If the defendant denied the charges, the prosecution was given an opportunity to present proof. The defense also prepared its own argument and the defendant was provided a court-appointed lawyer. There is some disagreement as to the earnestness of these public defenders; some historians view them as highly professional, whereas others see them as compromised by conflicts of interest.[20]

There were several methods of defense available to a defendant. One was the use of *tachas*, in which defendants named people who held enmity toward them and who might therefore have made their denunciations out of spite. Special witnesses were brought in to confirm or deny this attitude. If a defendant could prove the "mortal enmity" of his accusers, he had a chance of partially redeeming himself. This was moot, however, if the defendant failed to guess the individual or individuals who had denounced him.

The defense could also summon positive character witnesses to build up an image of piety and ecclesiastical devotion. Even if a defendant successfully established his accuser's enmity, a demonstration of his own good moral character was still necessary for acquittal. After selecting the witnesses, the defendant created a list of questions they were to be asked in hopes that they would make positive statements. The defense attorney, however, was not permitted to ask the questions. Instead, the process was conducted by special examiners affiliated with the court. In one of the asymmetries of the trial proceedings, defense witnesses could be cross-examined, while prosecution witnesses could not.

At the conclusion of the trial, lawyers, theologians, and scholars deliberated on the guilt and sentence of the accused in what was called the *consulta de fé*. If insufficient evidence was found for conviction, the trial was usually suspended rather than closed: even though the defendant was free to go, the case could be reopened at any time. In the exceedingly rare case where a defendant was found innocent, the verdict was announced privately at the trial. The overwhelming majority of cases, however, resulted in guilty verdicts.

Punishments for guilty offenders varied widely. There were three levels: penances, reconciliation, and burning at the stake. Penances tended to be issued for lesser heresies such as blasphemy and bigamy and reconciliation for major heresies, such as Judaizing. Although penances tended to be milder than reconciliation, both included physical hardships in addition to fines and spiritual requirements. The penanced and the reconciled were required to wear bright yellow smocks called *sanbenitos* for several months or more, in order to publicly broadcast their shame. After the required span of time elapsed, the smocks were hung from the rafters of the local church as a perpetual reminder of

their bearers' transgressions. Other penalties included imprisonment, fines, exile, scourging, mandatory church attendance, and
being sent to a monastery or convent for several years.[21] Scourging, which entailed a minimum of one hundred lashes, with two
hundred the customary number, was especially common.[22] Those
reconciled also forfeited all property acquired since their indiscre-
tion, even if it had happened decades before. Additionally, they
were barred from a range of occupations, including advocate,
landlord, apothecary, spice dealer, physician, surgeon, bleeder,
and public crier.[23] They were also forbidden from holding public
office.[24] The reconciled were banned from wearing gold or jewels,
from carrying arms, and from riding in carriages or carts or on
horses. These restrictions on occupation, transportation, and
dress were also extended to the convicts' progeny.

Burning at the stake was generally reserved for two categories of defendants: those who were found guilty but refused to
admit or repent their transgressions, and relapsed heretics. However, there were exceptions to this rule, particularly in the early
decades of the Inquisition. Defendants who confessed could
avoid the stake only if the inquisitor believed them to have confessed fully and to have sincerely repented. An inquisitor who
believed that sincerity was feigned had wide leeway to condemn
a repentant heretic to the stake.

Men and women condemned to die who sincerely repented
before their executions were strangled before being burned.
Others were burned alive. In either case, the condemned were
remanded to the secular authorities—a process referred to as
"relaxation"—who then carried out the punishments.

One of the earliest judgments was made against Isabel, identified as the wife of Lope de la Higuera, denounced for observing the Sabbath and following Jewish dietary restrictions and
other customs. On February 24, 1484, the inquisitors ruled,

We find that we must declare Isabel, wife of *bachiller* Lope de la Higuera, to be a heretic and apostate. She has incurred a sentence of greater excommunication, and all the other spiritual and temporal punishments contained in the laws against heretics, as well as the loss and confiscation of her goods. We relax her to the virtuous gentleman Juan Perez de Barradas, knight of Cieca, royal magistrate in this city and its territory; and we also relax her to this territory's governors and magistrates, and to any other judges of any other cities, villages and places within these kingdoms and outside of them, wherever the aforesaid Isabel might be found, so that they may do with her what they can and should do by law. We thus pronounce judgment through this sentence.[25]

Isabel, who had presumably fled prior to the arrival of the inquisitors, was sentenced to death upon her discovery.

Regardless of the specific punishments levied, all those found guilty were required to participate in a spectacle known as an *auto de fé*. Autos de fé were public ceremonies in which the penanced and reconciled were shamed and the hopeless were executed. All were required to walk in a procession while their crimes were read aloud to the spectators. Finally, those condemned to the stake were consumed by flames.

COERCIVE INCENTIVES

In its first two decades, before the Edict of Grace was replaced by the Edict of Faith, the Inquisition was implemented by the authorities as a coercive system aimed at achieving social control and eliciting denunciations. The Inquisition's approach in these early years helped overcome two major challenges: organized resistance and challenges to its legitimacy. The contention surrounding its creation reinforces why eliciting denunciations was especially challenging during this time period.

There are some indications that organized resistance to the Inquisition may have emerged as early as the first tribunal in Seville in 1482.[26] Better evidence exists regarding subsequent tribunals, however. In the city of Teruel, the conversos were quite powerful, and in 1484 city leaders closed the city gates to the arriving inquisitors. The city council declared that the Inquisition was in violation of their citizens' civil liberties. Ferdinand responded by penning a letter threatening that if his "orders are not completed, the disobedient shall receive such a punishment as to forever remain an eternal memory and example."[27] This proved insufficient; the city opened its gates only when Ferdinand brought in troops from both Aragon and Castile.

Valencia and Barcelona also resisted the Inquisition in 1484. Barcelona was more successful; it barred inquisitors from that city for three years. Segovia similarly defied the Inquisition in 1485, led by the converso bishop Juan Arias Dávila. This resistance, however, was short-lived and ultimately the bishop was denounced and put on trial by the Inquisition.

Barring inquisitors was not the only means of resistance. On September 15, 1485, inquisitor Pedro Arbués of Zaragoza was assassinated while kneeling in prayer at the city's cathedral. His murderers hoped that this would halt the functioning of the Zaragoza tribunal. A similar plot was hatched in Toledo in 1485, when the tribunal there was transferred from Ciudad Real. In this case, however, the conspirators were betrayed and six men were hanged for their participation. Regardless of the form that resistance took, Ferdinand and Isabella's response was clear: the Inquisition would not be deterred. The Inquisition was not just a method of controlling conversos, but also of demonstrating the power and sovereignty of the monarchs.

This forcefulness, however, did not solve the problem of denunciation. Even if the Inquisition could impose itself upon a locality, it still relied on information provided by local residents to identify heretics. Simply appearing in a new city was insufficient. As historian Henry Kamen has explained, where ordinary people "refused to cooperate, the tribunal was impotent."[28] And the widespread perception of the Inquisition as externally imposed and potentially illegitimate would have made eliciting that cooperation all the more difficult.[29] This is especially true considering that individuals maintained a profound sense of loyalty to their local village. It was the village that provided their sense of identity, not the kingdom as a whole.[30]

How, then, did the authorities overcome perceptions of illegitimacy and convince villagers to cooperate and turn in their neighbors?[31] In the first two decades of its operation, the Inquisition used a strategy of fear and coercion. The very arrival of an inquisitor was meant to frighten the villagers and induce them to confess and denounce. As Tomás de Torquemada, the first inquisitor general of the Spanish Inquisition, instructed, inquisitors should "proclaim a clear warning" during their initial appearance.[32]

The linchpin of this terror was the Edict of Grace, which, by linking confession with denunciation, put enormous pressure on conversos to come forward to incriminate themselves and others, in hopes of escaping the Inquisition's harshest punishments. The authorities made the consequences of not cooperating exceptionally clear. Inquisitors were especially harsh during this time, and burning at the stake was at its peak. It has been estimated that three-quarters of all executions during the 356 years of the Inquisition took place in the first fifty years.[33] Of the accused brought before the tribunal of Valencia between 1478 and 1530, 41 percent of those whose sentences are known were condemned to burn at the stake.[34] The greater the likelihood of such extreme outcomes, the stronger the pressure on individuals to come forward to confess and denounce.

The Inquisition was also utterly inflexible and even a slight deviation from the rules could put potential supplicants beyond hope of redemption. The seriousness of these outcomes can be seen in the case of Juan de Chinchilla, a tailor in the city of Ciudad Real. In 1483, he appeared before the Inquisition to confess during the period of grace but was told that the inquisitor had already retired for the day. He begged an official to admit him and the official promised to summon him later. Having never successfully reported his confession, he was arrested after the grace period had ended. His explanation fell on deaf ears and he was condemned to burn at the stake.[35]

Beyond the intense pressure created by the harsh and inflexible incentives embodied in the Edict of Grace, the authorities may have been strategic in their placement of the Inquisitorial office for each tribunal. In Ciudad Real, the office was situated near where the majority of conversos lived.[36] Thus, conversos may have been able to observe who spoke with the inquisitors, although they did not know the content of those meetings. The more people they witnessed presenting themselves, the greater the likelihood that they themselves had been denounced. This must have increased the pressure on those who had not yet confessed to contribute their own confessions and denunciations.

Compounding these pressures was the fact that all conversos had likely committed and witnessed a variety of heretical behaviors, which were ubiquitous among the population of the time. Christians (both conversos and Old Christians) were largely ignorant of correct church doctrine during this era. The Bible and Mass were in Latin and thus unintelligible to ordinary citizens, and local priests were not well educated and were isolated from the central church bureaucracy. Eighty percent of the population resided in rural parishes and each village tended to worship its own saints, along with maintaining traditions of superstition and folklore. This is supported by the records of the Toledo tribunal; from its inception in 1485 until 1550, only 37 percent of defendants could recite the four basic prayers of Christianity accurately, regardless of the charges against them.[37] A woman reporting a denunciation in the village of Gumiel de Hizan described the following scene:

> María, wife of Pedro Maestre, citizen of Quintana del Pidio . . . was baking bread . . . when the subject of the Inquisition came up . . . and María said "For my life, I'm afraid." And the others asked "Why?" She replied, "Because they say that they ask for the Pater Noster and the Ave Maria and the Credo and the Salve Regina and other things, a man [*sic*] will be afraid." To this Juana, wife of Juan Perez, said, "Cursed be the fear I have now. The whole thing's a rip-off."[38]

María and Juana were frightened that their ignorance of Christian doctrine was sufficient to warrant the punishments of the Inquisition. Indeed, in this instance expressing that fear in an impolitic way was enough to get Juana denounced.

Furthermore, the authorities were interested in the most minor transgressions. Even curse words spoken in the heat of anger could be considered sufficiently blasphemous for conviction. In Aranda in 1500 the surgeon Master Bernal was denounced for yelling during a game of bowls, "Get there! Get there! May Jesus Christ never flourish!"[39] In Coruña in 1495, Bernaldino Pajarillo reported how Juan de Santillana cried out in anger during a similar game: "I reject the whore of a God!"[40] These epithets were "devoid of any heretical intent,"[41] yet blasphemous statements were the most widely persecuted crime in the early modern period, far more than Judaizing.[42] No leeway was given for widespread ignorance or slips of the tongue. All conversos, therefore, would have felt intense pressure to confess their sins and turn in their neighbors.[43]

Together, these factors surely impelled many people to confess and denounce. And the more people who cooperated, the greater the pressure was on those who had not yet come forward. This may have created a feedback loop, where pressure increased as more individuals confessed and denounced, which led to more confessions and more denunciations, which further increased pressure on others. Perhaps this is why, in Ciudad Real, the rate of confessions and denunciations increased and then peaked at the end of the grace period.[44]

Not only was there intense pressure to come forward, but the pressure to behave properly persisted indefinitely. People who confessed and denounced became perpetually beholden to the Inquisition. By confessing, a person provided the inquisitors with verified documentation of heretical behavior. This evidence could then be used against him if the Inquisition ever suspected him of further heresy—in which case, he would be tried as a relapsed heretic and face far more severe punishment. Such is what happened to Marina Gonzalez; after confessing in 1484 to upholding various Jewish traditions and being penanced, she was retried in 1494. The prosecutor claimed that "she returned, like a dog to its vomit, to commit the very errors she abjured." Unable to defend herself successfully and facing a sentence of execution as a relapsed heretic if she confessed, Marina was ultimately condemned to burn at the stake.[45]

Confessors needed not only to behave flawlessly as Christians after confessing, but also to remain in the good graces of the Inquisition. They could be called on to provide evidence or testimony against others and it was not in their interest to refuse. Saving oneself required more than initially denouncing oneself and others; those obligations persisted in perpetuity.

Through fear, incentives, and perpetual obligation, the Inquisition used coercion to enact social control during its first two decades. So strong were these pressures that, despite widespread opposition to the Inquisition, conversos turned each other in in massive numbers. In Ciudad Real, two full books of testimony and 315 pages of a third were filled during the Edict of Grace between October 29 and November 11, 1483.[46] On the island of Majorca during the 1488 Edict of Grace, 424 people came forward to confess and denounce, as did 900 under the Edicts of Grace in Valencia in the late 1480s.[47]

THE RECRUITMENT OF VOLUNTEERS

By 1500, the Inquisition had spread throughout Spain and become a more normal part of Spanish life. Organized opposition had largely faded.[48] The Edict of Grace was discontinued and was replaced by the Edict of Faith.

With the new edict, the strong authority-based incentive to confess and denounce was removed. Individuals could still come forward, but they no longer received protection from the Inquisition's harshest punishments. Given this lack of pressure, one might expect individuals to have stopped participating altogether. But this was not the case: denunciations continued in large numbers throughout the kingdoms. The motivations for doing so shifted, however: rather than denouncing to gain protection from the authorities, individuals did so to selectively harm others within their communities. With the changing of edicts, the coercion model was replaced by the volunteer model.

Certain institutional features facilitated the making of socially opportunistic denunciations during this period. In particular, these protected denouncers from retaliation or hardship for their participation, or else they increased the likelihood that the people denounced would come to harm.[49] In other words, these institutional features gave denouncers the power to cause inevitable damage to others without repercussion. Of course, these features were not implemented intentionally for this reason. Rather, the authorities' zeal for information and presumption of guilt unintentionally enabled it.

It is important to acknowledge that these institutional features existed prior to 1500 when the coercion model was in effect. However, they were not particularly salient during that time period. Because pressure from the authorities to confess and denounce was so strong, the decision to participate was based largely on considerations of self-preservation. Only after 1500 did individuals have the luxury of considering the ways in which the Inquisition could serve their local interests.[50] In other words, the behavior of denouncers transitioned from defensive (vis-à-vis the authorities) to offensive (vis-à-vis their neighbors), and the importance of various institutional features shifted accordingly.[51]

One key way in which socially opportunistic denunciations were facilitated was through the secrecy in which the Inquisition shrouded them. As has already been mentioned, denouncers' identities were carefully kept secret from the people accused. This permitted opportunistic witnesses to accuse others with little risk of retaliation from the people they denounced, the accused's friends and family, or the community at large. This only functioned, of course, to the extent that secrecy was truly maintained. Fortunately for current-day scholars, it is possible to gain some insight into this from trial records. Recall that the primary method that accused persons used for their defense was the naming of tachas: people in the community they thought wished them harm and whose testimony should be discredited. If a defendant could correctly identify his denouncer and prove "mortal enmity," his chances of being exonerated increased.

Tachas provide a simple test of how well anonymity functioned in practice. If individuals knew who accused them, they should have been able to pinpoint those people easily and then focus on discrediting them. However, if they did not know who their accusers were, they would likely name as many people as possible in the hopes of catching their unknown accusers in a wide net. Historical evidence shows the latter case to be much more common.

Defendants often named long lists of people in their tachas, many of whom had nothing to do with the denunciations at all. This can be seen in the cases of two women from 1516. In the trial of Isabel López, there were six prosecution witnesses. In her tachas, Isabel named ninety-two different people. In the trial of María López, there were five prosecution witnesses, but she listed fifty-six different people in her tachas. This is not the behavior of people who had any idea who their accusers were.[52] Similarly, Diego Sánchez was prosecuted in the 1494 tribunal of Toledo for eating "squabs on a Saturday and eggs on Lent and remov[ing] fat from meat." He recounted "a long series of quarrels . . . which he had had with members of his family and others," but in the process successfully identified only one of the two witnesses against him.[53]

In addition to naming tachas, defendants could also name positive character witnesses. Yet on various occasions, they called the person who had denounced them—something that would not occur if those denounced knew their accusers' identities. For example, in Toledo in 1513, "in the trial of Mayor González, wife of Pero Nuñez Franco, prosecution witnesses were called by the defense counsel without the family having the slightest idea that they had testified for the prosecution."[54]

Overall, anonymity appears to have been robust, and that secrecy allowed individuals to denounce with little fear of retaliation or stigma within the community.[55] This may have been especially important in a context where village identity was so strong. Secrecy helped protect denouncers from the ostracism that can arise in tight-knit communities and allowed them to denounce their enemies with impunity.[56]

The trust that the Inquisition placed in denouncers also facilitated socially opportunistic denouncing. Denouncers were assumed to be acting in good faith, and their testimony was accepted and dutifully recorded without cross-examination. Furthermore, denouncers' characters and motivations were never questioned. There were no background checks and they were assumed to be reporting honestly regardless of their social standing or notoriety. Nicholas Eymerich, a fourteenth-century Aragonese theologian and inquisitor who helped create many of the Inquisition's rules, supported this practice of accepting all testimony, which was codified in the guidelines: "In answer to the question of whether criminals, known perjurers, or persons of infamous reputation should be allowed to testify for the prosecution, Eymerich answered in the affirmative because 'the crime of heresy is of such gravity.'"[57] Indeed, even the testimony of excommunicates and the insane was readily accepted.[58]

This faith in denouncers went so far that the Inquisition almost always granted them immunity from punishment in the rare cases where they were discovered to have accused spitefully or falsely. Although there are a few isolated cases of such people being punished, the great majority were assured of going free.[59]

This immunity may have made socially opportunistic denunciations especially attractive.

Certain institutional features also served to increase the likelihood that those denounced would be punished, making it easy for socially opportunistic denouncers to harm their targets. For one, standards of evidence were minimal: all testimony was accorded merit, no matter how conjectural or obscure. The Inquisition did not require denunciations to be based on eyewitness accounts. Hearsay evidence was perfectly acceptable and duly led to an investigation. For example, inquisitors in Aranda looked into the following denunciation: "Sancho, son of Pedro Vilalva . . . citizen of Aranda . . . said that he heard Bartolomé Sánchez, chaplain of the archpriest of Aranda, swear that Ortíz, priest of Vaavón, sleeps with his mother."[60]

Even if a heretical act was directly observed, no consideration was given for the duration of time that had passed or the condition of the denouncer's memory. People considered to be good Christians could be convicted for having made an alleged heretical remark in the distant past. There are records of denunciations for crimes that occurred up to fifty years previously. For example, in 1502 inquisitors learned of a crime from a quarter-century before: "Gonzálo Alonso, citizen of Aranda, said that twenty-five or twenty-six years ago . . . Francisco Mexías said that . . . those who do not suffer in this life will not burn in the next . . . And because he hadn't remembered this before, he hadn't reported it previously to the inquisitors."[61] The denouncer, Alonso, maintained that he had forgotten about this exchange, yet when he reported it to the inquisitors he had no difficulty conjuring up the conversation's specifics. Regardless, this denunciation was dutifully recorded like any other. A person could easily be convicted on the flimsiest of evidence, increasing the likelihood that those denounced would come to harm.

Not only were evidence requirements minimal, but inquisitors had an additional motivation to convict. An acquittal was perceived as a sign of dishonor for themselves. People taken to trial were expected to be found guilty. Indeed, between 1484 and 1530, the tribunal of Valencia only acquitted 12 people out of 1,862, or 0.6 percent.[62]

Even if a person were fortunate enough to be one of the few not convicted, he still faced substantial hardship. Individuals were often arrested soon after being denounced, yet they might not be informed of their crime or taken to trial for a period of weeks to years. Legally, they were not supposed to be arrested until after a formal indictment had been made, but the courts often did so prematurely, forcing them to spend more time in prison. A survey of Valencia prisoners in 1566 found inmates who had been there as long as two and a half years, with an average of three months before sentencing.[63] Not only did this restrict their freedom, but the obligation to pay for their own incarceration could quickly strain finances. No consideration was given for the welfare of the families of the denounced, and their property was sequestered for the duration of the trial in order to prevent them from liquidating their assets before a verdict was reached. This meant that a defendant's spouse and children had no access to their own wealth. There are records of formerly prominent families reduced to begging.[64]

Once a denunciation was voiced, hardship was inevitable, regardless of the verdict. Even if an accused individual was somehow acquitted in a timely manner that did not create too much hardship for himself and his family, he was still likely to be punished. Those acquitted could still be scourged and penanced merely for committing the crime of arousing suspicion. For example, Beatriz Beltraz was put on trial for Judaism in 1489 at

Zaragoza and successfully defended herself by discrediting her accusers and presenting twelve witnesses who swore to her Christian devotion. Nevertheless, the inquisitors declared her to be "vehemently suspect" and, because such suspicions could not be left unpunished, they penanced her.[65]

By implementing institutional features meant to facilitate the discovery and punishment of heresy, the Spanish Inquisition unwittingly created opportunities for socially opportunistic denouncing. Even though the Spanish authorities did not generally welcome such behavior, they nevertheless facilitated social control by accepting a steady flow of denunciations after the implementation of the Edict of Faith. Spanish constituents surely felt compelled to obey the Inquisition's precepts so as to avoid giving others an easy excuse to denounce them. In this period, the overall goals of the authorities succeeded even while their day-to-day operations were co-opted for the resolution of private disputes.

FROM GRACE TO FAITH: 554 DENUNCIATIONS IN SORIA

As has been argued, coercive pressure under the Edict of Grace elicited denunciations based on self-preservation, and specific institutional features facilitated socially opportunistic voluntary denouncing under the Edict of Faith. What remains to be seen is whether this bifurcation is truly descriptive of denouncer motivation. In other words, did denouncers in these two periods behave as predicted by the two models? Were people focused on saving themselves and appeasing the authorities under the Edict of Grace, and then striving to harm their rivals under the Edict of Faith?

A particular set of denunciations discovered in the Archivo General de Simancas in Valladolid, Spain, provide insight into these questions.[66] These records detail Inquisition activity from the diocese of Soria and Burgo de Osma in the northern part of Castile, near the Aragon border. Soria, the village where a large number of these denunciations originated, can be seen in the north central part of figure 2.2. Amassed in more than 150 folios, the denunciations include several hundred records from a *Book of Declarations* collected by inquisitors between 1486 and 1502 as they visited the villages within this territory. These records represent the initial denunciations made before the commencement of an investigation or trial. By closely examining them, it is possible to gain insight into the motivations of denouncers.[67]

To analyze these records, I translated them from fifteenth-century Spanish and coded their various components. The original data represent 444 appearances before the Inquisition by individuals seeking to make denunciations, sometimes about more than one person. By separating out each individual denunciation from the records, the data ultimately comprise 554 denunciations made by one individual against another. Each denunciation ranges from a few sentences to over a page in length.

The denunciations cover the period 1486 to 1502, near the beginning of the Inquisition, and include the Jewish expulsion in 1492. The denunciations reflect this event: Jews occasionally appear as denouncers in the records that predate the expulsion. Most of the denunciations occur in two periods: 1488 to 1492 and 1500 to 1502. This likely does not reflect the actual prevalence of denunciations in this region during this period, as the register is incomplete and lacks several folios. However, apart from certain years' data being missing, there is no reason to believe that denunciations are systematically missing in any other way. The frequency of denunciations by year in these records can be seen in figure 2.3.

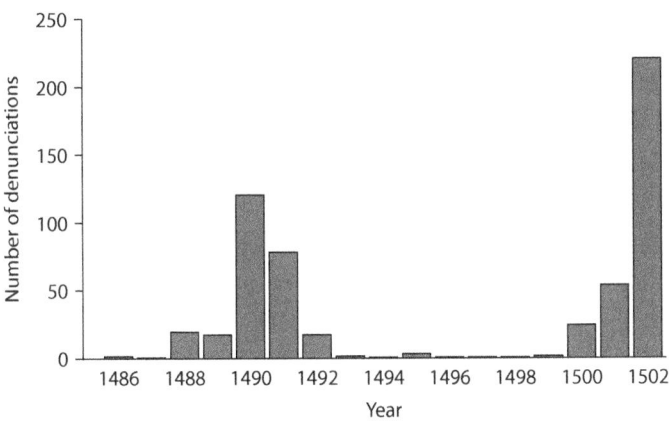

FIGURE 2.3 Number of denunciations by year.

These data also straddle the institutional change from the Edict of Grace to the Edict of Faith. As mentioned previously, conversos eventually realized that the Edict of Grace was a false promise. The fact that most of the data from this period come from the earliest years of the Inquisition indicates that the conversos had not yet realized the inquisitors' subterfuge. This ensures that a comparison between the two time periods effectively compares coercive incentives with voluntary denunciations.

There was widespread participation in denouncing throughout the region. Denouncers came from 115 different villages, while those denounced resided in 97. The majority of denunciations, however, were by people who lived in Soria or Aranda, both of which had large converso populations.[68] Residents of Soria made 184 denunciations (33 percent), and residents of Aranda made 65 (12 percent). The remaining 305 denunciations were spread among the other villages.

As was mentioned before, the early Inquisition was ostensibly interested in secret Jewish behavior by conversos, so it would be reasonable to expect that the majority of denunciations would be for such crimes. However, this was not the case, and the denunciations from the Soria and Burgo de Osma corpus demonstrate the range of behaviors for which people were denounced. As historian John Edwards exclaimed, "virtually every theological and philosophical option which has so far become available to humankind was espoused by someone in this region of Spain in the late fifteenth century."[69]

This diversity makes categorizing these records difficult. To account for the difficulties in categorization, I follow the schema outlined by historian Monsalvo Antón, who examined this same corpus of denunciations.[70] He detailed four categories of alleged crimes: Judaism, superstition, blasphemy, and Christian skepticism. The results of this classification can be seen in table 2.1.

Forty-one percent of the 554 denunciations fit within the category of Judaism, showing that it was one of the main crimes for which people were denounced and of primary interest to the

TABLE 2.1 Distribution of Denunciations by Category

Category	Number	Percentage
Judaism	229	41
Superstition	11	2
Blasphemy	54	10
Christian skepticism	238	43
Other	22	4
Total	554	100

authorities during this time period. One example took place in Soria on August 2, 1491:

> Leví Matroniel, tailor, resident of Soria . . . said that around 40 years ago he was passing by the house of Juan Sánchez de Almacán, treasurer, on a street near his house in this city and he heard Juan Sánchez worshipping from a book in Hebrew in the way that Jews usually worship . . . Juan Sánchez prays and follows the law of the Jews.[71]

Most of the denunciations in this category, however, do not involve literal Jewish worship by conversos. They include following Jewish customs, such as dietary laws, Sabbath observance, the celebration of Jewish holidays, the use or possession of Hebrew language and texts, nostalgia for Judaism, and sending money to a synagogue. In the village of Ojacastro on the 23rd of February 1490,

> Diego de Uclés, resident of that village . . . said that he was in the house of García de Cortes, resident of Cuenca, on Santybañes street, and saw García de Cortes and his wife Guiomar and the mother of García de Cortes fasting until the night on a Thursday and at nighttime they ate meat. And the witness said that he knew it was a major Jewish fasting day.[72]

Also included in this category are eight denunciations against individuals expressing regret for converting to Christianity. In 1502, the tailor García Lopez allegedly said, "When we were Jews, we were bored stiff by one Passover each year, and now each day seems to be a Passover and feast-day and it's all a burden and excessive . . . Before, the festivals were subject to us, but now we are subject to them. And when we were Jews we were masters, but now we are captives."[73]

The second category includes superstition and witchcraft. These are practices or expressions that have to do with magic rather than religion, and include things such as magical remedies and attempts to divine the future. Denunciations for such offenses are relatively rare in these records; only eleven fit within this category. One was reported in Soria in 1490, when Catalina de Violante was denounced for helping Catalina Sánchez determine if her lover—the parish priest Pedro Fernández de Berlanga, who was on a trip to Rome—was still alive. Catalina de Violante made an image out of stone or oak in a wire pan of a boy holding a small rod. From the image she determined that Pedro Fernández was indeed alive and was coming along the road.[74]

The third category includes blasphemous outbursts or epithets, often expressed in the heat of anger, during a game, or in jest. They are formulaic expressions, such as "I reject God" or "I do not believe in God." Ten percent of denunciations fall into this category. Goncalo, a resident of Soria, was denounced on July 19, 1490, for repeatedly saying "I reject God and Saint Mary" and mocking them in various ways.[75] A similar incident was reported on August 2, 1491:

> Juan Esteban, blacksmith, resident of Calatañacor . . . said that three years ago . . . when he was living in the village of Gómara . . . that one night Juan de Aranda, the mayor of Gómara, started to play a game with a king's tax collector in the house of Juan Esteban's master. During the game he heard Juan de Aranda exclaim "I don't believe in God and the seven pairs of angels closest to him!"[76]

The fourth category—Christian skepticism—actually includes slightly more denunciations than those alleging Judaizing. However, grouping these denunciations together is somewhat artificial; it is these denunciations that include the wide range of beliefs and statements that Edwards referred to. Antón differentiated them into three subcategories: behavior or statements showing skepticism toward Christianity, behavior or statements showing skepticism toward the church, and behavior or statements showing skepticism toward the monarchy. Although skepticism toward the state and statements against the Inquisition are fairly rare in these records, skepticism toward the beliefs and practices of Christianity is widespread. These denunciations include statements indicating doubt about the afterlife, skepticism that Christianity was the sole means of salvation, endorsements of materialism, doubts about the omnipotence of God, and deeming all religions similarly valid. Together, this category includes 238 denunciations, or 43 percent of all records, demonstrating that the authorities were dealing with heresy that went far beyond Judaizing. These alleged crimes range from explicit statements to implicit behaviors. One denouncer's interpretation of skepticism is somewhat subtle:

> María, daughter of Pedro García, citizen of Santisteban . . . said that fourteen months ago in the aforementioned village the Inquisitors were present and they reconciled to our faith Rodrigo de la Moneda, and that they asked him the articles of our faith and asked if it was believed that Mary was a virgin . . . and everyone responded and said that they believed it; and the witness saw that the wife of Ferrand Gonzales, furrier, citizen of Santisteban, who was next to the witness, shook her head without saying anything, and it appeared to the witness, in shaking her head, that she did not believe it.[77]

More explicit skepticism was voiced by Isabel, the wife of Pedro Alonso, while speaking about the sacrament of Mass. After the denouncer said that the sacrament was truly God in the altar,

Isabel allegedly responded, "I know that what they elevate at the altar is not God but his image."[78]

Some doubted more than just particular teachings or beliefs of Christianity. For example, the priest Juan Rodríguez mused that there were three laws—Christian, Jewish, and Muslim—and no one knew which was better.[79] Others doubted the omnipotence of God. Juan of Curiel, a resident of Gormás, appeared before the inquisitors on April 13, 1502, and reported that one year before he was having a conversation with Martín Pérez, the butler of the Count of Castro. Martín remarked, "God does not have the power to do good to anyone . . . we see many times that people, serving God, experience misfortune and do not thrive, while others, not serving God and doing many bad things, we see become rich and fortunate in this world."[80]

Others took a more materialistic philosophy of life. The cleric Diego Mexías was reported in Aranda on June 7, 1502, for exclaiming "that there was no Heaven or Hell, that there is nothing except birth and death, and having a nice girlfriend and plenty to eat."[81] Expressing a somewhat different view, Miguel de Gomara allegedly declared that "there was no other glory than dealing in money."[82]

Finally, there are twenty-two denunciations that do not fit neatly into any of the aforementioned categories. These include three reporting Muslim behavior, though this small number is not surprising considering that most converts from Islam lived further to the south. There are also thirteen denunciations made for nonreligious crimes.

Given the variety of allegations, there is widespread debate among historians over what to make of the content of these and other denunciations. Some have taken them at face value, arguing that they signify widespread heretical views and Judaizing behavior.[83] Others have viewed the alleged behaviors as symptomatic of widespread ignorance on the part of those denounced.[84] A third group has simply viewed them as false denunciations made for opportunistic reasons,[85] while others have argued for a combination of these three perspectives.[86] This debate reflects the difficulty in assessing motivation from records like these and from trial transcripts. The seemingly petty nature of many of the denunciations and the prevalence of those unrelated to Jewish worship or Jewish customs suggest that opportunism and perhaps ignorance were primarily at play. However, closer evaluation of patterns of denunciation reveals more specific motives: that individuals denounced out of self-preservation and to appease the authorities during the Edict of Grace and for social opportunism during the Edict of Faith.

In order to present the evidence for this conclusion, it is first necessary to discuss exactly who made these denunciations and against whom they were made. Only then can we properly understand the incentives that potential denouncers were facing. Most of the denunciations do not state the religious background of the denouncer, but some do indicate the background of the person denounced. The text explicitly indicates that 63.5 percent of those denounced were conversos, were accused of crimes relating to Judaism, or both. Interestingly, 61.4 percent of those denounced for Jewish crimes are not explicitly identified as conversos, meaning that the converso label was not meant to distinguish them from the other individuals in the records. In fact, those denounced are almost assuredly conversos, as conversos made up 91.6 percent of those tried in Valencia between 1484 and 1530 and 99.3 percent of those tried in Barcelona between 1488 and 1530.[87] Noting that many of the denunciations describe Jewish customs, historians who have studied the Soria records in particular are convinced that most of those targets were conversos as well.[88]

It is somewhat less clear who the denouncers were. There were three relevant population groups within this region in the early years of the Inquisition: Jews, Old Christians, and conversos. About 15 percent of the records indicate a Jewish denouncer, which is evident from their distinctly Jewish names. These denunciations all occurred during or prior to 1492, when the Jews were expelled from Spain.

Unfortunately, there is no similarly direct way to know whether the remaining denouncers were Old Christians or conversos. Indirect evidence, however, suggests that it was conversos denouncing one another. Denunciations in the city of Ciudad Real during the same time period were made primarily by conversos, as were denunciations in the tribunal of Valencia.[89] Contact between conversos and Old Christians was largely limited to work and business interactions.[90] Conversos maintained their own churches and social lives, and they tended to intermarry. The contemporary writer Alonso de Palencia declared that they acted as a "nation apart."[91] The large number of denunciations for alleged crimes that took place within the confines of someone's home therefore provides further evidence that denouncers in these records were conversos. It is highly likely that the Soria files represent mostly denunciations made by conversos against conversos, an assertion that John Edwards, who also examined these files, has endorsed.[92]

Determining the affiliation of denouncers is important because Old Christians and Jews were not subject to the same authority-based incentives that the conversos faced under the Edict of Grace. Jews were not under the jurisdiction of the Inquisition, so they gained no protections by participating.[93] Old Christians were not the target in those early years, so they similarly would not have felt the intense pressure to confess and denounce. Only for conversos was the shift from the Edict of

Grace to the Edict of Faith meaningful. Only for them did it indicate a transition from the coercion model to the volunteer model. Therefore, in order to focus only on conversos, I have removed the denunciations made by Jews.

As mentioned in the previous chapter, denouncers in the coercion model do so out of self-preservation as they strive to appease or satisfy the authorities. To accomplish this, they tend to target members of particular groups or to report particular crimes that the authorities consider most desirable: in this case, conversos secretly practicing Judaism. Denouncers who provided more information would also have been more likely to please the authorities, so multiple denunciations should be relatively common. Denouncers in the volunteer model, however, denounce their neighbors in order to harm and gain advantage over those they dislike. Therefore, they would most likely have denounced individuals within their locality whom they encountered regularly and who were similar in status.

Table 2.2 evaluates these expectations by comparing the early period (1486–1499), in which conversos faced coercive incentives under the Edict of Grace, with the later period (1500–1502), when voluntary denunciations were encouraged under the Edict of Faith. For this analysis, I use chi-square tests of independence to determine whether differences between the two time periods are statistically distinguishable.[94]

If denouncers were indeed responding to authority-based incentives in the earlier period, they should have been more likely to denounce for those offenses of primary interest to the authorities. The data are consistent with this hypothesis: 46 percent of denunciations in the early period were for Jewish practices, compared to 27 percent in the later period. In other words, denouncers were almost twice as likely to denounce for Jewish behavior in the earlier period than in the later one.[95] Furthermore,

TABLE 2.2 Coercive Versus Voluntary Denunciations
in the Soria Files, 1486–1502

	Pre-1500 (coercion model)	Post-1500 (volunteer model)	χ^2
Prototypicality			
Jewish practices	46%	27%	15.13***
Bad reputation	9%	1%	18.09***
Number denounced			
Multiple people	23%	13%	4.93*
Geographic proximity			
Same village	48%	63%	9.40**
Mean distance between villages	108 km	73 km	3.42***†
Relationship closeness			
Close relationship	27%	51%	24.55***
Distant relationship	56%	29%	33.50***
Status homophily			
Same occupational status	46%	55%	0.01
Same gender	68%	80%	8.01**
N	171	297	

* $p < .05$
** $p < .01$
*** $p < .001$
† This number is the result of a t-test, as distance is a continuous variable.

denouncers occasionally indicated if the person they were denouncing was widely known as a "bad Christian." As María added to the end of her denunciation against Pedro Sánchez in 1490, "he was a bad Christian and was publicly known as such."[96] Such comments appeared in 9 percent of all denunciations before 1500, but only 1 percent after 1500. This labeling is consistent with earlier denouncers trying to reinforce their helpfulness to the authorities; calling the accused a "bad Christian" appears to be a rhetorical device added to denunciations that otherwise read similarly to later ones that do not feature this verbal flourish.

If denouncers were responding to coercive incentives, we can expect that they would also have been more likely to denounce multiple people in the early period than they were in the later period. Indeed, in the period before 1500, 23 percent of individuals denounced more than one person. In the period starting in 1500, however, only 13 percent of them denounced more than one person. Almost double the percentage of denouncers in the early period denounced multiple people, whereas those in the later period were much more targeted in their denunciations.

By contrast, denouncers in the later period seeking to harm particular others could be expected to denounce more locally, especially targeting those they encountered regularly. Regular interaction not only allows negative ties to develop and be sustained; it also means that an individual stands to benefit when a particular rival or enemy is punished. Therefore, we can expect individuals to have denounced people who lived near them and with whom they had closer relationships.

To test the first part of this prediction, I examined the geographical distance between denouncers and the people they denounced. In the Soria files, 63 percent of denouncers in the post-1500 period denounced someone from the same village, compared to 48 percent of denouncers in the pre-1500 period. Denouncers in the later period indeed showed a local bias in their denunciations. This finding is further corroborated by looking at the mean and median distance between villages in cases where the denouncer accused someone from a different village. The difference in the median distance is particularly striking: in the pre-1500 period, the median distance was 96 kilometers; in the post-1500 period, it was only 30 kilometers. Similarly, the mean distance was 108 kilometers before 1500 and 73 kilometers after.[97]

The prediction above also suggests that denouncers under the volunteer model could be expected to target those with whom they had closer relationships. Relationship closeness can be inferred through a close reading of the context in which alleged crimes took place and the ways in which the denouncer sometimes characterized his or her relationship with the person denounced. I define a "close relationship" as one in which the two parties were in business together, were coworkers, had direct conversations with each other, were housemates, had been in one another's houses, interacted frequently, or were relatives.[98] One such denunciation was reported in Roa on January 23, 1502, when an individual denounced his former housemate:

> Sancho . . . resident of Aranda . . . said that he knows how Alonso de la Reyna, cleric, resident of Aranda, sleeps with María de Torres, and Alonso's father also sleeps with her. Alonso de la Reyna's father said to him: "Bad man, don't sleep with this woman who I have slept with," and still Alonso had to be with her. And Sancho knows this because he lived with Alonso and saw it many times.[99]

"More distant relationships" include denouncers who were two degrees of separation from the person they denounced (e.g., a friend of a friend), who overheard or saw the crime but did not interact directly with the person denounced, who heard about the crime secondhand, or who denounced someone who was in town only temporarily. One such denunciation was made in Soria on July 17, 1501. On that day, Mosé Asayuel appeared and said that about two or three years before Manuel Rodrigues had come to his house and begged to spend one night there. Manuel said he was from Toledo, where he had a nice house and a daughter. Later he begged for some food to eat. Mosé gave him food and thought that the visitor appeared to be Jewish.[100]

Using these categories, there is a clear difference between the two time periods. In the earlier period, almost twice as many denunciations (56 percent) were made against more distant relationships as against closer ones (27 percent). In the later period this pattern is reversed, with 29 percent of denunciations made against more distant relationships and 51 percent against closer relationships.[101]

Under the volunteer model, denouncers can also be expected to denounce people of similar status, as similar status can lead to status conflict. Denouncing someone of similar status also provides the greatest opportunity for relative gain. To examine this, I looked at status in two ways: occupation and gender.

The denunciation records indicate the occupation of denouncers 49 percent of the time and those denounced 65 percent of the time. Occupation is a good indicator of status during this time period and occupations within this corpus encompass the full range of positions in Spanish society. Forty-seven unique occupations are listed for denouncers and fifty-two for those denounced. The three most common occupations for both parties are priest, notary, and shoemaker.

Unfortunately, while many denunciations include the occupation of the denouncer or the person denounced, only thirty-seven in the early period and twenty-eight in the later period include both. This means that any results are tentative, especially since the reason for occupation not being systematically recorded is unknown. Given the paucity of occupation data, I categorize occupations into three types: low-status industry jobs, which include shoemakers, carpenters, and weavers; high-status professional jobs, which include physicians, lawyers, and priests; and traders, who would have fallen in the middle of the status hier-archy.[102] Using this categorization schema, 46 percent of denounc-ers in the earlier period denounced someone of similar status, while 55 percent did so in the later time period. Although this difference is not statistically significant, it is in the expected direction, with more intra-status denunciations in the later period.

A second measure of status is gender. Women had lower sta-tus than men during this time period; this is evident in the denunciations themselves where many women are identified by their relation to their husband. Fortunately, gender is consistently identifiable in the data. Across both periods, a man denouncing another man was the most common denunciation, occurring in 65 percent of the records. Of the remainder, 11 percent were between women, 10 percent consisted of a man denouncing a woman, and 14 percent involved a woman denouncing a man. However, these types were not evenly distributed between the two periods. Based on expectations from the volunteer model, there should be more within-gender denunciations in the later time period. This was indeed the case, with 68 percent being within-gender in the early time period and 80 percent starting in 1500.

Together, the different rows of table 2.2 provide cumulative evidence that individuals denounced out of self-preservation in the earlier time period and for social opportunism in the later one. A focus on appeasing the authorities shifted to a focus on harming particular others. Consistent with this, there were six denouncers who admitted to "past enmity" with the individuals they denounced. All six of them denounced in the later time period. For example, after reporting Pero de Juan Martines for a blasphemous statement, a denouncer admitted that "a few times there was enmity because Pero de Juan Martines had tried to do harm to him." The denouncer assured the inquisitors, however, that "now there was no enmity, and he did not report this because he wanted to harm Pero de Juan Martines, but because it is the truth and he wanted to clear his conscience."[103]

Another example of past enmity was reported by Juana García of Aranda, who testified that about four years prior, the cleric Diego Mexías began bragging and boasting to her and her daughters. When Juana scolded him for behavior unbefitting a member of the clergy, he told her that there is no "paradise or hell, nor anything to believe besides birth and death and men getting what they desire." She continued her denunciation by declaring that "she did not report out of hatred, although after that occurrence she was mistreated by the suspect and his brother and his uncle."[104] Although it is impossible to say to what extent past enmity truly motivated these denunciations, Juana García does not come across as particularly convincing.

We can also expect that many denunciations in both periods were false, as both coercive and voluntary denunciations are motivated by self-interest. This expectation cannot be evaluated directly, but the records contain several clues as to how people felt about the Inquisition, along with their thoughts about the truthfulness of the denunciations. Alvaro de Prado was denounced in Aranda on October 22, 1501, for voicing such a sentiment:

> Pedro de Frías, resident of Aranda . . . said that this month of April, he was speaking with Gaona and others in the house of Pedro Barbero, and they were speaking about the Inquisition; and Alvaro de Prado, resident of this village, said "I vow to God, in Castile more than fifteen hundred people have been burned by false witnesses." And that . . . Gaona sent signals for him to shut up but others wanted him to say more.[105]

Diego from the same village was denounced for saying something similar, as he allegedly "swore to God that most of
those that burned by the Inquisition burned from false
witnesses . . . that if he did not say it, there were another hundred who would." When Diego was urged to be quiet, he
claimed that Alonso Traspaso, a former resident of the village,
had been burned because of false testimony.[106] Rodrigo de San
Martín said that he swore to God and his virtues that none of
the many heretics burned had been burned for heresy, that
they had no more guilty than the angels in the sky, and that
the inquisitors had gone with the devil.[107]

These complaints about false denunciations correspond well
with the opinions of several historians that such denunciations
were indeed prevalent.[108] Some contemporary writers were also
in agreement. Fernando de Pulgar, the royal chronicler at the
court of Ferdinand and Isabella, asserted, "There were in this city
some poor and vile Jewish men who because of enmity or malice
gave false testimony against one of the conversos, saying that
they had seen him Judaizing."[109] Although the prevalence of false
denunciations is impossible to assess quantitatively, the next
chapter provides more direct evidence about falsehood under the
two models.

One additional result particular to the Spanish Inquisition is
consistent with the theoretical differences between the two models: the denunciation of the dead. Perhaps surprisingly, many
individuals in the Soria files denounced someone who was already
deceased. The authorities were interested in such denunciations
and commonly put the accused on trial posthumously. In fact,
Grand Inquisitor Torquemada warned inquisitors in 1485 that
their prosecution of the living should not lead them to neglect
the prosecution of the dead. One such denunciation from 1490

does not indicate when the denounced individual passed away, but considering how long ago the alleged crime occurred, it may have been some time before: "This day appeared before the Inquisitors Pero Sánchez de la Puente de Ravanera, resident of Soria, and said that about 40 years ago, he saw many times Juan Sánchez de Almacán, resident of Soria, deceased, make Jewish orations in Hebrew, keeping the Sabbath prayers."[110] The prevalence of such denunciations in the Soria files can be seen in table 2.3.

In the earlier period, a higher percentage of denunciations were of someone who was deceased: 25 percent before 1500, compared to only 5 percent in the later period. This accords well with the theoretical models. Under the volunteer model, we can expect denunciations to be made against living individuals, as denouncing the dead neither causes them harm nor confers relative advantage.[111] However, denouncing deceased individuals in the coercion model allowed villagers to demonstrate their eagerness to provide information to the authorities.[112]

TABLE 2.3 Denunciations Against the Living and Deceased

	Pre-1500 (coercion model)	Post-1500 (volunteer model)	χ^2
Living	129	283	38.72***
Deceased	42	14	

* p < .05
** p < .01
*** p < .001

MOBILE DENOUNCERS AND LOCAL DENUNCIATIONS

One of the macro implications of the two models is that the volunteer model should require less effort from the authorities. Whereas the coercion model requires the active imposition of pressure, the volunteer model permits the authorities to be more reactive. This may seem like a meaningless distinction in this particular context, as inquisitors traveled around collecting denunciations under both the Edict of Grace and the Edict of Faith. However, there is one way to evaluate this particular implication: by examining the willingness of denouncers to travel to another village to make their reports. If the Edict of Faith truly corresponded to less effort needed from the authorities in order to elicit denunciations, then denouncers should have been more willing to seek out inquisitors under the Edict of Faith than under the Edict of Grace. In other words, coercive pressure should have required the direct presence of the inquisitor, while the desire for social opportunism should have motivated some denouncers to seek out an inquisitor on their own.

The visitation schedule of the inquisitors can be largely reconstructed from these records. Each denunciation not only mentions where the denouncers and those denounced resided, but also the village in which the denunciation was recorded. Although denouncers and the people they denounced lived in approximately one hundred different villages, denunciations were only recorded in thirty-five. This means that some people were indeed willing to travel to another location. Their propensity to leave their villages to denounce is displayed in table 2.4.

In the period before 1500, denouncers were slightly more likely to denounce in their own village when the inquisitors arrived

TABLE 2.4 Denouncers' Willingness to Travel

	Pre-1500 (coercion model)	Post-1500 (volunteer model)	χ^2
Did not travel	90	122	5.39*
Traveled to denounce	81	175	

* p < .05
** p < .01
*** p < .001

than to travel to another village where the inquisitors were situated. Starting in 1500, however, 59 percent of denouncers traveled in order to denounce, a significant difference between the two periods. Denouncing in one's home village was most prevalent in the early period, while traveling to denounce was most common in the later period. Despite experiencing less pressure to denounce, denouncers were willing to put forth more effort to do so. Coercive incentives, on the other hand, were most effective when applied directly.

This result is especially intriguing when combined with the geographic closeness results in table 2.2. Denouncers under the Edict of Faith were more willing to travel in order to denounce people from their local village. In other words, denouncers became more mobile at the same time that denunciations became more local. The Edict of Faith required less effort from the authorities because individuals worked proactively to harm their neighbors; the drive for social opportunism was strong.

CONCLUSION

Henry Kamen has stated that "the major achievement of Ferdinand and Isabella was to bring peace and order to Spain."[113] Having started with two kingdoms racked by civil war and rife with internal tensions, the royal couple successfully consolidated power and enacted social control throughout their territory, much of it accomplished through the Spanish Inquisition.

The Inquisition was not, however, a monolithic entity that persisted unchanged throughout the decades. Rather, it was a collection of rules and practices that evolved over time. One of the most important steps in this evolution was the shift from the Edict of Grace to the Edict of Faith. On its surface, this change may not have seemed especially meaningful, but the analysis in this chapter has demonstrated that the patterns in which people denounced shifted fundamentally in its wake. A defensive motivation of self-preservation was replaced by an offensive motivation of social opportunism.

Despite this shift, the Inquisition was effective during both time periods. In both, large numbers of denunciations reached the inquisitors. This steady flow of information allowed them to root out heresy and deter other people from committing similar crimes, enacting social control.

The Edict of Grace was effective because it presented individuals with a stark choice: cooperate with the authorities and receive a milder punishment, or not cooperate and risk a brutal one. Many people were unwilling to take this risk, preferring self-preservation—and the requisite denouncing—over the possibility of ending up penniless or condemned to the stake.

The Edict of Faith was effective without the use of authority-based incentives because it protected denouncers while ensuring that the people they denounced would come to harm.

Secrecy prevented retaliation, while trust from the authorities meant that denouncers' characters or motivations were never questioned. The zealousness of the inquisitors ensured that practically anyone denounced would come to harm. Many people found this environment convenient for the expression of personal grievances.

Although both edicts were effective, they varied in terms of strengths and weaknesses. The Edict of Grace created powerful incentives that helped overcome local resistance in the earliest years of the Inquisition. In this way, the perceived legitimacy of the institution was almost irrelevant, as the authorities were able to acquire denunciations through intimidation and terror. As a means of gaining local information rapidly from a resistant populace, the coercion model as manifested in the Edict of Grace was highly effective. This may have been why it was reintroduced in the 1560s and 1570s when the Inquisition began a forceful drive against Christians with Muslim heritage, known as *moriscos*. This had immediate results: an Edict of Grace in Valencia in 1568 led to 2,689 moriscos denouncing themselves and turning in others.[114]

The Edict of Faith was perhaps successful because it was not instituted right away, but only after the populace had largely accepted the Inquisition as a part of Spanish society. Once the Inquisition became viewed as more legitimate, individuals may have been able to view it less as an externally imposed intrusion and more a normal feature of public life, as well as a convenient means of resolving private disputes. In other words, either coercive incentives were no longer required to spur participation from a recalcitrant populace or the desire to harm others was so appealing that the Inquisition's legitimacy was less important. In either case, the desire to harm others was sufficiently motivating that denouncers were more likely to travel to denounce under the Edict of Faith than under the earlier Edict of Grace. Perhaps this is why, by the second decade of the 1500s, witnesses were required to swear that they held no animosity toward the person denounced, as such denunciations had become increasingly prevalent.[115]

Overall, this chapter has shown how the use of coercive incentives resulted in different behaviors and motivations than encouragement without incentivization within the same historical setting. The next chapter presents another instance of the coercion and volunteer models, but in a very different context: Russia at the start of the Romanov dynasty, in the first half of the seventeenth century. This setting provides more direct evidence of denouncer motivation and the prevalence of false denunciations under both the coercion and volunteer models. In this case, however, different segments of the population were subject to each of the models rather than there being a shift in procedures over time. Further, the two models manifested themselves in different ways: denouncers in the coercion model were subject to positive, rather than negative incentives; and denouncers in the volunteer model experienced a much less conducive environment for social opportunism.

3

ROMANOV RUSSIA

In 1613, after a fifteen-year period of war and famine known as the "Time of Troubles," a sickly sixteen-year-old named Mikhail Fedorovich Romanov was named the new tsar of Russia.[1] He inherited a land occupied by Polish invaders to the west, Swedish invaders to the north, and a pretender to the throne in the south. He faced the task of reinstituting the rule of law, rebuilding the army, and bringing prosperity back to a devastated countryside. Despite the seemingly insurmountable obstacles confronting him, Mikhail successfully consolidated power and launched the Romanov dynasty, which would rule Russia for the next 304 years.

One of the tools he used to accomplish this was known as the Sovereign's Word and Deed. Operated out of the Service Chancellery, it was established to encourage local residents to report treasonous behavior to the central authorities. When an individual knew of a statement that maligned or rejected the tsar and his legitimacy, that was a Sovereign's Word; when an individual knew of an action meant to harm the tsar or his authority, that was a Sovereign's Deed. This chapter examines Sovereign's Word and Deed reports from a period spanning the first decades of the Romanov dynasty, from Mikhail's coronation in 1613 through the first four years of Aleksei Mikhailovich's reign, which began in 1645. During this period, central authority was exceptionally weak and especially focused on social control.

Although the institution of the Sovereign's Word and Deed remained constant throughout this time period, different subgroups of the population experienced it in very different ways. Prisoners and others in custody believed that if they could provide valuable information to the authorities or speak directly to the tsar, they would be relieved of their immediate hardship. Free individuals, on the other hand, gained no authority-based benefits from denouncing, nor did they suffer consequences for withholding information. Thus, the early Romanov dynasty contains instances of both coercive pressure and voluntary action. I evaluate their differences in 453 denunciations reported during this time period. These records go beyond those seen in the previous chapter, providing details about the ensuing investigations, the verdicts, and the punishments meted out. In some cases, denouncers even described in their own words their motivations for coming forward.

Through a comparison of denunciations made by free individuals and those in custody, I find evidence for the coercion model, where prisoners denounce in the hope of being relieved of hardship, and the volunteer model, where free individuals denounce in order to harm others within their local communities. In the latter case, the results demonstrate how, even in voluntary environments where institutional conditions are not particularly favorable to social opportunism, recent interpersonal conflict and heightened emotional intensity propels individuals to come forward to harm their neighbors.

HISTORICAL BACKGROUND

Russia was a place of extreme turmoil at the turn of the seventeenth century, so much so that the fifteen-year period from 1598 to 1613 is known as the "Time of Troubles." In 1598, Tsar Fedor Ivanovich died without leaving an heir and for the next seven years his brother-in-law Boris Godunov ruled over Muscovy. Politically, however, the ruling elite began to collapse in 1601, and from 1601 to 1603 a devastating famine left massive numbers of peasants starving. After Godunov died in 1605, three different rulers managed to briefly gain control of the land, only to lose their grips on power. Foreign invasions by Poland and Sweden amidst civil war resulted in a severe dislocation of the population along with widespread destruction of entire villages. A map of Russia during this time period can be seen in figure 3.1.

Only in 1612 did some modicum of stability return to the region. Native Muscovites recaptured Moscow, which had been taken by Poland. With the city again under Russian control, messengers were sent throughout the territory calling on representatives to come and choose a new tsar. Several hundred individuals from a cross-section of the Russian citizenry answered the call.[2] On February 7, 1613, after much debate and intrigue, the Assembly of the Land of Moscow chose a sixteen-year-old youth, Mikhail Fedorovich Romanov, to rule Russia.

Mikhail's ascension was quite obviously a compromise.[3] He was young, sickly, and had "limited gifts."[4] He was also not an obvious choice in terms of lineage. Yet he was the only person about whom the various social classes could agree, and his perceived insignificance and weakness likely contributed to his being selected.[5]

FIGURE 3.1 Muscovy, 1613. Unlike modern states, the borders of Russia during this time period were not fully delineated. Although explicit borders existed with established states to the west, the lands to the east and south of Russia were a frontier occupied by various nomadic groups. This territory was not organized into states and lacked clear boundaries (Khodarkovsky 2002).

Adapted from Crummey (1987, 262).

The new tsar did have a politically savvy father, Filaret Nikitich, who was a captive in Poland during the time of Mikhail's ascension. In 1619, Filaret was released from prison and returned home to become the patriarch of Moscow and Russia. He quickly emerged as the de facto ruler of Muscovy; he and Mikhail jointly heard petitions and issued decrees, and were both referred to as the "Great Sovereign."[6] The Romanov dynasty, which would last for three centuries, had truly begun.

In the early years this legacy was anything but assured. The regime had to reinstitute the rule of law in a land where anarchy had essentially reigned for fifteen years. The army needed to be rebuilt and continuing internal unrest to be stamped out. Swedish forces occupied parts of Russia to the north, while Polish forces occupied areas to the west. The authorities had only tenuous control over the southern frontier region and new pretenders periodically appeared and asserted their claims to the throne. As one historian put it, Russia was "a wasteland of ruins, rubble and corpses from the Arctic Ocean to the southern steppes of Astrakhan and into Ukraine, and from the eastern European border to the foot of the Urals. Cities and villages were burned and depopulated and desolate."[7] There were also widespread rumors that the Romanovs' claim was not, in fact, legitimate.

Quite understandably, Mikhail and Filaret's primary concern was to consolidate power and prevent the same fate from befalling them that had ended the reigns of the most recent tsars. To do this, they sought to inspire allegiance across social classes, including provincial officials, soldiers, and even peasants. Part of this agenda included an emphasis on reviving and expanding a legal institution known as the Sovereign's Word and Deed: the obligation to report any act or expression of treason against the tsar. Before the Romanovs, this was a duty exclusively of elites, but Mikhail expanded it to all residents of Muscovy.[8] This expansion can be first observed in the oath of allegiance to the new tsar, where people of every rank pledged to fight anyone who conspired against the sovereign and to report them to the authorities if capturing them was not feasible. They would make a similar oath in 1645 at the coronation of Mikhail's son Aleksei.

This expansion of the Sovereign's Word and Deed would prove effective. Individuals from all social categories came forward to report the transgressions of their neighbors. The central authorities paid scrupulous attention to the most minor denunciations, which allowed the nascent dynasty to monitor the populace and stamp out any perceived threats to its power.

PROCEDURES OF WORD AND DEED

Cases of the Sovereign's Word and Deed were handled locally, with guidance provided by the central authorities at the Service Chancellery in Moscow. This was a very loose centralization; procedures of Word and Deed were never formally written down and there was some local variation. However, the general steps by which denunciations were received and processed can be inferred from the case records.

In order for an inquiry to be opened, a formal denunciation had to be made. This could be done orally or in writing, though most were made verbally and in person at the office of the local administrator, known as the *voevoda*.[9] The voevoda was the person charged with investigating crimes of Word and Deed, so a denunciation made initially to another official would quickly be relayed to him. Once such a crime was reported, the voevoda was required to open up an investigation immediately.[10]

The purpose of this initial inquiry was primarily to establish the denunciation's accuracy and truth. The voevoda sought to understand the basic facts of the allegation, including the identities of the denouncer and the person denounced, what the alleged crime was, where and when it took place, and if there were accomplices involved or witnesses who could testify about the event. The voevoda also attempted to determine if the denouncer was trustworthy and whether the crime was malicious or accidental in nature.

The first step of the inquiry was to take the relevant actors into custody: not only the defendant, but sometimes the denouncer and witnesses as well.[11] If the case was minor, the denouncer and witnesses would be put in the custody of another person or permitted to remain free under a surety bond (which could not be redeemed if the individual in question absconded). In more serious cases, the denouncer could be arrested and put in jail along with the person denounced.[12]

Two types of interrogation could be used during this initial phase. In most cases, the individuals involved were questioned separately. Much more rarely, the interrogation included a confrontation in which the denouncer repeated his accusation to the alleged perpetrator.

The first person to be interrogated was invariably the denouncer. Officials sometimes conducted a background check to determine whether he or she was trustworthy, but this appears to have been a rare occurrence.[13] Then the defendant and any witnesses named by the denouncer were questioned. During this stage of the investigation, the defendant could plead innocent, guilty, or partially guilty. He could also name witnesses for his defense; however, this rarely happened and may have been discouraged by the authorities.

After the basic facts of the case had been gathered and the interrogations were complete—a process that usually took one or two days—the voevoda sent a report to Moscow that included all findings, along with detailed transcripts of the questionings. When the tsar's officials had reviewed it, they either pronounced judgment or gave additional instructions to the voevoda regarding how to continue the investigation.[14] These instructions could include orders to threaten or apply torture, though these were rarely given.

When it did occur, torture usually consisted of beating with a knout—a rawhide whip—or scorching with fire or hot pincers. The information gathered during such sessions was considered legitimate. Torture could be directed against either the denouncer or the person denounced. When it was used against the denouncer, it was almost always because he refused to answer the investigator's questions. Those denounced were most likely to be subjected to torture when witnesses corroborated the denouncer's account but the defendant denied the crime. Stoicism in the face of torture could be an important defense against accusations of wrongdoing.

If torture or the threat of torture was utilized, another report with the new results was sent to Moscow. This correspondence between local and national officials continued until the central authorities were satisfied with the investigation and felt ready to pass judgment. Overall, individual cases tended to take about a month, largely because of the time required to send messages between Moscow and the different localities. Cases could be especially drawn out in more distant regions along the frontier. If a guilty verdict was returned, local officials were often instructed to mete out the punishment in public, in front of the town's entire population. Punishments ranged from reprimands to imprisonment to beatings to exile or death, with the majority consisting of a beating along with about a week in jail.[15]

Overall, the system of denunciation was largely voluntary. Although denouncing was technically an obligation for people who witnessed a crime, there were no authority-based incentives prompting ordinary individuals to come forward. Local residents were well aware of this fact: those who knew of crimes but did not denounce "showed no fear . . . of being accused of disloyalty themselves."[16] This is especially evident among witnesses; there is no evidence of their having been punished for not reporting the crimes themselves. Nor did denouncers seem overly concerned when they did not make their denunciations right away, despite the requirement that they report misdeeds immediately. The Sovereign's Word and Deed therefore fits well with the volunteer model. Individuals could denounce freely if they so desired, but there was no punishment for not denouncing and no reward for doing so.[17]

This voluntary system persisted throughout the entire period under investigation with no variation in institutional structure. Within this environment, however, there was a particular group of individuals who *did* experience an authority-based incentive to cooperate and denounce others: those already in the custody of the authorities or in the process of being taken into custody. These included prisoners and suspects under investigation for unrelated crimes. Prisoners believed that if they provided information to the authorities or managed to assist an official higher up than the local voevoda, they would be released from jail. This belief appears to have been widespread.[18] Similarly, if someone being beaten, arrested, or interrogated by the authorities for an unrelated matter cried out knowledge of a Sovereign's Word or Deed, the beating, arrest, or interrogation would come to a halt and an investigation would ensue. This provided a respite, at the very least.

Together, prisoners and people taken into custody represent a category of individuals who experienced the Sovereign's Word and Deed as a coercive system with authority-based incentives. They believed that if they assisted the authorities, their negative situation would improve. What follows is a discussion of the ways in which the perceived authority-based incentives elicited denunciations among those in custody, and how particular institutional features facilitated the reporting of voluntary denunciations by those who remained free.

COERCIVE INCENTIVES

Unlike the Spanish Inquisition under the Edict of Grace, authority-based incentives were not applied intentionally to those in custody in Romanov Russia.[19] The authorities never offered benefits for denouncing or punishments for withholding information. Nonetheless, there was a perception among the imprisoned population that reporting a violation of Word or Deed could result in a reduced prison sentence or even exoneration. Similarly, people beaten, arrested, or interrogated for unrelated matters believed that if they declared knowledge of a Sovereign's Word or Deed, the current hardship would cease. As a result, these groups experienced an unintentional instance of the coercion model. The perception of authority-based incentives alone was sufficient to affect behavior, regardless of whether that perception was accurate. In reality, the vast majority of prisoners gained no benefits from the authorities in return for their denunciations. Local administrators were in fact strictly forbidden from sending denouncers to Moscow without special orders, and none of the denunciations examined in this chapter involve a denouncer who successfully made it to the throne room.

The authority-based incentives found in Romanov Russia were distinct from those used in the Spanish Inquisition in another meaningful way. Incentives come in two types: positive and negative. Positive incentives indicate that something beneficial will occur if a particular action is taken (i.e., a reward), while negative incentives indicate that something undesirable will occur if a particular action is *not* taken (i.e., a punishment). In the Spanish Inquisition, the Edict of Grace elicited denunciations with the threat of a negative outcome that could be avoided through confession and denunciation. For those in custody in Russia, however, there was no threat of additional hardship. Instead, individuals were already experiencing hardship for an unrelated matter and viewed denunciation as a means of improving their situation—gaining release from prison or ending a beating, arrest, or interrogation. Yet these positive incentives and the negative incentives seen in the previous case study are identical in an important respect: both are authority-based in nature. Both, therefore, lead denouncers to orient themselves toward gratifying the authorities in the hope of eliciting a particular response.[20]

The incentive to denounce existed for those in custody because their circumstances were so dire. Russian prisons were often unhealthy and overcrowded, with prisoners dying from hunger and "bad air"[21] or being kept in darkness and isolation. Disease ran rampant. In the words of historian Robert Hellie, prisons were "intolerable cesspools of oppression and starvation."[22] People who were arrested or interrogated faced painful beatings that could leave them maimed or dead,[23] and torture was always a possibility. For these groups, the perceived incentives were less illusory, at least in the short term. Because the authorities were so interested in information regarding crimes of Word and Deed, they would halt the arrest, beating, or interrogation if an individual cried out knowledge of such a crime. However, after the investigation the initial hardship would inevitably resume.

FINDING VOLUNTEERS

Certain institutional features may have facilitated or hindered the reporting of voluntary denunciations in the first half-century of the Romanov dynasty. As described in previous chapters, two types of institutional features affect the likelihood that people will denounce and thus the volume of denunciations reported within a voluntary environment: those that protect denouncers from retaliation or hardship for their participation and those that increase the likelihood that the people denounced will suffer and come to harm. Together, these enable socially opportunistic denouncing. However, institutional features were much less conducive to social opportunism in Romanov Russia than they were during the Spanish Inquisition. Russian officials were neither as protective of denouncers nor as harsh with the people denounced. Because of this, fewer individuals should have been willing to come forward to report transgressions.[24] This is not to say that those who did come forward were not motivated primarily by personal vendettas and rivalries. Rather, it was simply more difficult—but in no way impossible—to achieve such goals.

The authorities did try to make denouncing as easy as possible. One of the ways they did this was by accepting denunciations from everyone, including women, slaves, and non-Russians.[25] Denunciations were also welcome from convicts, and not just those imprisoned for minor crimes; the authorities dutifully investigated accusations by people jailed for brigandage, murder, and arson. Sentence length did not matter; even denunciations from people who had languished in prison for over a year were looked into.

But giving denouncers the benefit of the doubt only extended as far as receiving the initial report. After that, the content of the denunciation and the background of the denouncer could be investigated. Whereas in the Spanish Inquisition denouncers' testimony was accepted without question, in Muscovy they could be incarcerated or even tortured, though the latter only occurred if the official believed that the denouncer was not revealing everything that he knew.

During the Spanish Inquisition, maintaining the secrecy of denouncers' identities facilitated denunciations, as this protected them from community ostracism and reprisals. Such protection does not appear to have been prioritized to the same extent in Muscovy. Occasionally a denouncer and the person denounced were made to repeat their testimony in each other's presence, though this practice was uncommon. Witnesses could also be interrogated in front of the denouncer, though these people were almost always named by the denouncer and thus likely to be sympathetic to his cause. Perhaps the clearest indication that denouncers' identities were not kept as secret was the fact that they could be detained and put into custody. It seems unlikely that community members would fail to notice such an occurrence. Overall, it seems likely that at least some denouncers' identities were publicly known.[26]

Muscovites appear to have been relatively safe from punishments for false denunciations. Only in 1649 was an explicit law against this put into effect, and even that appears to have been rarely enforced.[27] Most of the men and women found to have denounced falsely went unpunished.

In Russia, the consequences of being denounced were milder than in the early decades of the Spanish Inquisition. A guilty verdict was not guaranteed. Russian authorities tried to be diligent in determining the truth of accusations, and in the event that a denunciation was determined to be false, the accused person went unpunished. Those who were found guilty were penalized, but not to the extent seen in the Inquisition. Some defendants were only reprimanded, though this was likely done publicly and may have had associated status costs. The majority of the people convicted received harsher punishments than this— indeed, some could be quite severe—but overall many escaped with a nonlethal beating and a week in jail. Even if found not guilty, however, those denounced generally suffered to some extent. They were incarcerated for the duration of the investigation, being either placed under guard or put in jail, and that surely constituted a real cost.[28] Additionally, those denounced could be tortured to elicit confessions, though this was uncommon.

Indeed, concern over the consequences of being denounced were real. In 1643, when Vasilii Polianskii heard that he had been denounced by a priest named Moisei Luk'ianov for making a lewd hand gesture and cursing the tsar, he promptly went into hiding. When questioned about his whereabouts, his wife explained, "My husband went to Moscow two weeks before Christmas. My neighbor, the boiar's son Anton Danilov, arrived here from Moscow and told me that my husband was living in Moscow. But prior to his trip to Moscow my husband lived at home with me." Polianskii eventually surrendered in Moscow, where he was beaten with cudgels as punishment for his infraction.[29]

Overall, the institutional features of the Sovereign's Word and Deed demonstrate some degree of suspicion toward denouncers and uncertainty as to whether a target would suffer, suggesting that opportunistic denunciations would be less prevalent than in other environments. Yet some early writers disputed this account. Adam Olearius, who documented his travel through Muscovy in the seventeenth century, reported that in "cases of hostile and spiteful informing, especially in cases concerning offense to His Majesty, the accused, without inquiry, argument, or reply, was sentenced to punishment and reduced to poverty, or was executed. . . . Cases of this sort among the Russians are countless."[30] Or, as Pierre-Charles Levesque put it over a century later, "The most respectable citizen could be arrested on the accusation of the lowliest pauper. A severe punishment awaited the calumniator, but if he was vigorous and a little sensible, he was sure to bring his enemy to loss."[31] A third writer, Nicolas-Gabriel Le Clerc, claimed that denunciation "was a sure means to do away with many victims of hate, ambition and personal interest."[32] Together, these writers indicated that in actuality it may have been easier to denounce for opportunistic social purposes than the previous discussion suggests.

Regardless, it remains clear that the Sovereign's Word and Deed indicated milder consequences for those denounced and less protection for denouncers than under the Spanish Inquisition. In other words, the potential costs of denouncing were higher and the expected benefits were lower. At best, denouncers faced substantial uncertainty as to how they would be treated after making a denunciation, and whether the person denounced would experience hardship.

So what led people to surmount this hurdle and denounce one another? It required the denouncer's desire to harm a particular member of the community to outweigh the risk of failure or hardship. As will be seen, emotional circumstances such as arguments or fights may have provided the impetus necessary for individuals to denounce with little thought to the consequences.

THE FREE AND THE IMPRISONED:
453 DENUNCIATIONS IN MUSCOVY

The denunciations described in this chapter come from the archives of the Service Chancellery of Moscow, the majority transcribed and published by Nikolai Iakovlevich Novombergskii in 1911.[33] Eighty-one additional denunciations come from a variety of other sources and were compiled, along with the records from Novombergskii, by Mark Lapman in 1982. Together, this aggregates to 411 case files spanning the period from 1605 to 1649. These files contain summary reports sent to Moscow, testimony transcripts, directives, and the final decisions made by Muscovite officials. Although not every case contains each of these components, each component exists in several hundred of the cases. There does not appear to be any systematic reason why cases are missing particular components.[34]

These are not the complete records for this time period. A massive fire occurred in Moscow in 1626 and destroyed almost all of the previous records. This explains the dearth of denunciations during the first years of the period of analysis. Otherwise, it is reasonable to assume that losses have been random.[35]

These denunciations do not always consist of one individual accusing another. Occasionally they involve one individual accusing more than one person, or two individuals jointly accusing a third. I have separated them so that every observation includes a single denouncer and a single person denounced. This raises the total from 411 denunciations to 453. The following analyses are based on this full set of 453 denunciations between individuals.

Figure 3.2 displays the distribution of denunciations over the period of observation. Denunciations generally increased over time, with the years from 1645 to 1649 having more than

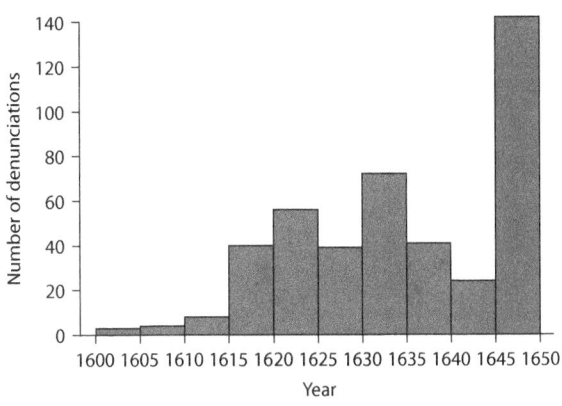

FIGURE 3.2 Number of denunciations by year.

any other time period. The next highest peak was from 1630 to 1634. The period with the fewest denunciations was during the earliest years of the 1600s, although this number may be artificially depressed by the fire in 1626 that destroyed many of the records.

The increasing number of denunciations over time could be due to Muscovites' greater awareness of the Sovereign's Word and Deed and increased understanding of how it functioned. The peak at the end of the 1640s corresponds with Aleksei Mikhailovich's ascension to the throne upon his father Mikhail's death in 1645. However, it is unclear if this was truly a driver of further denunciations, and it is somewhat precarious to put too much weight on these overall trends. Other Russian archives are known to house 404 additional denunciations. Although these show the same geographic distribution as the other records, they are more evenly distributed throughout the decades.[36]

Denunciations originated in all parts of Russia. The 453 examined in this chapter come from 99 different districts from central Moscow to the outer frontiers. (Districts were administrative units that included a number of villages and towns, along with an administrative center.)

Not only did denunciations come from all parts of Russia, but the people who made them came from all social categories. Eight distinct social groups are represented within these files, ranging from nobles to peasants. Other groups are provincial hereditary servitors, Cossacks, bondsmen, musketeers, church-people, and townspeople.[37] These social categories were very important; social status was usually specified in both legal and private documents, and it formed the "unquestioned cornerstone of the political order."[38] The distribution of these social categories within denunciations can be seen in table 3.1.[39] Social groupings are available for 325 denouncers and 253 of those denounced.

At the top of the social hierarchy were the nobles. Nobles were the power elite and had extensive landholdings, often worked by hundreds of peasant households. Next in status were the provincial hereditary servitors, who received an annual salary from Moscow and also controlled land farmed by peasants. They served as heavy-formation cavalry whenever their services were needed. Next came lower-ranking members of the armed services: musketeers and Cossacks. These groups lived off annual salaries in return for their military service, and although they tended small plots of land granted to them, they did not have the right to exploit peasant labor. Their control of their land was contingent on lifelong service in the military. Cossacks, some of whom were runaway peasants, were slightly lower on the social hierarchy than musketeers. After them came the townspeople, who would have made their livelihoods through handicrafts or trade. At the very bottom were peasants and bondsmen, who did

TABLE 3.1 Denunciations by Social Status
of Denouncer and Denounced

Status	Denouncer	Percentage	Denounced	Percentage
Nobles	39	12	32	13
Provincial hereditary servitors	62	19	53	21
Churchpeople	35	11	31	12
Musketeers	37	11	22	9
Cossacks	52	16	35	14
Townspeople	19	6	20	8
Peasants	45	14	38	15
Bondsmen	36	11	22	9
Total	**325**	**100**	**253**	**100**

Note: Percentages are rounded to the nearest whole number.

not have land of their own and instead farmed the fields of those higher up in the hierarchy. Churchpeople had their own hierarchy based on their status within the church: top officials owned land and serfs, while parish priests led lives similar to those of peasants. This group had the benefit of not having to pay taxes or provide military service. Little social mobility was possible across categories in this time period; as the century progressed, peasants were increasingly limited in their freedom of movement and gradually turned into dependent serfs.[40]

As can be seen from the table, not only did denouncers and those denounced come from the full range of positions in Russian society, but a similar percentage of both were members of each social category. Across all eight social categories, there is never more than two percentage points' difference between a category's proportion of denouncers and its proportion of those denounced. This provides prima facie evidence that denunciations were not directed consistently up or down the status hierarchy, but rather were reported by and against all social categories. Mikhail Romanov's expansion of the Sovereign's Word and Deed from an obligation held by nobles to an obligation for the entire population appears to have had its intended effect.[41]

Diversity also appears in the crimes for which people were denounced. As in the cases recorded by the Inquisition, denunciations in Muscovy were based primarily on verbal statements, many of which seem almost inconsequential. There was no clear understanding among the populace in the seventeenth century regarding the exact meaning of the Sovereign's Word and Deed, and this is reflected in the crimes for which people were denounced: they ranged from unsuitable language, administrative and economic crimes, and religious transgressions all the way up to treason and uprisings. The distribution across categories can be seen in table 3.2.[42]

Verbal statements make up 63 percent of all denunciations reported to the authorities. These include declarations by the accused of being the tsar or claiming to be a member of the tsar's family, suggestions that someone or something was better than the tsar, comments made about the tsar's legitimacy to rule, mentions of previous pretenders to the throne or praise of non-Russian rulers as being superior to the tsar, or unwillingness to take an oath or drink to the health of the tsar. Almost one-third (31 percent) of the denunciations in this category consist simply of insults made against the tsar. Actual statements include "You will find on me the same beard as on the Sovereign,"[43] "My feet

TABLE 3.2 Denunciations by Crime

Crime	Number	Percentage
Language	180	63
Treason	34	12
Uprising	31	11
Administration	19	7
Economic	17	6
Religious	4	1
Total	**285**	**100**

are better than Aleksei Mikhailovich's,"[44] "It seems to me that the tsar is not tsar by birth,"[45] "I spit on the tsar's business,"[46] and "I will not drink to the tsar's health."[47] The convict Savva Gnedushev was denounced for saying, "I sit in darkness and poverty now, but when I get out of jail I will be tsar over all of you common men."[48]

In one case, two Cossacks named Ivashko Vezema and Ortem Zharenyi had an argument near the voevoda's headquarters in Mozhaisk in August 1626. Vezema told Zharenyi that he was sick of Zharenyi's boasting and had made reports about his behavior to the sovereign in the past. Zharenyi responded by saying, "I wipe myself with your reports." For this Vezema denounced him, as the reports would have contained the sovereign's name and wiping oneself with the tsar's name could have been considered a punishable offense. An investigation ensued and Zharenyi was questioned. He explained that, although he had indeed made the statement, he was only referring to Vezema's oral reports, which could not have properly contained the sovereign's name. The authorities concluded that Vezema had misrepresented Zharenyi's words and ordered Vezema beaten with cudgels.[49]

The next most common categories of denunciations were treason and uprising, together totaling 23 percent of all denunciations. Treason generally referred to defection or running away: it applied to servitors who left their roles and peasants who vacated their lands. The former indicated disloyalty to the tsar, while itinerant peasants were presumed to be bringing information to foreign enemies. Examples of denunciations for treason come from Grishka Titov, who denounced two people: Matvei Kursakov, for allegedly inviting a Lithuanian spy into his home and providing him with information, and Gavrilka Zamietnin— Kursakov's accomplice—for planning on moving his family and possessions to Lithuania.[50]

Denunciations about uprisings allege involvement in rebellions. However, twenty-two of the thirty-one denunciations of this type were reports by nobles in their administrative capacity— *voevody* reporting on the region under their authority or traveling as representatives of the central government. As such, these reports should not properly be considered Word and Deed cases in the same manner as the others; they did not involve ordinary individuals reporting spontaneously to the authorities. Denunciations for uprisings reported by other social classes make up only 3 percent of all records. One of these was reported by a convict in Livny, who denounced a Cossack for confiding: "The sovereign does not give sufficient grants to us, and, therefore, a conspiracy of one hundred men or more has arisen among us."[51]

Several denunciations were also made for administrative or economic crimes. Although these would not be properly characterized as Word and Deed cases, they were sometimes denounced and investigated as such. Accusations of administrative crimes involved mainly bribery or corruption, though a few were for suppressing or failing to investigate alleged crimes of Word and Deed. For example, Fedor Lodyzhenskii, the voevoda of Kursk, was denounced for letting brigands out of jail for cash, and for making money from the sovereign's supplies.[52] About half of the economic denunciations were made against people who knew the location of various treasures, such as silver ore deposits or a stone "that glows in the darkness of night."[53] The others were allegations of counterfeiting money or stealing from the tsar's warehouses or treasuries. For example, Gregorii Siniaev was accused of making false coins and then trading them for legitimate ones.[54]

Finally, a few denunciations were made for what could most properly be characterized as religious transgressions. These were denounced as Word and Deed violations, but were determined to fall under the jurisdiction of the ecclesiastical authorities.[55]

With these records, it is possible to classify denunciations not just by allegation, but also by outcome. Cases often include information about the subsequent investigations, along with verdicts and punishments. The verdicts will be discussed in greater detail later in the chapter, but in the aggregate 56 percent of denounced individuals were found to be guilty. This represents a much lower conviction rate than in the early years of the Spanish Inquisition, when denunciations were almost guaranteed to be sustained. Among denunciations with guilty verdicts, 219 records detail the punishments meted out. These can be viewed in table 3.3.

Of the people punished, 21 percent received nothing more than a reprimand, which was likely made in public. The remaining 79 percent received more substantial punishment. A full

TABLE 3.3 Denunciations by Punishment

Punishment	Number	Percentage
Reprimand	45	21
Cudgels	71	32
Knout	39	18
Imprisonment	14	6
Exile	15	7
Death	11	5
Multiple severe	24	11
Total	**219**	**100**

50 percent of those convicted received a beating, either with cudgels or the knout. Sixteen percent of those who received a beating also spent at least a week in jail. Twenty-three percent of those found guilty were given especially severe sentences, either exile or death. The "Multiple Severe" category refers to individuals who faced death or exile in combination with other severe punishments.[56] In sum, the convicted faced about the same likelihood of a reprimand as a severe penalty (exile, death, or multiple severe), and about half of those convicted received a beating.

Now that the records of Word and Deed have been introduced in the aggregate, we can examine how the behavior of those in custody facing coercive incentives differed from that of free individuals for whom denouncing was voluntary. To make this comparison, the thirty-nine denunciations made by nobles first need to be removed. Denunciations by nobles were made in their role as administrators or envoys, not as independent citizens. As such, they tend to be reports about uprisings that were taking place in areas under their jurisdiction.

A further three denunciations made before Mikhail Romanov came to power in 1613 have also been removed. These were reported before the scope of the Sovereign's Word and Deed was expanded, which makes them difficult to interpret considering they were not made by nobles.

Next, the denunciations are divided into those by free individuals and those by people in the custody of local authorities. The former category includes 234 denunciations. The latter category includes 113 individuals who were in prison at the time of their denunciation, 27 who were in the process of being arrested, 21 who were being beaten by the authorities as punishment for some wrongdoing, and 16 who were in the process of being interrogated. Because all perceived an authority-based incentive to denounce, I group them together into a single category of 177 denunciations. The ensuing analysis compares patterns of denunciations between the 234 free individuals and the 177 individuals in custody to show how their motivations differed.

Before proceeding, it is important to note that this comparison requires that the two populations comprise similar individuals and that the only meaningful variation be the existence of the perceived incentive for those in the coercive environment. If individuals in custody are fundamentally different from free individuals, then that variation could instead be the cause of any differences in denunciation patterns between the two groups. It is difficult to know to what extent people in custody and those not in custody differed, but it is not unreasonable to posit some differences between the two populations. On the one hand, it is possible that the people in custody were more liable to commit crimes; this greater willingness to violate the norms of society may have made them more willing to fabricate denunciations than free individuals. Those in custody may also have been more self-interested and less swayed by prevailing morality. On the other hand, there may have been little different between the two populations. There may be systemic reasons why particular individuals ended up in custody that are related only loosely to their propensity to commit crimes. Without knowing which of these is the case, it is nevertheless important to consider the ways in which potential differences may affect or bias the results.

Even if the people in custody did differ fundamentally from those who maintained their freedom, there is no clear reason to expect such characteristics to systematically affect the patterns of denunciations expected under the coercion and volunteer models. There is little reason to think that those in custody would have been more likely to try to appease the authorities if they were not in custody, or that free individuals were more likely to harm their neighbors regardless of whether they were free. Most likely, any differences between the two populations along the dimensions examined are indeed attributable to the presence or absence of authority-based incentives, which is a function of environment, not disposition.

The exception to this, as already mentioned, may be prisoners' willingness to violate honesty norms and more frequently make false denunciations. Even if this were so, the presence or absence of perceived incentives should still affect the *motivation* behind false denunciations, even if their relative prevalence is biased. With this in mind, it is now possible to proceed to the results.

Table 3.4 displays the results of the analysis comparing people in custody to free individuals during the first several decades of the Romanov dynasty.[57] Due to differences in the data sources and context compared to the Spanish Inquisition, some of the

TABLE 3.4 Coercive Versus Voluntary Denunciations
in Muscovy, 1613–1649

	In custody (coercion model)	Free individuals (volunteer model)	χ^2
Prototypicality			
Economic crimes	19%	1%	25.72***
Number denounced			
Multiple people	18%	3%	23.63***
Geographic proximity			
Same district	81%	88%	3.53+
Status homophily			
Same status	35%	45%	1.12
Same rank	56%	74%	0.34
Falsity			
Denounced falsely	74%	28%	39.82***
No name	32%	7%	20.35***
Motivation			
Speak to tsar	46%	6%	87.51***
Benefits from authorities	65%	18%	7.14**
Spite	2%	18%	5.56*
N	177	234	

+ p < .10

* p < .05

** p < .01

*** p < .001

comparisons are operationalized in different ways. However, they test the same fundamental concepts.

Under the coercion model, denouncers should denounce prototypically, which means they provide the type of information in which the authorities are most interested in hopes of gaining something in return. In the case of Muscovy, this would seem to be denunciations about treason and uprisings, which had the greatest potential to cause harm to the fledgling dynasty. Yet in the records, these crimes were no more likely to be cited by people in custody than by free individuals.

However, one type of crime received a different sort of attention from the authorities, despite not appearing to have been fundamentally more of interest to them than the others. Denunciations for economic crimes were the only ones that led to denouncers being sent to Moscow to present their testimony, rather than having the cases handled within the locality. It is unclear why this was the case, but those in custody had a particular interest in being sent to Moscow, as this would give them access to someone higher up in the administrative hierarchy from whom they could potentially secure their release, either by providing useful information or by pleading their case. Thus, although it cannot be properly described as prototypical in the sense used in the previous chapter, denouncing economic crimes reveals a similar motivation of seeking a particular response from the authorities. Given this, it is unsurprising that 19 percent of denunciations made by people in custody were for economic crimes, whereas only 1 percent of those made by free individuals were of this type.

Another way to appease the authorities is through the amount of information provided: the more there is, the more likely they are to be satisfied with a particular denouncer. There is strong evidence of this dynamic in the Muscovy files, where 18 percent of those in custody but only 3 percent of free individuals denounced more than one person.

In the volunteer model, denouncers are motivated by social opportunism, and free individuals are most likely to denounce those with whom they interact regularly and seek advantage over. One indication of whether people have regular contact is geographic proximity. In the Muscovy files, assessing this requires looking at the administrative district within which people lived, as specific villages are not reported. Considering that each district covers a fairly broad territory, it comes as little surprise that more than 80 percent of all denunciations by those in custody and by free individuals were of people within the same district. However, the trend is in the expected direction; those in custody denounced someone from the same district 81 percent of the time, while this level for free individuals is 88 percent.

Two individuals explicitly identified as neighbors were Eliseika Afanas'ev and Ivashko Grigor'ev, both peasants in the Fedorovskii settlement in the Dmitrov region. In 1637, the two got into a drunken argument. During their altercation, Grigor'ev took his one-year-old son into his arms and declared, "He is of the tsar's seed." Afanas'ev reported Grigor'ev, who confessed and pled that he had no evil intentions. He received a beating with cudgels for his crime.[58]

Not only should denunciations be geographically closer under the volunteer model, but they should also originate from closer relationships, specifically people who interact regularly with one another. The records provide little in the way of systematic clues about the relationship between denouncers and the people they denounced, so this expectation cannot be properly evaluated for a majority of the denunciations. For small subsets, however, a comparison is still possible. In fifty-two cases, the alleged crimes took place during a private dinner or feast. These events could have up to about twelve attendees, and participants likely knew each other fairly well. Consistent with expectations, 83 percent of these denunciations were made by free individuals, compared to only 17 percent for those in custody. There are also six cases between known family members: three between cousins, two between uncles and nephews, and one between a son-in-law and father-in-law, all people who would have come regularly into contact with one another, but might not have felt the intense bonds of a nuclear family. Of these six familial denunciations, five were made by free individuals. Together, this suggests that free denouncers more often sought to harm particular individuals whom they encountered regularly in their everyday lives.

One case between cousins is particularly illustrative. In Livny in October 1649, Stepanka and Pankrashka Mezintsev were visiting a mutual friend's home when they began to argue. During the argument, Pankrashka mentioned that his brother, Pantelei, had burned a store of rye belonging to Stepanka. In reply, Stepanka shouted: "Get away from me, I'll deal with you through God, the Sovereign, the voevoda and the guba elders." Pankrashka responded by cursing those authorities, which Stepanka then reported to the authorities as a violation of Word and Deed.[59]

The volunteer model should also result in more denunciations between people of similar status, which can lead to animosity and status competition. In the denunciation records, the social group of both the denouncer and the person denounced is recorded in 164 cases. Within these, those in custody denounced someone of the same status 35 percent of the time, while free individuals denounced someone of the same status 45 percent of the time. Although this difference is not statistically significant, it is in the expected direction, with free denouncers making this type of denunciation more frequently.

It is also possible to take a closer look within certain social categories at the rank of those involved in denunciations. Rank was important to churchpeople, musketeers, and Cossacks, and it is sometimes indicated in the case files. A musketeer could either have no leadership responsibilities, be a leader of ten musketeers, be a leader of fifty musketeers, or be a chief musketeer. Similar gradations of rank existed for Cossacks and churchpeople. There are thirty-four cases involving individuals within those three social categories where the rank of both parties is known. Overall, 56 percent of those in custody within this subset accused someone of the same rank compared to 74 percent of free individuals. Again, this trend is in the expected direction.

The Muscovy files also provide information about whether denunciations were deemed after investigation to be true or false, along with some explanations given by the denouncers themselves regarding their actions. This provides a different type of evidence that was unavailable in the examination of the Spanish Inquisition in the previous chapter. Before comparing true and false denunciations between the two populations, however, it is important to note that this should not be construed as an exact accounting of how often denunciations were falsified, as it is unlikely that investigations were able to uncover falsehood perfectly. Similarly, the explanations given by denouncers as to why they denounced falsely should not be accepted with full credulity. Nevertheless, differences between the two groups are still revealing.

Overall, the authorities concluded that 74 percent of denunciations made by people in custody and 28 percent of those made by free individuals were fabricated.[60] Recall that there is no particular expectation as to whether the coercion model or volunteer model should have more false denunciations, just that they should be present in both. And as mentioned previously, it is possible that people in custody were fundamentally more predisposed to make false statements. Even focusing on free individuals, however, this means that more than one out of every four denunciations was concluded to be false.[61]

Looking more closely at the specifics of falsehood is particularly enlightening. In some cases, a denouncer never named the person he was accusing. This happened in 32 percent of all denunciations made by people in custody and in 7 percent of those made by free individuals. This disparity is revealing; certainly it would make little sense for free individuals, if they were motivated by local animosities, to declare knowledge of a Sovereign's Word or Deed without providing the perpetrator's name. People in custody, on the other hand, could be expected to use unspecified denunciations strategically, in an attempt to gain access to an official higher up in the administrative hierarchy who might then free them from incarceration.[62]

It is possible to gain direct additional insight into the motivations of denouncers from their own demands and explanations. For instance, 46 percent of those in custody demanded that they be allowed to provide their evidence directly to the tsar. This was another attempt to gain access to someone higher in the administrative hierarchy in the hopes of obtaining particular benefits. The case of Fed'ka Semenov shows his attempt at this particular strategy. Below is the text of a letter sent to Moscow by the local voevoda regarding this case:

> In our time, Sovereign, in this year of 1648 on the ninth day of January the Sevsk gatekeeper Iskushko Ignat'ev came into our headquarters and told us, your slaves, that the convict, Fed'ka Semenov, had cried out from the jail and claimed to have knowledge of a sovereign's word . . . And we questioned him, Sire, about what sovereign's word he, Fed'ka, claimed to know . . . And he, Fed'ka Semenov, told us, your slaves, under questioning that . . . the word he knew was against his master, the landowner Leontil

Potriasov. But he claimed it was impossible to discuss his charge with us. And we, your slaves, ordered him thrown back in jail as before to await your order, Sire . . . And on this subject, Sire, we will act as you instruct us.[63]

Unfortunately for Fed'ka Semenov, the authorities in Moscow were not interested in meeting him in person to discuss his denunciation. They responded with the following:

> When this decree reaches you, then you should ask Fed'ka Semenov what sovereign's deed he has on his mind and order that he write it down in his own hand or have his spiritual father do so and give it to you sealed. Then you, by our decree, should have the document sent to Moscow. But do not send Semenov himself to Moscow. However, if Fed'ka Semenov is illiterate and will not talk to his spiritual father, then you should tell him to reveal the sovereign's deed to you in private, and you should write it down in your own hand. Only if he does not reveal our deed to you alone are you then, by our decree, authorized to torture him in the inquiry.[64]

Fed'ka Semenov finally admitted that the denunciation was false and that he was simply trying to get out of jail.

Compared to people in custody, free denouncers were quite different. Only 6 percent of the latter demanded to present their evidence directly to the tsar. As they were seeking primarily to harm other local actors, it did not matter who investigated the case.

In cases where people admitted ultimately to false denunciations, they sometimes gave reasons for this behavior. Although the reliability of these is questionable, differences between the two populations are nevertheless revealing.

Sixty-five percent of denouncers in custody admitted that they were trying to gain benefits from the authorities, such as relief from a beating or release from jail. Conversely, only 18 percent of free individuals admitted that they were seeking similar benefits. As one prisoner put it,

If I were allowed to go to Moscow, then someone in Moscow would take me out of jail. Here there is no one to intercede for me. . . . By claiming to know of a sovereign's word, I hoped to get out of jail. If I had been allowed to go to Moscow, I would have confessed this and not accused them [the defendants]. My thoughts were evil due to feelings of guilt, desperation and a longing to see the light of day.[65]

Another prisoner was substantially more desperate in his plea. The following comes from a petition written in the summer of 1646:

To the Tsar, Sovereign and Grand Prince, Aleksei Mikhailovich of all Rus. Your slave, the prisoner Fedotko Korovaev of Riazan', Vasilii's son, petitions you out of the darkness . . . In this year, Sire, in 1646, while sitting in jail I claimed to have knowledge of a sovereign's word and the voevoda, Dmitrii Ovtsyn, wrote to you about this to the Service Chancellery in Moscow. And in response to his dispatch your sovereign decree was sent from the Service Chancellery ordering that I be interrogated. And I, your slave, was interrogated according to your decree. But your final sovereign judgment regarding me has not come, Sire, and I sit in vain, without guilt dying of hunger and hardship . . . But even though I have done nothing wrong, the elders will not let me go without orders from you. Dear Sovereign, bestow on me, your imprisoned slave, a sovereign decree ordering my release so that I, your slave, sitting in jail will not perish from cold and hunger. Tsar, Sovereign, I beg of you, Please.[66]

The same motivation applied to those being taken into custody or beaten. In a small village owned by the Chudov Monastery, a large group of peasants were sitting down to a feast on April 1, 1638 when a commotion arose and Petrushka Miagkoi began beating Semionka Varaksa. Running away, Varaksa fled into the street and cried out that he knew of a Sovereign's Word and Deed. When questioned by the voevoda, he admitted that he had nothing to report: he had cried out to avoid the beating and did not have any knowledge of a political offense.[67]

Although many false denouncers pled insanity or drunkenness as the motivation behind their actions, some—18 percent of free individuals but only 2 percent of those in custody— admitted being motivated by spite. The prevalence of spite by free individuals can be further seen in specific denunciations, and not just in ones found to be false. One example took place in 1635, when Stepanka Denisov and Olferko Shuvaev had a dispute over a piece of land. During the argument, Denisov dared Shuvaev to go to the voevoda to resolve the dispute. Shuvaev replied, "I thumb my nose at you and the voevoda." Denisov responded that he would take the dispute all the way to Moscow, to which Shuvaev retorted, "The one on whom you're counting . . . He doesn't scare me at all." Denisov then went to the voevoda and denounced Shuvaev for indicating that he was not frightened of the sovereign. The authorities found the alleged behavior to have been truly committed.[68]

In nine denunciations, an insult against a particular individual was extended to include the tsar, including three defendants who allegedly "gave the finger" to the person with whom they were arguing and said "This is for you and the Sovereign."[69] Such behavior is a clear indication of animosity. Eight out of these nine denunciations were made by free individuals. The verdict is also known for six of them: five were deemed to be true. Individuals often gave their enemies the ammunition with which to denounce them honestly; failing that, a denunciation could always be fabricated.

Together, the evidence suggests that denunciations made by people in custody were attempts to gain freedom, whereas those reported by free individuals were motivated by social opportunism. In Romanov Russia, as during the Spanish Inquisition, the coercion model and the volunteer model are supported as descriptions of denouncer motivation under different institutional conditions. However, there still remains a puzzle of why free individuals in Russia found denouncing worth it. As described earlier, people could face hardship and imprisonment for making a denunciation. The person accused might be found not guilty or could go free with only a reprimand. The costs of denouncing could be substantial and the benefits uncertain. Nevertheless, people denounced to harm their neighbors.

The case files provide clues to this puzzle. In many instances—including several of the examples provided in this chapter—denouncers were spurred by a precipitating and emotionally charged event. These events, which often involved fights or an argument, provided the extra impetus to denounce for socially opportunistic reasons. The voevoda of Khotmyshsk described such behavior in a letter to Moscow in 1648:

> After fighting, people make [political] denunciations against [one another]. When they sober up, they retract their denunciations and petition you, sire, and bring to me their confessions explaining that they do not remember anything that happened when they were drunk. And whoever among any of the ranks of people in Khotmyshsk, serving out their responsibility to you, sire, has falsely claimed knowledge of a political offense in drunkenness and in the heat of argument, I have reported to you but have had no orders from you.[70]

It is possible to observe such a pattern of behavior in the denunciations. The records indicate when an alleged crime occurred during a fight, which would have increased the hostility among combatants and onlookers and heightened the emotional intensity for those present. The records also indicate how long it took after an alleged offense was committed for it to be reported to the authorities. If emotional intensity and overt hostility motivated individuals to denounce in this setting, then denunciations by free individuals should arise more often during fights and be reported immediately while tensions remained high. The results of this analysis can be seen in table 3.5.

While only 12 percent of denunciations by people in custody allege criminal behavior during a fight, 33 percent of those made by free individuals do so. Such denunciations were far more

TABLE 3.5 Fighting and Elapsed Time to Denounce

	In custody (coercion model)	Free individuals (volunteer model)	χ^2
Circumstances			
Fight	12%	33%	22.89***
Elapsed time			
Same day	15%	33%	4.88*
By next day	29%	47%	4.31*
N	177	234	

* $p < .05$

** $p < .01$

*** $p < .001$

Note: These results are similar when only prisoners are included in the "In Custody" column.

prevalent in the latter setting and likely provided the emotional intensity and animosity necessary for individuals to risk the potential hardships associated with denouncing and make a report. This heightened emotion applies to those directly involved in the fight and to spectators, who likely supported one disputant or the other. For example, two peasants entered into an argument over tax assessments during a village meeting in Isakovskoe in 1620. One peasant, Kirilov, suggested they take their dispute to Moscow, and the other, Overkiev, made a disparaging comment about the tsar's father in response. Kirilov intended to report this treasonous statement but Overkiev then beat him, leaving him lame. It was Kirilov's son who ultimately reported Overkiev for his remark.[71]

The elapsed time between an alleged crime and its reporting provides further evidence that emotional intensity spurred voluntary denunciations. This figure is available for 166 of the denunciations. One-third (33 percent) of denunciations by free individuals were reported on the same day as the alleged crime compared to only 15 percent by those in custody. Looking at denunciations made by the end of the following day maintains this pattern: almost half of denunciations were reported within one day by free individuals, compared to 29 percent of denunciations by those in custody.[72]

One of the denunciations is particularly illustrative of this dynamic. While drinking heavily together on February 9, 1649, Kondrashka Kozhukhov made a disparaging remark about his cousin Vas'ka's father, which led to an intense argument. The offended cousin went immediately to the voevoda to complain about this disrespect and Kondrashka followed, making an accusation of Word and Deed against his relative. The cousins continued to argue with each other throughout

the voevoda's investigation, exclusively about property matters, and revealed no information about political crimes. The
voevoda eventually threw them both in jail until they sobered
up. Six days later, on February 15, they presented a joint petition to the voevoda, claiming that they had reconciled and
begging forgiveness.[73]

Overall, heightened emotional settings led to quick denunciations by free individuals; such settings made them more willing
to accept the risks of denouncing in the hopes of harming a
neighbor.[74]

CONCLUSION

Despite the difficulties facing Mikhail Romanov when he came
to power at age sixteen in 1613, he and his father successfully
launched the family dynasty on a trajectory that would remain
ascendant for over three hundred years. Through the use of the
Sovereign's Word and Deed and other policies, Russia stabilized
over the course of the seventeenth century.[75]

Despite this success, the Sovereign's Word and Deed presents
a very different institution from that conceived in Spain two
centuries prior. In Russia, the authorities imposed potentially
burdensome costs on those who came forward to provide information. Denouncers' identities were not protected, nor was their
general well-being assured. Their targets were not guaranteed
punishment, as the authorities expended real effort toward dis-
tinguishing between what was true and what was false. Nevertheless, people denounced. For people already in custody, the
perceived possibility of improving their situation or gaining
their freedom was sufficient to elicit denunciations. For free

individuals, intense emotions resulting from fights and confrontations helped denouncers to overcome their reticence and report opportunistically on their neighbors.

In 1649, perhaps because the political situation was more stable and the tsar's grasp on power more secure, the authorities grew tired enough of the prevalence of false denouncing to do something about it. A law code was released in which three of the twenty-two articles on "The Tsar's Honor and How to Safeguard the Tsar's Health" were about consequences for false denouncing. Article 17 decrees: "If someone has initiated an important case involving the sovereign or a treason charge against someone, but did not support it, and it is established about that conclusively that he deliberately initiated such a [false] case against someone: inflict on that informer [the sanction that] the person whom he accused would have deserved."[76] Article 14 in particular touches on some of the denouncer motivations described in this chapter:

> If slaves of any category proceed to initiate a treason case on their own behalf; but subsequently they themselves proceed to say that they know of no treason case, but that they had initiated the treason case to escape a beating by someone [the accused], or they were drunk; beat them with the knout for that, and having beaten them with the knout, give them back to their owners.[77]

It is unclear what impact these codified consequences had on the prevalence of denouncing. According to historian Angela Rustemeyer, they were infrequently enforced.[78] Regardless, the institution of the Sovereign's Word and Deed persisted until 1762, when it was abolished during the reign of Catherine II. Her reason for the decree was most revealing: "It was in the name of people falsely and maliciously denounced that her decree was dedicated; she noted how individuals from almost every walk of life were freely able to destroy their masters and enemies out of spite and revenge."[79] As is apparent from the denunciations, Catherine II was only partially right. Although individuals did not generally use the system to destroy their masters, they were more than happy to do so to harm their enemies.[80]

The next chapter shifts to a more modern context to demonstrate the presence of similar dynamics: Nazi Germany in the twentieth century. Despite the Nazis' use of sophisticated propaganda, motivations to denounce did not change with the passing of the centuries. Nazi Germany is representative of the volunteer model, and the chapter focuses in particular on officials' attempts to reconcile their desire for local information with their dislike of false and petty reports. As will be seen, this was a dilemma that they never successfully resolved.

4

NAZI GERMANY

After years of striving for power, Adolf Hitler was appointed Chancellor of Germany on January 30, 1933. Less than a month later, the Reichstag building—the home of the German Parliament—burned to the ground from what appeared to be arson. Hitler immediately blamed the fire on a communist plot to overthrow the government and used the incident as an opportunity to suspend civil liberties across Germany. This cemented his rise to power, as he began reorganizing the laws, the courts, and the police to consolidate his authority and start Germany on the path toward totalitarianism.

One of the ways that this transition was brought about was through the creation of the Gestapo, the secret police tasked with discovering, investigating, and eradicating all hints of treason against the new regime. So successful were they at their jobs that for decades historians referred to them as "omniscient, omnipotent, and omnipresent."[1] As laws became more restrictive and surveillance more universal, Germans had to be careful about the words they spoke and the people with whom they interacted. Even the tiniest indication that someone did not fully support the regime could lead to his or her arrest, torture, and possible execution.

Yet, according to more recent historians, the much-feared secret police were so few in number that there was only one Gestapo officer for every ten thousand residents of Germany.[2] Instead, the ubiquitous surveillance felt by the populace was due largely to widespread denunciations made by ordinary citizens. Although exact numbers are unknown because most of the records were destroyed, historian Klaus-Michael Mallmann reported that in 1937 alone, 17,168 individuals were denounced for violations of the law against treachery—only one of the many laws that a person could be denounced for violating. The total number of denunciations reported throughout the twelve years of the Nazi regime was likely in the millions.[3]

These denunciations were made in an environment that accords well with the volunteer model. There were no negative consequences for not denouncing and no authority-based rewards for coming forward. Instead, people made their accusations at their own discretion throughout the duration of the regime. Despite a lack of variation, this setting offers two key benefits for the study of denunciations. First, it provides insight into whether the use of sophisticated propaganda was able to affect denouncer motivation and lead to more ideologically driven behavior. Second, many communications between Nazi officials regarding denunciations survive. These reveal the role of the authorities in structuring institutions of social control, along with the internal debates that this process engendered.

This chapter details the institutional features that facilitated this period's remarkably large volume of denunciations through an examination of several studies looking at over eight hundred denunciations across different regions of Germany. As predicted by the volunteer model, German denouncers were motivated primarily by social opportunism. Yet, despite the fact that the authorities quickly became aware of this, it was something they found themselves unable—and unwilling—to change.

HISTORICAL BACKGROUND

In 1920, the National Socialist German Worker's Party—commonly known as the Nazi Party—was created on a platform of nationalism and anti-Semitism. Hitler became the party's leader in 1921, and in November 1923 he led an unsuccessful uprising against the government. For this, he was imprisoned for high treason and the Nazi Party was banned from Germany.

Yet Hitler only spent a year in jail for his crimes. After his release in December 1924, he convinced the authorities to reinstate the Nazi Party, promising that it would only seek power through legitimate means. By 1928, this had proven unsuccessful; in that year's national election, the Nazis received less than 3 percent of parliamentary votes.

Crises in Germany, however, reshaped German politics. The Great Depression that had begun in 1929 led to widespread unemployment and economic distress, and by 1932 an estimated one in three German workers was unemployed.[4] Simultaneously the political system began to collapse, with no government able to gain a parliamentary majority in the Reichstag after 1930. Worries about the breakdown of traditional values had also been growing ever since the fall of the imperial monarchy.[5] Together, these crises fueled the rise of extremist parties and made the Nazis' message increasingly appealing, especially among members of the middle class and people who had not previously voted.[6] However, the Nazis held some appeal for all social groups; they became the "catch-all party of social protest."[7]

Widespread dissatisfaction with the direction of the country thus garnered Hitler's party more than 18 percent of the popular vote in 1930, making the Nazis the second-largest party in the Reichstag. When they won 33 percent of the seats in November 1932, Hitler was appointed Chancellor of Germany as part of a coalition government—a triumph for the Nazi Party after its years-long struggle for legitimacy.

The coalition meant that the Nazis had limited power with which to enact their reforms. The Reichstag fire in 1933 provided the perfect excuse for them to take stronger action. Although it remains unclear who perpetrated the fire or if it was intentionally planned by the Nazis themselves, what is known is that on the night of February 27, just one week before the next parliamentary elections, the building that housed the German parliament burned to the ground. A Dutch communist named Marinus van der Lubbe who was nearby was charged with setting the fire.

Hitler's reaction was swift and unequivocal. Calling the fire part of a communist plot to overthrow the government, he urged the president to announce the Reichstag Fire Decree, which tightened laws against political crimes and suspended civil liberties, including protections against extended detainment. This led to the immediate and violent suppression of communists, socialists, and trade unionists throughout Germany. After the March elections gave the Nazis 45 percent of the seats in the Reichstag, Hitler convinced the body to pass the Enabling Act of 1933, which gave the cabinet the right to enact laws without parliament's consent or participation. This democratic vote essentially gave Hitler dictatorial powers.

From this beginning, the government passed laws that increasingly restricted the freedom of German residents. Decrees in 1933 and 1934 criminalized statements or expressions made against the Nazis and other organizations of the Third Reich. Such expressions, no matter how careless or innocuous, could now be strictly punished. Police were empowered to spy on private communications, arrest people without charging them, and conduct searches and seizures of private homes.

These new laws were bolstered by two concurrent developments. By March 1933, Special Courts to prosecute cases of treason were established in every regional capital; these not only curtailed rights to a defense, but also forbade appeals. In the same year, preexisting police forces were modified and transformed to create the Gestapo, a new force that was more centralized and acted outside of the traditional jurisdiction of law. Within months of the Reichstag fire, Hitler had implemented a system in which repressive laws were enacted, a judicial system was set up to hear violations of those laws, and a secret police was established to funnel violators into the new courts. Almost instantaneously, a police state was born.

Figure 4.1 displays a map of Germany in 1933 at the time of Hitler's ascent to power. Over the course of the next twelve years, Germany would come to occupy much of Europe.

Despite these maneuvers and his party's widespread violence, Hitler's initial grip on power was somewhat tenuous. This was especially true because the Nazis were not trying simply to rule; they were actively attempting to dismantle and replace the political and legal structure of the German state. Their precariousness can be seen in the process by which they consolidated power. Their first several years of governance could best be described as power-sharing between the Nazis and the old conservative forces in state and society.[8] Although they were quick to establish their own courts and police force, these remained separate from the preexisting courts and police. Only gradually did the Gestapo and the Special Courts extend their authority: in

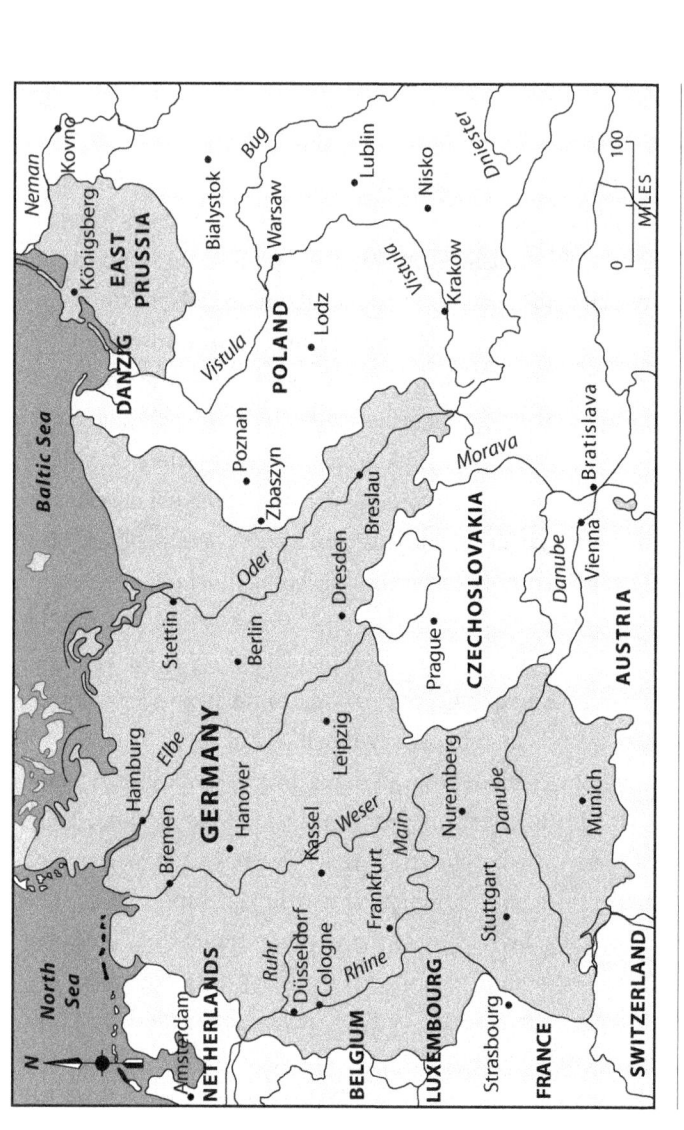

FIGURE 4.1 Germany, 1933.

Courtesy of the US Holocaust Memorial Museum and adapted.

1936, the preexisting political police forces were subsumed under the Gestapo, and by 1938 any crime could be prosecuted in the Special Courts so long as it was sufficiently "grave and reprehensible."[9]

But controlling the courts, the police, and the laws was insufficient for complete and secure power. In order to ensure full compliance and prevent undesired behavior, the Nazis needed a way of obtaining information from the populace. To do this, they encouraged Germans to come forward and denounce their neighbors for any wrongdoing against the state. This was promoted as following in the spirit of *Volksgemeinschaft*, or German national community to uphold and help enforce collective unity.[10] By denouncing and condemning outsiders or transgressors, a new racial folk community could be created to replace modern individualism and isolation, all united behind Hitler himself.[11]

NAZI PROCEDURES OF DENUNCIATION

In order for a person to make a denunciation, he first had to contact the authorities in some way. In Nazi Germany, there was no formalized procedure for doing this. Denunciations could be made directly to the Gestapo or to various party and state organizations. They could be made in person or by letter, and letters could be signed or anonymous. Many written denunciations were sent to party officers such as welfare administrators, precinct captains, or district leaders. In Düsseldorf, denouncers could also file their reports at "advice centers," which sought to build bridges between the party and society.[12] Sometimes localities distributed questionnaires to residents and encouraged them to name any transgressors in their communities. Denunciations were even mailed to newspapers, which sometimes published them. All of these methods were accorded equal credibility. Regardless of where or how a denunciation was made, it was generally passed on to the Gestapo.[13]

Once the Gestapo received a denunciation, they inevitably followed up. The procedures used for investigations varied, but they included spying on the suspect, monitoring mail, and questioning neighbors and witnesses. The Gestapo could also arrest the suspect and take him in for questioning. The arrest itself could be dangerous; instructions to officers to get tough with antisocial elements led to an increase in the number of people shot or injured while allegedly resisting arrest.[14]

When suspects were brought in for questioning, they first filled out a form providing detailed information about their family, their job and career, and their religious and party affiliation.[15] After that was complete, the interrogation ensued, ranging from verbal questioning to more forceful techniques, sometimes involving physical violence or torture. Suspects did not have recourse to a lawyer.

After the investigation was complete, there were several possible next steps. The best-case scenario for a suspect was to be released, with or without a warning. The files of the alleged transgression and its investigation would remain, however, and people who were released could still be placed under indefinite police surveillance.

Suspects might also be placed in "protective custody," which served as a form of arbitrary incarceration. Technically the Gestapo headquarters was supposed to approve of all protective custody cases, but this appears to have been largely pro forma. The custody could be as short- or as long-term as the investigating officers recommended. Once placed in protective custody, a suspect could languish there indefinitely without access to a lawyer, a trial, or any sort of legal appeal. A particularly harsh form of protective custody was to be sent to a concentration camp.

Finally, suspects could go to trial, usually before a Special Court administered by three judges who presided over each case. No juries were used and the judges took an active role in examining witnesses and calling for evidence.[16] Technically, standards of evidence required three witnesses to corroborate any charges, but this was left largely to the discretion of the Gestapo and the courts. During a trial, defense attorneys had no right to demand proof of the charges and the judges themselves decided which evidence was to be considered. Judges were instructed to not focus on the details of the particular law in question or whether legal procedures were being followed carefully. Instead, they were encouraged to decide a case rapidly and, as the propaganda minister Joseph Goebbels declared in 1942, "based less on law than on the fundamental idea that lawbreakers are to be eliminated from the community of the *Volk*."[17]

Defendants who were found guilty were either sentenced to time in prison, sent to a concentration camp, or executed. Judges generally had broad latitude in deciding which punishment to assign and defendants had no right to an appeal. Severe punishments could be imposed even if the defendant was accused only of making a verbal statement that disagreed with some aspect of the Nazi agenda, and they grew increasingly harsh with the advent of war in 1939. On average, cases that went to court during the 1930s took about three months from the time of the initial denunciation until the final verdict, and about six months during the war years of the 1940s.[18]

It is important to note that individuals' experiences with the Gestapo and the court system could vary dramatically depending on who they were. For members of marginalized groups such as communists, socialists, and Jews, the experience tended to be substantially harsher. "Ordinary" Germans who were convicted were more likely to be sentenced to prison, while Jews were more likely to be sent to concentration camps.[19] Denunciations against ordinary Germans were also more likely to be dismissed by the Gestapo and the courts without any punishment being meted out.[20] Even for these suspects, however, the fact that there was no right to a lawyer or to a fair trial meant that there was a great deal of uncertainty throughout the process.

Overall, this was a voluntary system. Although it held considerable power, the Gestapo was generally a "reactive" police force.[21] Rather than actively identifying suspects, officers often relied on citizens to come forward and denounce. As the former Cologne Gestapo chief Emanuel Schäfer testified in his postwar trial, the Gestapo "let things come to them."[22] To some degree, this was out of necessity, as its members were few in number and did not have the resources to conduct widespread surveillance. However, it was also by choice; the Nazis were more active when it came to identifying and policing marginalized groups, but they seemed content to encourage ordinary citizens to self-monitor.[23] They offered no rewards for denunciations and no punishment for people who knew of deviant behavior but did not report it. Denouncing was purposely never codified into law as a requirement. Instead, the Nazis encouraged volunteers and eagerly investigated whatever information was willingly provided.

In addition to there being no actual authority-based incentives to denounce, it is also unlikely that Germans perceived any. Denouncing was not seen as a particularly reliable way of getting in the authorities' good graces and deriving future benefits. The Gestapo was far more interested in denunciations than in the individuals who brought them, and they sometimes viewed denouncers as questionable moral figures.[24] If a person wanted to gain direct benefits from the Nazis, a better course of action was to join the Nazi Party or become otherwise involved in their cause. Heinrich Weber of Hildesheim, for example, described how during the Nazi years his father attended "educational evenings" designed to instruct community members about National Socialist doctrine. Weber's father attended these meetings not because he was a loyal Nazi, but because he feared the Nazis would call for a boycott of his painting business if he did not.[25] Such shows of support and compliance were a far more reliable path to pleasing or appeasing the Nazis than making denunciations.

Several key institutional features contributed to the widespread reporting of voluntary denunciations throughout Germany. Due to their insatiable desire for information about the populace and the perpetually expanding scope of laws regulating behavior, Nazi authorities unwittingly created an institution that facilitated socially opportunistic denouncing on a massive scale.

AN ARMY OF VOLUNTEERS

The German authorities did everything they could to facilitate the reporting of denunciations and ensure that it was easy and costless for the denouncer. Their eagerness to uncover and punish wrongdoing also guaranteed that being denounced resulted in a great deal of fear and uncertainty, even if defendants were ultimately exonerated.

The first way that the Nazis protected denouncers was by making anonymous denouncing available. The Gestapo investigated anonymous allegations with the same zeal they devoted to reports from identifiable sources. Even if a denouncer went to them in person, it was at the Gestapo's discretion whether that person's identity would be revealed to the person denounced. There was no procedure in place requiring them to act one way or the other, but they did seem to honor requests for anonymity, which would reduce a would-be denouncer's fear of sanctions from the community or retaliation from his or her target.

Anonymity was also available by other means. For example, in 1943 anonymous letters were sent to the authorities in Düsseldorf complaining about a thirty-five-year-old saleswoman named Miss Wollenberg. When these letters failed to engender the desired response, a further letter followed up:

> We have been writing repeatedly . . . but till today the letters have not been followed up. I would now like to very politely request you to urgently take up the matter of Miss Wollenberg, employed in the firm Brenningmeyer. Miss Wollenberg has relations with men from the Gestapo that involve intimate matters. Her father is a full Jew, so are her mother and brothers. Frau Wollenberg comes to Litzmannstadt where she gets news and objects that are smuggled. Frau Wollenberg is also oriented against the present government, which comes out in her talks. . . . Frau Wollenberg does not deserve a place as salesgirl in the firm. There are definitely more upright women who can take her place. Miss Wollenberg is extremely refined and cultivated and has put hurdles on the way of many colleagues.[26]

This letter was signed by "Two salesgirls from the same firm." The names given were Frau Hess and Miss Persil.

The Gestapo investigated and concluded that, despite not being Jewish herself (she was adopted), Miss Wollenberg was guilty of becoming "Jewish in her ways" and she was dismissed from her job.[27] The denouncers, on the other hand, remained mysterious. When the Gestapo tried to contact them to gather additional information, Frau Hess denied having written the letter; she had in fact left the firm some time before. The

second woman could not be traced. It is likely that the denouncers had in fact disguised their identities in order to attack a
colleague.

Even when accurate names were provided, the lack of specificity in many denunciations—for example, allegations of being
a "friend of the Jews"—may have made it difficult for those
denounced to ascertain the identity of their accusers. Similarly,
many Gestapo files describe "suspicious behavior" as the sole
reason for initiating an investigation. In many respects, the
Gestapo was focused more on investigating individuals identified by denouncers than on investigating particular crimes.

Denouncers were also assured of having their reports taken
in good faith and not being second-guessed because of their
backgrounds or motivations. The Gestapo was far more interested in the information contained within a denunciation than
on the identity or characteristics of the denouncer. Denouncing
was not limited to any particular economic or social strata, and
even though certain denouncers were noted as being mentally
deficient, their testimony was still accorded merit.

Even if an ulterior or instrumental motive was evident, denunciations were still considered plausible and were investigated.
Students who had been punished in school could denounce the
very teachers who had punished them. Jilted lovers could
denounce their former partners to the police. The following clear
example of a personal vendetta was investigated:

> In December 1937 allegations were made about the behavior of
> Mayor Hoffmann of Leidersbach, near Würzburg. Not for the
> first time, the accuser was a disenchanted Party member, a drunk
> with a police record, and rarely in regular employment. The prob-
> lem probably started, according to the dossier, when some years
> earlier Hoffmann had disciplined the denouncer for appearing

drunk in SA uniform; since then the man had sought revenge, and pursued the mayor with a series of denunciations.[28]

Even known false denouncers were still accorded attention. In 1935, a family in Würzburg reported their neighbor, Hans Fichtel, for saying "To hell with the Swastika flag!"[29] The Gestapo investigated, despite the family's being well known to the police for previous false denunciations.

Not only did the Gestapo investigate such dubious reports, but this emphasis on information over motivation went so far as to generally prevent any action from being taken against false denouncers. Karl Hof of Zeil admitted that the damning testimony he had provided during a 1941 investigation was untrue:

> I planned that I would take revenge on this man at the first and best opportunity . . . I considered that the time had come for me to avenge myself on Pastor Bach, which is why I made the statements already known to you. In answer to why I put things together in this way, I can only say that it just popped into my head, that is, I had not thought it over beforehand.[30]

Despite his blunt confession that he had fabricated his prior testimony, Hof was not punished.

In addition to protecting denouncers, certain institutional features facilitated the harming of the people denounced. One of the mechanisms for this was the Gestapo's acceptance of all types of reports as valid. The scope of crimes was so great that credibly denouncing a particular individual became astonishingly easy, especially as the Nazis passed increasingly restrictive laws. Perhaps the most enlightening example of just how petty denunciations could be, and just how culpable everyone was, was the Gestapo's response to denunciations for behavior that had not been illegal at the time of its occurrence. They looked into anti-Hitler statements made before Hitler came to power in 1933. Associations with Jews in the past were also taken seriously, even if they had been terminated with the ascension of the Nazis. A Würzburg postman was denounced in 1936 for subletting part of his four-room apartment to a Jew before 1935, when that activity had not yet become illegal.[31]

Even behavior that was illegal at the time of its occurrence was never clearly defined. The boundary between legal and illegal behavior was vague, as the regime attempted to isolate and later eliminate not just Jews, but also "handicapped," "antisocial," and "mentally ill" individuals. The latter category came to encompass all sorts of behavior, including prostitution and poor housekeeping.[32] Simply listening to foreign radio stations was considered a crime, as was the ill-defined category of "malicious gossip." In the former case, denouncers often described "the way people spoke" as leading to the suspicion that their information came from foreign radio broadcasts.[33] Individuals could have each other investigated on the basis of vague suspicions without reporting any concrete facts at all.

Decades after the Nazi regime ended, historian Eric Johnson conducted a study asking 188 survivors in Cologne whether they had participated in illegal activities under Hitler. Almost every single person answered in the affirmative, with 53 percent having listened to illegal radio broadcasts, 27 percent having told illegal jokes, and another quarter having shared news about the Jewish extermination. Only one of the 188 respondents described being involved in active resistance, yet any one of them could have been punished had the Nazis been aware of their activities.[34]

Thus, anyone could be credibly denounced, and being credibly denounced generally led to hardship. Being denounced immediately brought one to the scrupulous attention of the Gestapo, which included a high likelihood of experiencing some degree of difficulty, regardless of one's innocence or guilt. The use of torture during interrogations became sufficiently common that the courts grew resigned over time to defendants appearing with obvious marks of bodily harm.[35] Investigators were also free to take their time, as laws of protective custody stipulated no constraints on how long a person could be held.

Defendants who made it to court were often no better off than when they were in the hands of the Gestapo, as the courts were highly politicized. In 1939, Karl Engert, the vice-president of the People's Court—the most important of the Special Courts— emphasized its biased nature when he "demanded that its members must be politicians first and judges second."[36] The judges in the regular courts were little different.

Even if a case was dismissed by the courts, this did not mean that the defendant was out of danger. The Gestapo sometimes rearrested people immediately after their acquittals and sent them to concentration camps. This became so prevalent that instructions were written in 1939 that required them to wait until after the acquitted defendant was at least outside of the courtroom before making the arrest. By the third day of the war, the Gestapo was also authorized to execute "guilty" individuals spared by the courts. Below is one such example:

> A milker working on a farm near Düsseldorf was denounced on October 3, 1939, for listening to Radio Moscow and for making unflattering comments about life in Nazi Germany. He was soon interrogated and his case was sent to the Special Court, but by November 20 the court said there was too little evidence to proceed to trial . . . But the Gestapo was not content with this decision, and, in an example of police justice . . ."corrected" the court's

verdict by placing the accused in protective custody on December 2. Just over a week later he was sent . . . to a concentration camp . . . his death was reported on November 6, 1940.[37]

Even if a suspect's innocence was ultimately recognized by both the Gestapo and the court and no "enhanced interrogation" techniques were used, the process could still create substantial hardship. Simply receiving a postcard from the Gestapo to meet with them at 8:00 p.m. to "answer a few questions" was assuredly terrifying.[38] Margaretha R. suffered much more: after being denounced for making illegal remarks in 1943, she was put in jail for three months. She tried to petition the state prosecuting attorney to let her go free while she awaited trial, "for her husband was severely ill and she needed to care for him and their three children. [Her lawyer] also reminded the prosecutor that Gerhard V.'s denunciation had arisen from a motive of revenge."[39] The plea was denied. She stayed in jail another two months until eventually the case was thrown out without a trial.

Furthermore, there were potentially negative consequences to being found innocent. The Supreme Labor Court of the Reich upheld the right of employers to fire employees without notice if they had been denounced by a local Nazi party leader, even if the denunciation was demonstrably false. The reasoning for their judgment was the "established doctrine" that unfounded criticism or unfounded suspicion alone carried enough weight to be sufficient grounds for dismissal.[40] Similarly, business owners could lose their companies. Denounced individuals were also likely to be monitored by the Gestapo from then on, as the mere fact that they had been denounced made them permanently suspect. In fact, they usually had to sign a declaration warning them that they would face "state police measures" if they were ever denounced again.[41]

Thus, in Nazi Germany being denounced placed a person in immediate jeopardy in a highly uncertain environment that could potentially have long-lasting effects. Which officer happened to be working a case and his current mood could have a disproportionate impact on the consequences.[42] Even though ordinary Germans were treated with more consideration and lenience than were members of maligned populations, they too were at the capricious mercy of their investigators. Regardless of how many cases were dismissed or how quickly certain individuals were exonerated, being investigated by the Gestapo was assuredly unpleasant and often caused suffering to those accused.

Because people who were denounced often suffered while the well-being of denouncers was protected, this created an environment highly conducive to the reporting of socially opportunistic denunciations. Several historians have sought to understand the motivations behind denunciations in Nazi Germany, making it possible to assess cases across a number of different regions. As will be seen, it was not propaganda or ideology that spurred people to denounce, but the opportunity to resolve local conflicts and gain relative to one another.

PUTTING THE GESTAPO TO WORK: 883 DENUNCIATIONS IN GERMANY

Although the Nazis produced voluminous records, only a limited number are still available. Many of the Gestapo records were destroyed at the end of World War II, which is why it is difficult to provide the total number of denunciations reported during the Third Reich. Even where a number of files remain, there are widespread omissions. For example, in Würzburg officials managed to burn all files of individuals whose names began with the letters "A" through "G" or with "V."[43] Some of these missing records, however, can be recovered from other sources. Nearly twenty thousand records of the Cologne Special Court survive, documenting the cases of almost thirty thousand defendants.[44] These files include copies of the associated Gestapo investigations; however, they omit cases that did not eventually go to court and that were handled entirely by the police.[45]

Within the corpus of extant case files, it is necessary to determine which cases started from denunciations rather than the Gestapo's own investigative police work. Although this is clear in many files, in some cases the origin is difficult to determine. Among cases that clearly originated from denunciations, historical researchers who study this topic take different approaches: some look at denunciations within Gestapo files, while others focus on denunciation letters originally sent to party officials. A third group analyzes court cases that began with a denunciation. Due to their different questions and foci, some scholars also purposefully exclude or include certain crimes or certain types of denounced individuals. Most select a particular region to evaluate. The approach taken in this chapter is to present all of these together and demonstrate how, despite the variety of regions represented and the different selection criteria and idiosyncrasies of each sample, the resultant patterns are remarkably consistent.

The records used come from nine different samples put together by six different historians. In regard to region, Reinhard Mann, Vandana Joshi, and Jan Ruckenbiel focused primarily on samples of denunciations from Düsseldorf, although Ruckenbiel added the nearby counties of Geldern and Kleve. Robert Gellately looked at files in Würzburg and later at Düsseldorf, Neustadt, Lower Franconia, the Rhine-Ruhr, and the Palatinate. Gisela Diewald-Kerkmann focused on Lippe, and Eric Johnson analyzed denunciations from Krefeld and Cologne.[46]

Within these regions, the aforementioned historians further constrained their samples. Mann excluded certain crimes from his data, including denunciations relating to racial offenses, emigrants, foreign workers, prisoners of war, separatism, and espionage. Diewald-Kerkmann analyzed denunciations reported directly to the Nazi Party, rather than to the Gestapo. For some of his analyses, Johnson examined only Gestapo case files and Special Court cases in which the denounced individual was Jewish. Gellately looked specifically at crimes relating to race defilement and friendship to Jews, and later focused on the crime of listening to foreign radio broadcasts. Joshi looked exclusively at crimes dealing with Jews, foreign minorities, and communists, along with individuals accused of malicious gossip, with a particular focus on female denouncers. Ruckenbiel examined crimes of opposition and malicious gossip.[47]

Together, these samples help to reveal patterns of denunciation in Nazi Germany, and where they agree they provide robust evidence through corroboration. Although all samples do not provide equal insight into every aspect of the denunciations discussed below, together they provide enough detail to elucidate denunciation's general dynamics within this particular context.

The most common method by which denunciations were reported to the authorities was verbally and in person. In one study, 52 percent of denunciations were reported in this way, compared to 33 percent made through written letters.[48] Another study found that 42 percent of denunciations were reported in person, compared to 22 percent that were sent in writing.[49] In both studies, these sets of letters were signed. Perhaps surprisingly, there seems to have been a dearth of anonymous letters; across four studies, anonymous letters account for only 3 to 6 percent of all denunciations.[50]

The scarcity of anonymous letters is somewhat surprising, as anonymity would seem to have helped protect citizens from retaliation. However, it is unclear how many of the signed letters and in-person denunciations included a request for anonymity. It is also unclear how many people gave a false name at the bottom of signed letters. Interestingly, it was more common for rural denouncers to write anonymously than urban denouncers.[51] Perhaps members of tight-knit communities were better able to guess who had denounced them, and therefore denouncers were more likely to take this precaution.

The files also reveal basic information about denouncers. They were predominantly male (70 to 80 percent).[52] People of all ages denounced, with almost all denunciations made by individuals between the ages of twenty and sixty.[53] They held a variety of occupations, ranging from unskilled laborer to skilled laborer to shopkeeper and businessman. They were sometimes members of the Nazi Party or other Nazi groups and sometimes had no political affiliation. Denouncers appear to have come from the full spectrum of German society.[54]

It is difficult to succinctly categorize the crimes for which people denounced each other in Nazi Germany, as the ever-increasing scope of regulations meant that all sorts of behaviors were considered transgressive. One historian identified fifty-two different categories of crime among the Gestapo files in Düsseldorf.[55] Among these categories, the most prevalent crimes had to do with communist activity, Jews, emigrants, and malicious gossip.[56] A more parsimonious way to categorize crimes is to place them into three broad categories: the continuation of or association with forbidden or marginalized groups, including political parties and religious organizations; nonverbal transgressions such as having or disseminating forbidden documents and listening to foreign radio; and verbal forms of nonconformity. Verbal nonconformity included slander against the Nazi party, party leaders, or Hitler himself; critiques of National Socialism; complaints about living standards or the war; support for freedom of expression; or support for other countries, parties, or Jews.[57] Examples of denunciations for each of these three categories are included below.

The following is a typical denunciation for association with marginalized groups. On July 29, 1940, a twenty-two-year-old clerical worker named Gertrud Weiss arrived at the Gestapo headquarters in Würzburg to denounce twenty-seven-year-old Ilse Totzke, an unemployed woman living on an inheritance. Among several crimes Totzke was alleged to have committed, Weiss reported her for having sympathy for the Jews, along with occasionally having a female visitor of about thirty-six who "looked Jewish."[58]

The next example is in the nonverbal transgressions category. Maria von Lingen was a countess in Silesia and ran the household while her husband was away at war. In the summer of 1942, Maria's friend Jane visited from Munich while Maria was away in Italy; she listened to BBC radio broadcasts and left the dial on the illegal station. The following morning, Maria's household staff found this evidence. Three of them—the nanny, the housekeeper, and the kitchen maid—denounced Maria to the authorities.[59]

The third example is for a verbal crime. In 1943, Dutch pianist Karlrobert Kreiten was on a concert tour in Germany and stayed at the home of a friend of his mother's in Berlin. During a meal at her house, he allegedly called Hitler "brutal, sick and insane" and declared that the Nazi era would soon be over. The woman denounced him for this remark and accused him of "giving aid and comfort to the enemy" and "undermining morale."[60]

The files also include information about whether accused individuals were found guilty and what punishments they suffered. In general, about half of the cases resulted in nothing more than a dismissal or a warning. The rest either went to trial or the suspect was put in protective custody.[61] Consequences were harsher for members of marginalized groups; among all Krefeld Gestapo cases, about 50 percent of individuals escaped with a dismissal or a warning; this figure was 34 percent when the suspect was Jewish.[62] The Gestapo in practice was not always as brutal as its reputation, but Nazi justice was unpredictable.

Several historians of Nazi Germany have analyzed the investigations and testimonies associated with denunciations in order to determine what the denouncers hoped to accomplish by making their reports. Before discussing these results, however, it is important to emphasize the difficulty of such an endeavor. Even though the Gestapo was more interested in the content of denunciations than in denouncers' motivations, denouncers still had an incentive to appeal to Nazi ideology and conceal any ulterior motives if they wanted to maximize the likelihood that the person they denounced would be punished. Thus, it is possible that researchers have undercounted the number of denunciations that were made for personal reasons. That being said, the results should nevertheless be indicative of general trends, especially if the percentage of personally motivated denunciations is substantial. These findings are shown in table 4.1.

The first column lists the region of Germany from which each sample is drawn and the historian who examined the files. The second displays the number of denunciations evaluated in each sample, while the last three columns indicate each scholar's determination of which denunciations were motivated by loyalty,

TABLE 4.1 Assessment of Motives in Studies of Denunciations in Nazi Germany

Region (source)	Total denunciations	Percentage loyalty motive	Percentage personal motive	Percentage unknown motive
Düsseldorf (Mann 1987)	213	24	37	39
Lippe (Diewald-Kerkmann 1995)	292	30	38	32
Krefeld (Johnson 1999)	105	35	39	27
Cologne (Johnson 1999)	32	23	54	23
Düsseldorf, Geldern, and Kleve (Ruckenbiel 2005)	241	18	31	51
Total	**883**	**26**	**37**	**37**

Note: Percentages are rounded to the nearest whole number.

which by self-interest, and which have motivations that are difficult to determine. Loyalty motives, which indicate clear support for the Nazi regime, range from 18 to 35 percent of the denunciations in each of the samples.

Regarding personal motives, recall that denouncers did not receive any sort of benefit or compensation from the authorities for their reports, nor did they gain protection from future harm. Thus, personal motives were social motives: the desire to harm or remove a particular member of the community. These were denunciations motivated by social opportunism. In each of the samples, personal motives are attributed to 31 to 54 percent of denunciations.

In each of the five samples, personal motives were responsible for more denunciations (an average of 37 percent) than were loyalty motives (26 percent). Put another way, about 50 percent more denunciations are attributable to the former than to the latter. This trend is especially stark when looked at from the opposite perspective: despite ubiquitous propaganda, roughly three-quarters of denunciations had nothing obvious to do with expressly supporting the Nazi agenda.[63] There appears to have been widespread adoption of denunciations for their own use by Germans all across the country.[64]

The last column of the table indicates denunciations that are not easily categorizable as loyal or instrumental. It is difficult to tell what the motivations were: they neither uphold the importance of Nazi ideology nor betray a self-serving motive.[65]

Particularly notable in table 4.1 is the consistency of the results despite the idiosyncrasies of each sample. The two samples examined by Eric Johnson include only denunciations made against Jews. With Jews targeted as victims by the Nazis, it may seem logical that denunciations against them would more likely be ideological. However, this does not appear to have been the case; denunciations against Jews were just as self-serving in nature as denunciations for other crimes.

Among those denunciations that were personally motivated, it is possible to further categorize the reasons why people denounced. Personally motivated denunciations can be generally divided into three categories. The first includes quarrels and conflicts, which often occurred between neighbors and sometimes between current or ex-lovers. The second category involves economic rivalries and professional competition. The third indicates social jealousy, where an individual wanted to harm a social or romantic rival in order to gain relative to them. All three types appear to have been prevalent and all three fit under the umbrella of social opportunism.[66] All represent attempts to harm particular individuals and benefit from their punishment. Sometimes these types occur in combination with one another. Examples of each of the three types are included below.

A neighborly conflict is revealed in a letter from 1943, which barely even tries to couch the neighbor's crimes in political terms:

> As a soldier's wife (a prolific mother with six children) I hereby make a request to sternly warn my neighbor, a full Jewess, for once. It has been observed that the Jewess has adopted a particularly provocative stance in the last few months of the war, in spite of the fact that I have already put up with it for so long. Ever since my husband became a soldier (he was earlier block warden) the situation has become unbearable. The Jewess pours two barrels of liquid manure on the hedge on hot days so that one cannot sit outside. I work a lot outside and even eat there. She continuously belches with open mouth making me feel sick. This goes on the whole day. But she does not do this while talking to others, which she does rather pleasantly . . . On top of this is the preferential treatment the Jewess enjoys when the firewood is being distributed in the nearby bunker.[67]

The letter was signed by three women. Upon investigation, it was discovered that Frau Rosenthal (one of the denouncers) and Frau Schimmel (the person denounced) had once been great friends and visited each other often. However, Frau Schimmel had also been Frau Rosenthal's landlord, and Frau Rosenthal had borne a grudge ever since Frau Schimmel attempted to evict her from her apartment. The above letter came to the attention of the Gestapo shortly after that event.

A 1938 quarrel between long-time friends Arthur Winkler and Josef Weigand in Würzburg became so contentious that Winkler charged Weigand's wife with libel. Enraged, Weigand denounced Winkler for malicious gossip—specifically for having suggested that a local Nazi Party leader had associated with Jews before 1933. The Gestapo investigated and determined that the charge was baseless.[68]

In an example of social jealousy, a resentful wife turned in two young women she suspected of having too close a friendship with her husband:

> The wife of a Frankfurt regional-court associate judge who was jealous of her husband's friendship with two Jewish girls . . . asked the Gestapo "to evacuate the Jews to the east, so that her husband no longer had the opportunity to meet them" . . . As the head of the Frankfurt Jewish Section reported, "The two Jewish girls, which [sic] were not registered as 'Jews' by either the National Association of Jews or by the Gestapo or by the residents' registration office but only became known to us from a verbal and telephone report, were sent to the east with the next transport."[69]

Similarly, a jealous neighbor from Lambach wrote a letter in 1940 denouncing her next-door neighbor for "having become rich and possessing things that did not go with her status as a saleswoman." The denouncer attributed this good fortune to friendship with a Jew five years before. The Gestapo investigated and found the charge to be unsubstantiated.[70]

An example of an economically motivated denunciation was made in 1940, when a man named Luis appeared at the local Gestapo office and accused his business rival, a Jew named

Gerschenkron, of doing business with various telegraph offices. A law had been passed in 1938 barring Jews from economic life, so this would have been considered illegal. Gerschenkron's house was raided, but the investigation found no evidence of illegal activity. Dissatisfied with this result, Luis returned to the Gestapo to report that Gerschenkron was using a pseudonym for his business. This turned out to be true and the business was forced to close, giving greater opportunity for Luis's own to thrive.[71] Similarly, a man was denounced to the Würzburg Gestapo in 1938 for having purchased his wine business from a Jewish owner. The letter was anonymous but its author indicated that he was a "German competitor." Upon investigation, it was determined that, although the business had indeed been purchased from a Jew, the transaction had followed the letter of the law.[72]

Together, these three types of personally motivated denunciations fit well with the prediction that social opportunism should motivate denunciations in the volunteer model. Certainly it appears that most denouncers knew the person they denounced, often well. Across several studies, being neighbors was the most common relationship between the parties.[73] Similarly, individuals were most likely to denounce people of similar status, the relationships most likely to involve conflict and jealousy.[74]

Further evidence of socially opportunistic denunciations can be seen in the prevalence of false denunciations. Although most of the aforementioned scholars do not report this statistic, Robert Gellately has provided the percentage of denunciations that were deemed to be false or baseless by the Gestapo after their investigations. For this sample, he specifically examined the crimes of "Race Defilement" and "Friendship to Jews," which encompass all activity involving sexual relationships with Jews, friendliness to Jews, verbal comments that seemed favorable to Jews, or any nonacceptance of Nazi racial doctrines. The results of this analysis can be seen in table 4.2.

Of the 175 case files examined, 36 percent of denunciations relating to "Race Defilement" and 45 percent of those for "Friendship to Jews" were found to be false or baseless—even though almost everyone was guilty of some crime under Nazi law. Clearly, denouncing a specific individual was far more important than reporting a crime honestly. Overall, 41 percent of all denunciations were deemed to be false.[75]

Tracking the crimes of "Race Defilement" and "Friendship to Jews" over time is also revealing. In Würzburg, the number of denunciations for these crimes reached its peak at the end of the 1930s, yet at this point Jews were isolated and ordinary Germans did not have much opportunity to interact with them. Yet German citizens continued to denounce one another for Jewish crimes. These reports did not arise from a deep concern about pro-Jewish activities in the community; denunciations for racial crimes were simply a means of resolving private jealousies and

TABLE 4.2 Denunciations of "Race Defilement" and "Friendship to Jews" in the Würzburg Gestapo Case Files (1933–1945)

Crime	Total denunciations	False or baseless denunciations	Percentage false or baseless
"Race Defilement"	84	30	36
"Friendship to Jews"	91	41	45
Total	**175**	**71**	**41**

Source: Table from Gellately 1990, 164.

disputes. An example of a denunciation for improper contact with Jews illustrates this well:

> On 9 September 1939, the Gestapo in Würzburg was alerted by neighbors that 17-year-old Anna Reising, of Würzburg, was having visits from a "suspicious man". The Reising house was thereupon placed under surveillance. The family and neighbors were subsequently brought in, although it turned out that the man was neither particularly suspicious nor Jewish, but Anna's boyfriend. She explained that the whole uproar was really about a toilet:
>
> "As I have already mentioned, with those people [the denouncers] there is always an argument, and in fact only because of the matter of the toilet. Fourteen of us had to use one toilet, while only two of them used another. We finally managed to get it established that their toilet was to be used by us and other parties in the house, and since that time hatred has existed. We have not spoken to these people for 10 years."[76]

Overall, Germans used the Gestapo's eagerness to find and punish illegal behavior to serve their own purposes, especially to harm social and economic rivals and to resolve private disputes. This occurred all over Germany and became similarly common in the territories conquered during the war.[77] Such co-optation on a massive scale was not unknown to the German authorities and Hitler himself began complaining about it as early as 1933. The following section details the ways in which the authorities dealt with—or failed to deal with—unwanted denunciations, which helps to illustrate the tenuous yet mutually beneficial relationship that developed between local Germans and the central authorities.

A SYSTEM OF UNEASY COOPERATION

If the Nazis expected German citizens to denounce out of ideo-logical support for the regime, this illusion was shattered almost immediately. No clearer indication is there than Hitler's 1933 dec-laration that "We are living at present in a sea of denunciations and human meanness." Only months into his first year in power, he was already aware of the fact that Germans were not denounc-ing in the way that he intended.

Other officials were also well aware that denouncers were not behaving as desired and made statements to that effect throughout the course of the regime. Top Nazi official Her-mann Göring echoed this sentiment in 1939. Although he was satisfied with the progress of the removal of Jews from society, he expressed dismay at "German fellow citizens" being denounced "because they once bought something in a Jewish store, lived in the same house as Jews, or otherwise had had business relations with the Jews." Regardless of how important it was to explain to the people the need to remove the Jews from the German econ-omy, that should not have led to "the spying out and denunciation of such long-past events."[78] Reinhard Heydrich, the director of the Gestapo, complained in 1943 that his agency had become something between a "maid for all occasions and rubbish-bin for the Reich."[79]

Local officials were also aware of the problem. In Novem-ber 1941, the mayor of Theilheim was asked by the Gestapo to investigate a rumor relating to Jews in his town. The mayor refused, declaring that he was fed up with investigating com-plaints that inevitably failed to lead to any actual crimes.[80] As Werner Best claimed at the Nuremburg trials, "ninety percent of the cases were not worth dealing with."[81]

Given that the Nazis were well aware of the misuse of denunciations, this raises the question of what they did to curtail this undesired behavior. Their response can be summarized in a single word: ambivalence. Despite complaining repeatedly about petty and false denunciations, every time the Nazis made a move to slow down the torrent, they backtracked almost immediately. In April 1934, Germany's minister of the interior inveighed against denunciations based on local conflicts and demanded that something be done. Yet in the very same month, Reich Minister Rudolf Hess announced that "every Party and folk comrade impelled by honest concern for the movement and the nation shall have access to the Führer or to me without the risk of being taken to task."[82] In other words, Hess viewed prosecuting petty denouncers as antithetical to the Nazi agenda. Similarly, in 1943 the minister of justice wrote a letter to judges across Germany that decried the false denouncer as a scoundrel.[83] Yet he continued his letter by declaring that prosecuting thoughtless and careless denouncers could cause all denunciations to dry up, which was not in the interest of the regime.[84]

The Nazis' reaction to denunciations between spouses is particularly illustrative. In 1941, the Gestapo headquarters in Berlin sent a letter to all its local branches concerning the matter of denunciations between relatives. The letter gave an example of an actual case, where a man denounced his wife for espionage. The woman was jailed for an extended period of time while the case was being investigated. Ultimately, the authorities concluded that the accusation was baseless; the man had not lived with his wife for years and was hoping for a favorable divorce settlement. The letter concluded by urging investigating officers to question married men under oath as to whether divorce proceedings had already commenced or were contemplated. However, again the Nazis were unwilling to be overly forceful. A subsequent letter on the same topic by Minister of Justice Otto Thierack, while again warning against denunciations made between spouses for personal purposes, noted that denouncers might nevertheless put the police on the trail of criminal deeds.[85]

The Gestapo occasionally published reminders that they were not the complaint bureau for personal spitefulness or base denunciations. In 1937, authorities went so far as to place an article in the *Frankfurter Zeitung* announcing a reward of one hundred marks for information about false denouncers.[86] Such an unambiguous step, however, was atypical. Possibly the biggest change that the authorities made to curb unwanted denunciations occurred after the war started, when the Gestapo advised some people who had been falsely denounced to initiate legal proceedings against their denouncers.[87] Yet even this reflects the authorities' longstanding ambivalence; they did not prosecute or punish such denouncers themselves, but left it up to affected citizens to take action on their own. The Gestapo never took substantive action in terms of explicitly changing institutions of social control. In the words of Jan Ruckenbiel, the Nazis were perpetually "Janus-faced."[88]

Even when a crime actually took place, there was no legal mandate requiring witnesses to make a denunciation, though this matter was discussed internally. Gestapo director Reinhard Heydrich was strongly in favor of imposing penalties on those who failed to report relevant information. Eventually, however, the idea was abandoned so as to avoid undermining national solidarity.[89]

Unsurprisingly then, petty, self-serving denunciations persisted throughout the entirety of the regime, and the Gestapo continued to follow up and investigate them regardless of the denouncers' motivations. In the words of Reinhard Mann, "the incidence of false charges was so great in Nazi Germany that they constituted a real problem for the regime, one it never solved."[90] This quote somewhat overstates the issue; the incidence of false charges was a problem the authorities *chose* not to solve because the benefits of the established system of social control were perceived to be too great.

These benefits are not difficult to observe. Members of the Gestapo were few and far between, with estimates of the total number of officers across all of Nazi Germany in 1937 at no more than seven thousand. By 1941, this number had climbed to only 7,600 in a population of approximately 80 million people.[91] The Gestapo did have the cooperation of local police forces, but it was not unusual for branch offices to complain of having inadequate resources to fulfill their responsibilities.[92]

Accepting questionable denunciations was also necessary due to the failures of Nazi propaganda.[93] Had propaganda been more successful, a much larger proportion of denunciations would have originated from political rather than personal motives. Yet despite the Nazis' best efforts of "alignment," "ideological schooling," and "coordination"[94] and an emphasis on Volksgemeinschaft, Hitler never stopped worrying about having the support of the general populace. His concern was warranted: a nonscientific poll carried out in 1942 among Nazi Party members found that 69 percent were indifferent to the Jews and only 5 percent called for their extermination.[95] As one historian summarized, "Historical scholarship has been very attentive to signs of whether Germans internalized National Socialist ideology. The consensus is that they did not."[96] In fact, it has been suggested that the primary or only domain in which propaganda was effective was among the Hitler Youth, though even this has been contested.[97] The Nazi propaganda machine, often touted as a perfect inculcator of ideology, did not result in large-scale ideological denouncing. With a small secret police force and a nonzealous populace, the Nazis grudgingly accepted the trade-off of resolving private disputes in order to gain information, even if that information was of dubious quality.

The importance of denunciations for the Nazi system of social control can be seen in table 4.3. This displays the percentage of case files that were initiated by denunciations compared to other sources of information (such as investigations conducted by the Gestapo or other security organizations) according to multiple studies.

Across a variety of samples from different regions looking at different crimes, the findings are generally consistent. Case files arising from reports made by ordinary residents almost always outnumber those initiated by information from the Gestapo or other authorities. The difference is often substantial. Combining these samples, 49 percent of 3,397 case files were initiated by denunciations and 36 percent by information collected by the authorities, and 15 percent were of unknown origin. Indeed, denunciations made by the public were indispensable for the Nazi program of social control; a greater volume of suspicious individuals came to their attention that way than by any other means. Even self-interested denunciations could still contain real information and even false denunciations could have a deterrent effect on future behavior.

There is reason to suspect that these results undercount the true prevalence of denunciations in bringing individuals to the attention of the Gestapo. Reinhard Mann, whose sample reported one of the lowest percentages of denunciations from the populace, explained that including all of the case files that strongly suggest they were initiated through denunciations would inflate the percentage of such reports to at least 33 percent.[98] Furthermore, some proportion of the authority-initiated cases may be misattributed, as the reports that the Gestapo

TABLE 4.3 Origin of Case Files

Region (source)	Total cases	Percentage from denunciations	Percentage from authorities	Percentage unknown
Düsseldorf (Mann 1987)	845	26	61	13
Düsseldorf (Joshi 2003)	366	59	18	23
Würzburg (Gellately 1990)	175	57	32	11
Düsseldorf, Wurzburg, and Neustadt (Gellately 2001a)	226	73	17	10
Lower Franconia, Rhine-Ruhr, and Palatinate (Gellately 2001a)	444	54	32	14
Krefeld (Johnson 1999)	432	25	40	35
Cologne (Johnson 1999)	578	65	28	8
Düsseldorf and the counties Geldern and Kleve (Ruckenbiel 2005)	331	73	16	11
Total	**3,397**	**49**	**36**	**15**

Note: Percentages are rounded to the nearest whole number.

received from other authorities included citizen denunciations sent to those officials that were then passed on to the
Gestapo. It is difficult to know how many fall into this category, as the files do not always indicate where the organization that passed along the information obtained it. Regardless, it is clear that denunciations were a critical source of
information for the Nazis. Despite their frequent displeasure
at petty and spiteful denunciations, they begrudgingly welcomed them nonetheless.

CONCLUSION

On May 8, 1945, known as V-E Day, the Allied forces accepted
Germany's unconditional surrender, officially ending World War
II in Europe. Hitler was already dead from a self-inflicted gunshot wound eight days before. The Nazis' totalitarian experiment
was over, and with it their program of social control. Ever since,
scholars have sought to understand how Germany could change
so dramatically in such a short period of time.

Philosopher Hannah Arendt described totalitarianism as a
movement in which people become atomized, sundered from
their personal relations and directly engaged with the state.[99] In
this atomized condition, people are molded by propaganda and
directed toward perpetual revolution. The analysis in this chapter reveals that this was not the case in Germany: the Nazis
depended on local relationships in order to enact social control
and establish repression. Yet these were not the bonds of Volksgemeinschaft that they envisioned either. Although social relationships served as the foundation, individuals participated in
the social-control apparatus of the state not as a means of looking toward the future to create a great folk community, but as a

way of looking back to the past to destroy old rivals and enemies.

Yet through the aggregation of these individual acts of subversion, the regime benefited. The volunteer model in Nazi Germany helped to enact social control, facilitating the imposition of brutal repression. As Robert Gellately noted, "Without denunciation in Nazi Germany . . . there is no telling how many people might have helped Jews or members of other stigmatized groups or expressed solidarity with them."[100] Even though many denouncers did not support the regime strongly, their reports acted in regime-supporting ways by deterring illicit behavior and promoting the myth of the Gestapo.[101] Despite the failure of propaganda to create a population of Nazified ideologues, it was not internal conflict or rebellion that ultimately brought down the Nazis: it took the combined military power of much of the rest of the world.

The end of the Nazis did not signify the end of denunciations within Germany, however. Instead, the four occupying powers—the Soviet Union, the United States, the United Kingdom, and France—began a program of denazification where it was local citizens' "special task and duty" to report "the guilty" in their communities.[102] Over sixteen million questionnaires known as *Fragebogen* were circulated by the occupying powers, requesting personal information and encouraging respondents to report others for pro-Nazi activities. This facilitated the continuation of widespread denunciation throughout Germany. For example, in Soviet-controlled territory, Herr W., a teacher and director of an elementary school, was denounced for a number of pro-Nazi offenses, including having made a denunciation to the Nazis. He denied all charges and a neighbor explained that the whole thing was about firewood:

The trouble actually began, she testified, after the war, when the teacher requested the deputy mayor's help in securing firewood to heat the school. The deputy mayor . . . dismissed the request . . . The teacher then allegedly went directly to the local Soviet commander to request aid, a move that incensed the deputy mayor. . . . From this point on, "there was just hatred and hatred."[103]

Similar denunciations were reported in the territory controlled by the United States. A letter was sent in November of 1945 to a military government office in the town of Zweisel, not even attempting to mask the denouncer's motivation:

My son-in-law, Alois Grimm, has treated me badly. He promised to behave decently to my wife and me. We gave him our house, arable land, and 500 Marks. No sooner was he in the house when he began to act violent against me. My son-in-law was a strong supporter of the Nazi Party, he collected much money, and had the function of a *Blockleiter* . . . I cannot stand these maltreatments any longer . . . I have heard that the American Court of Justice has settled several such cases.[104]

The above two examples are typical. As a local mayor reported, people were denounced not "on political grounds, but for personal squabbles."[105] Similarly, the chief of the British Legal Division expressed concern about the "malicious denunciations" being made, and that "this practice of denunciations, which now threatens under the guise of denazification, is strongly reminiscent of Nazi methods."[106] The German Protestant Church's official position was that the program of denazification had "deteriorated into a program of revenge."[107] Although the crimes had changed, the institutional environment remained similar, which made it easy for people to report (or fabricate) wrongdoings that served their own purposes.

The end of the Nazis also precipitated a wave of denunciations outside of Germany. In France, this was part of the *épuration*, or purge, where former collaborators were sought out and punished. In occupied France an estimated three to five million denunciations had been sent to the Vichy authorities during Nazi rule.[108] After the German defeat this continued: "denunciation and some dubious score-settling proliferated."[109] Such postwar practices took place not just in France, but all over Europe.[110]

Indeed, denunciations continued unabated throughout the twentieth century and into the present day. Not only appearing in repressive regimes and postwar Europe, they pervaded and continue to pervade modern democracies in a variety of forms, including plea-bargaining, whistle-blowing, crime reporting, and counterterrorism efforts. After discussing the general implications of the previous case studies, the next chapter examines these modern forms of denunciation. Although they may be labeled with different names than the historical examples, the dynamics are often the same. The coercion and volunteer models persist into the present.

5

DENUNCIATIONS

Present and Future

B
eginning in the 1930s, authorities in the Soviet Union
began to encourage denunciations, with a particular
interest in reports of wrongdoing by officials. Individuals could provide information in a number of ways: directly to
the secret police, through letters sent to newspapers, or with
spoken testimony during "self-criticism" sessions. Responding to
this encouragement, many people came forward for the familiar
reasons already detailed in this book: a desire to gain the favor of
the authorities, to avoid negative consequences, or to cause harm
to a rival. As historian Sheila Fitzpatrick explained, "The Soviet
state was very responsive to denunciations. This responsiveness
meant that it was always vulnerable to manipulation by denunciation writers with personal agendas."[1] Although this dynamic
can take different forms, it can be found in many settings.
Denunciation occurs and recurs in predictable ways.

The previous chapters have explored some of these ways, demonstrating particular relationships between institutions of social
control and denouncer behavior. Across three culturally distinct settings spanning 450 years, these relationships have
proven consistent. This consistency—such that a villager during
the Spanish Inquisition might not have found Nazi Germany's

denunciatory system to be too foreign—lends support to the general theory laid out in the first chapter.

Specifically, different institutional forms of social control produce different motivations to denounce and different patterns of denunciations. Environments with authority-based incentives foster denunciations that attempt to placate or appease those authorities. These incentives can be either negative, as during the Edict of Grace in the Spanish Inquisition; or positive, as experienced by prisoners in Romanov Russia. So long as incentives are sufficiently strong or perceived as such, individuals will denounce others out of self-preservation or to gain positive rewards.

Voluntary environments, on the other hand, do not offer direct incentives from the authorities in exchange for denunciations. In such settings, individuals denounce in order to harm others within their local communities and gain relative to them. This desire to harm arises from personal arguments, economic rivalries, and social jealousies. Such denunciations become particularly widespread when two institutional conditions are met: when denouncers are protected from hardship and retaliation, and when the person denounced is likely to suffer. This explains why denunciations appear to have been far more prevalent under the Edict of Faith in the Spanish Inquisition and in Nazi Germany than in Romanov Russia. Denunciations did occur in Romanov Russia; however, these were impelled primarily by high emotion, which increased would-be denouncers' willingness to attempt to harm others, even if their actions also put themselves at risk of hardship.

What follows are various implications of these findings, starting with the broader impact these two models have on a society. Although both the volunteer and the coercion models enhance social control, the volunteer model does so in a more effective way by requiring fewer centralized resources and giving the illusion of greater public support. Providing more autonomy to individuals to direct the policing power of the state results in stronger social control. Yet this raises the question of what conditions lead to the occurrence of one model or the other in any particular regime. Two factors—legitimacy and urgency—likely help to explain this variation.

The remainder of this chapter moves beyond repressive regimes and considers denunciations in the present-day United States, especially in the form of plea-bargaining, whistle-blowing, crime reporting, and counterterrorism efforts. Each of these contemporary manifestations follows a logic similar to the coercive and voluntary denunciations that we have explored in other settings, though modern democracies generally implement more safeguards to prevent false denunciations. The coercion and volunteer models, however, are not the only ways in which widespread denunciations can occur. Accordingly, I introduce a third model—the prosocial model—which manifests in environments where individuals denounce for more than their own self-interest. The book concludes with a consideration of the future of denunciations. Although denunciations have played a constant role in human societies throughout history, the advancement of automated surveillance technologies raises questions about their persistence in the future.

FROM MICRO TO MACRO

The previous chapters have described some of the ways in which self-serving denunciations can be beneficial to authorities. Overall, in repressive regimes both the coercion and the volunteer models serve to enhance social control and consolidate power. Some of the information acquired is truthful, which helps the authorities to punish unwanted behavior. People facing coercive pressure know they are more likely to satisfy the authorities if they provide truthful information. Under the volunteer model, would-be denouncers know that they have a greater probability of harming their targets if they denounce them for true crimes. As a result, both coercive and voluntary denunciations have a strong deterrent effect among potential opponents of a regime, as public transgression puts them at greater risk of being denounced. Fear of being denounced likely compels many people to comply, even when actual support for the regime is weak.

Widespread denouncing also benefits the authorities because cooperation, even given for personal rather than ideological reasons, tacitly legitimizes the authorities' right to investigate and adjudicate complaints. This occurs regardless of whether citizens denounce truthfully or they privately oppose the regime; it is public opinion, not private, that undergirds political power.[2] Widespread denouncing may give a false impression of popular support for the authorities and their agenda, which can lead to the diffusion of regime-supporting norms.[3] In such an environment, people will express support because they believe that others support the regime, even if that belief is inaccurate.

Widespread denouncing also affects preexisting networks of social relationships in regime-supporting ways. It ruptures horizontal ties and erodes trust, as individuals are at constant risk of being harmed by anyone at any time. This leads to increasing social distance as people limit intimacy and contact with one another so as not to give others the knowledge or motivation to denounce them. At the same time, denunciations rigidify hierarchies, as government officials become the outlet for complaints. Ultimately, this can lead to an orientation of society away from cooperation and trust and toward hierarchy and obedience.[4]

Under both models, authorities can use denunciations to harm particular groups, even when those authorities do not command the ideological support of the populace. By emphasizing the identification of wrongdoing among certain groups or by punishing members of those groups more harshly, they can target social control toward particular ends. The case of the Spanish Inquisition demonstrates how denunciations served to control the *conversos*, even though most denunciations were intragroup, not intergroup. Similarly, by punishing members of marginalized groups more harshly, the Gestapo used interpersonal conflicts to marginalize those groups further.

Taken together, these benefits help to explain why authorities may maintain institutions of denunciation despite the prevalence of false and petty reports. The aggregate effects of many individuals denouncing—for whatever reason—leads to the emergence of social control. Such a system inhibits conspiracy and revolt: it empowers the authorities while preventing individuals from coordinating dissent.

THE TWO MODELS COMPARED

Although both models increase social control, we should expect that it will be imposed more efficiently and effectively under the volunteer model.[5] More resources are required for a regime to employ an active police force that maintains and enforces incentives (as in the coercion model) than to employ a more reactive and sparser police force that waits for denunciations to be reported (as in the volunteer model). This is particularly evident in the contrast between Nazi Germany and the contemporary Soviet Union. Nazi Germany maintained approximately one Gestapo officer for every ten thousand residents. The Soviets, who implemented a more coercive system, had one secret police officer for every five hundred residents during the same time period.[6] Both systems are commonly thought to have been effective, but the Nazis accomplished similar levels of control with a far smaller investment of manpower.[7]

One of the primary reasons for this greater efficiency is that the coercion model requires the constant presence of incentives in order for denunciations to persist over time. The volunteer model, on the other hand, is largely self-sustaining. Even if all existing local animosities have been reported, denunciations reduce generalized trust, which strains interpersonal interactions and relationships. Increased suspicion can give rise to new arguments, rivalries, and jealousies that motivate people to make more denunciations. This is the volunteer model's feedback loop, where denunciations and negative ties co-create one another.

The differing orientations of denouncers under the two models also have different implications for the communities in which the denunciations take place. Under the coercion model, the incentive structure is likely widely known. This means that members of the community tend to attribute other citizens' participation to authority-based incentives, especially if these are strong. Any dissatisfaction or anger that community members feel about widespread denunciations will, to some extent, be directed against the authorities for imposing those incentives. Denouncers themselves may resent the authorities for particularly coercive tactics.

Under the volunteer model, however, the lack of authority-based incentives suggests that members of the community will likely attribute widespread denouncing to personal choice: to the denouncer's desire to harm others or support the regime. Either way, observers can be expected to blame denunciations on the denouncers rather than on the authorities. Denouncers themselves may be grateful to the authorities for assisting in the resolution of private disputes. In the volunteer model, therefore, any blame or dissatisfaction with the generalized system of social control may be deflected away from the authorities and toward members of the local community who participate in that system.

We can expect a similar dynamic among people who consider denouncing but do not go through with it. In a coercive environment, those who resist pressure to denounce are in implicit conflict with the authorities; they are choosing to defy the latter's incentives and suffer the consequences.[8] In the volunteer model, people who do not denounce are not in conflict with anyone. Their orientation was never toward the authorities, so their inaction should have little impact on their perception of that relationship.

These differences suggest that the volunteer model does not align with a simple oppositional narrative of the authorities as oppressors and the citizens as those oppressed. By permitting ordinary citizens to direct individual acts of harm, the authorities take on the role of arbiters rather than instigators. Their reactivity is in a sense their greatest asset: social control is imposed through fear not of the authorities, but of one's neighbors. Under the volunteer model, denunciation becomes the means of both the people's empowerment and their subjugation. As a result, this model may ultimately support a more lasting and more stable repression.[9]

THE CONTEXTUAL DETERMINANTS OF SOCIAL CONTROL

From the authorities' perspective, the volunteer model would seem to offer clear benefits over the coercion model. Yet the coercion model persists and has been used throughout history. This raises the question of why authorities continue to adopt it and suggests that contextual factors may influence how institutions of social control are designed, regardless of their relative effectiveness.

This is not to suggest that authorities necessarily recognize the differences between the two models or that they are particularly deliberate when implementing institutions of social control. Indeed, it is likely that they often use whatever means of denunciation are most readily available. Inquisitorial procedures in Spain were borrowed largely from papal inquisitions, and Mikhail Romanov expanded the scope of the preexisting Sovereign's Word and Deed. Nevertheless, authorities can adjust institutional features to suit their preferences and probably do so strategically, based on their beliefs about what motivates denouncers. Two factors may be particularly salient in determining the form of social control that emerges within a given context. These factors are *legitimacy* and *urgency*.

A Matter of Legitimacy

The key determinant of whether a regime elicits denunciations by enacting coercive incentives is likely its legitimacy. In a regime viewed as legitimate, citizens willingly follow directives and laws and support the regime without needing to be coerced by threats of violence.[10] What matters here is not the citizens' willingness to follow directives, per se, but the authorities' *perception* of their willingness. If the authorities view the populace as generally supportive, they are more likely to elicit voluntary denunciations. If they believe the populace's support is questionable, they are more likely to impose coercive incentives.

Authorities who believe their policies are legitimate generally perceive widespread support for their platform and agenda

among either the general populace or the people whose support they need to remain in power. Such support need not be
universal: although some (or indeed a majority) of the population may not agree, the authorities believe that a large percentage favors them and their cause and that, if encouraged, will
voluntarily denounce to protect the existing power structure.
The case studies examined in this book bear this out. In Muscovy there was a history of reverence for the tsar, which the
expansion of the Sovereign's Word and Deed was intended to
access. Similarly, the Nazis won 44 percent of the popular vote
in 1933, far more than any other party; although this may not
have been the level they were hoping for, it nevertheless indicated the support of a sizeable fraction of the population. In
both cases, leaders expected their supporters to denounce voluntarily in support of the regime.

However, when authorities suspect their policies do not have
sufficient support, they are more likely to adopt coercive incentives. Initially the Spanish Inquisition was perceived by many
people as illegitimate, especially in its attempt to impose a Castilian institution on cities in Aragon, and inquisitors were barred
from some cities.[11] Faced with this lack of support, the Inquisition applied coercive pressure through the Edict of Grace in
order to elicit participation.[12] Although the use of coercive incentives may not be particularly appealing, authorities whose legitimacy comes into question likely feel that they have little choice
if they hope to enhance social control through denunciations.[13]

As has been shown even in legitimate regimes operating under
the volunteer model, however, individuals tend to denounce not
to support the regime, but rather to resolve local disputes. This
is why Hitler was surprised and disappointed when he discovered the real reasons why Germans made so many denunciations.
Yet authorities probably do not anticipate these dynamics. To the

extent that they are ignorant of the actual motivations of denouncers, legitimacy likely plays an important role in how institutions of social control are structured.

A Matter of Urgency

The type of social control enacted in a given regime also tends to depend on the urgency with which the authorities seek to consolidate power and impose control. The level of urgency likely determines whether they prefer denouncers (either voluntary or coerced) or informants. Unlike denouncers, informants are recruited by the authorities to monitor particular groups or individuals for an extended period of time. They file regular reports and are generally paid or compensated for their assistance, though they may also be coerced through threats or blackmail.

Both denouncers and informants provide local information from the populace; however, they represent very different forms of social control. When authorities want urgently to establish social control, they are more likely to encourage denunciations. When they have more time and less pressure, they are more likely to make use of informants.[14]

Consider the situations faced by Ferdinand and Isabella in Spain, Mikhail Romanov in Russia, and Adolf Hitler in Germany when they initially came to power. All had become rulers amid somewhat tumultuous circumstances. Ferdinand and Isabella both faced civil war in their kingdoms and they sought to unite Aragon and Castile for the first time in history. Mikhail Romanov took the throne after a period of political turmoil and devastating famine, and was chosen partially because he had "limited gifts."[15] Hitler, although elected through relatively legitimate means, sought to eradicate the preexisting system of governance and replace it with a dictatorship. In all three cases, the rulers were in uncertain positions and sought to consolidate and entrench their power by mitigating the possibility of uprising or dissent by the population.

Such circumstances illustrate the utility of denunciations when the need for social control is more urgent. When authorities are weak or lack stability, denunciations offer a rapid means of consolidating power. Both coercive incentives and voluntary encouragement can result in an immediate outpouring of crime reports.[16]

By contrast, a system based on informants takes more time and resources to establish. Whereas denouncers make spontaneous reports on their own, informants must first be identified, vetted, and then persuaded to participate. Procedures in the German Democratic Republic—the former East Germany—demonstrate how laborious this process can be. The Stasi (secret police) often initially identified potential informants because of their access to particular groups or organizations that the Stasi wanted to monitor.[17] Potential informants were then secretly investigated in order to understand their strengths, weaknesses, and interests. Next, a Stasi officer made contact and attempted to establish a relationship of mutual trust. Only gradually would political subjects be brought up. If the target responded appropriately, the officer would reveal himself and propose that the target become an informant. By 1989, there were an estimated seven hundred regulations regarding the proper way to recruit and handle informants.[18]

Every step in this process would have been unnecessary had the East German authorities instead relied on denunciations.[19] Because they insisted on using informants, the Stasi had to expend much of their time and resources on recruitment efforts. In this setting, however, there was little urgency. East Germany became a Communist country controlled by the Soviet Union in the aftermath of World War II, and Soviet troops remained in the country for the duration of its existence. With little need for swift action to stabilize a volatile situation, the East German authorities patiently created an army of informants.

Simply because such a system takes more time to establish does not mean that the information received from informants is necessarily more reliable.[20] In fact, there is strong reason to believe that informants behave similarly to denouncers in the coercion model, as they are also motivated by authority-based incentives.[21] Regardless, the difference in time and resources necessary to establish each system is clear. Repressive regimes needing to consolidate power quickly are likely to favor denunciations; in regimes where social control is not needed so immediately, the use of informants should be relatively more prevalent.[22]

Figure 5.1 presents these dynamics, showing the expected contrast between urgency and legitimacy and how we can expect this to manifest itself in institutions of social control. In settings with high urgency and high legitimacy, authorities are likely to encourage denunciations without the use of incentives. In settings with high urgency and low legitimacy, they are likely to use incentives to elicit denunciations. The less legitimate the authorities, the more likely those incentives are to be negative, as negative incentives tend to be more powerful than positive ones.[23] In settings with low urgency, authorities are more likely to use informants motivated by either positive or negative incentives.[24]

The distinction between high legitimacy and low legitimacy may apply not only to denunciations, but also to the use of informants. The extent to which informants are offered rewards as opposed to being coerced with threats varies. It is likely that

	High legitimacy	Low legitimacy
High urgency	Denouncers (Volunteers)	Denouncers (Negative incentives)
Low urgency	Informants (Positive incentives)	Informants (Negative incentives)

FIGURE 5.1 Types of social control and environment.

stronger incentives are necessary to recruit informants in low-legitimacy settings than in high-legitimacy ones. Therefore, in settings with low urgency and high legitimacy, authorities are more likely to offer informants positive incentives, whereas in settings with low urgency and low legitimacy, they are more likely to impose negative incentives. Concerns about legitimacy moderate both the strength of the incentives and their valence.[25]

DENUNCIATIONS IN THE BALANCE

Thus far, there has been an implicit assumption that there is a positive relationship between the volume of denunciations and the imposition of social control. In the coercion model, stronger incentives increase the volume of denunciations, which leads to more social control. In the volunteer model, more protections for denouncers and a greater likelihood of harm for those denounced lead to more denunciations, which again enhances social control. This is surely true for low and moderate levels of denunciations. Few denunciations have little effect on social control, as they neither punish nor deter misconduct. As denunciations increase, this also increases punishment and deterrence.

Where this relationship does not hold is at the other extreme, when denunciations become rampant. At especially high volumes, denunciations create chaos rather than control, terror instead of stability. When everyone denounces, the likelihood of any particular individual being denounced approaches certainty, which causes people to either focus exclusively on avoiding being denounced or flee the environment entirely. Two historical examples illustrate this effect.

During the Spanish Inquisition, the Edict of Grace served as such a powerful incentive in the early years that some converso communities practically disappeared. Not only were people denounced and punished, but many conversos fled from the inquisitors. In Seville, so many people escaped after the first arrests and later after the first victims were burned that Ferdinand and Isabella ordered all inhabitants of Seville and its archdiocese to remain in their houses. As described by Andres Bernaldez, who observed this first tribunal, "A penalty was imposed upon them, that they could not flee the city under pain of death, and guards were put at the city gates; so many were seized that there was no place to put them. Still, many fled to the lands of nobles, to Portugal, and to the land of the Moors."[26] The contemporary chronicler Alonso de Palencia characterized the city of Seville as "almost uninhabited" in the wake of the Inquisition between those who fled and those who were punished.[27] The vague and diffuse nature of crimes, along with denouncers' willingness to report whatever they thought would appease the authorities, impelled many people to leave, regardless of whether they had committed heresy. This was not the intent of the Inquisition; the objective was to punish and control heresy, not to drive large numbers of conversos from their homes.

A second example involves workers at one particular factory in the Soviet Union in the late 1930s. Soviet officials urged the employees to denounce "enemies of the people" and a strong culture of denunciation emerged.[28] This quickly expanded into full-blown terror:

> Throughout the spring of 1937, the political terrain became ever more dangerous and difficult to negotiate. Party members construed silence as evidence of enemy sympathies, demanded public criticism of victims as a demonstration of loyalty, employed the preemptive [denunciations] as an insurance policy and named their superiors in an attempt to deflect blame for their own associations with "enemies." They learned and adopted all of these strategies quickly. Yet the very behaviors that offered some measure of protection for the individual served only to implicate ever-larger numbers within the group. . . . Like drowning people, they tried to save themselves by struggling atop the bodies of their comrades and frantically pushing them underwater.[29]

Rampant denunciation resulted in chaos, as workers became focused exclusively on protecting themselves by sacrificing others. The factory—which was a key element in the country's economic plans—lost numerous shop heads, engineers, managers, and technical employees to false denunciations. The people who did remain were powerless: managers lost control of their workers and technical staff were terrified of making decisions. The factory fell short of its production targets in April, May, and June and failed to achieve its annual plan for 1937. Similar to some villages during the Spanish Inquisition, unchecked denunciations led to disruption and panic, not social control.[30]

These examples reveal the curvilinear relationship between the volume of denunciations and the extent to which social control is imposed. Initially, increasing numbers of denunciations facilitate the authorities' ability to control the behavior of their constituents. However, at extreme levels denunciations can result in a lack of control, as constituents engage in behaviors that disrupt more than they control, and are ultimately counter to the interests of the regime.

This relationship raises the question of why institutions of denunciation do not more often devolve into these extremes. Because denouncers' primary motivation is to gain personal or social benefits, they are not hindered by whether they have actual knowledge of misdeeds; they can always fabricate information. Yet in most settings with widespread denunciations, denouncers still make up a minority of the population: enough to enhance social control, but few enough to prevent chaos. One reason for this balance is the presence of a common social norm against denouncing.

Norms are standards of behavior that are enforced within groups. When they are violated, it is an affront to the community and anyone within the group is liable to administer sanctions. Norms serve as informal forms of social control, in contrast to the formal means of social control that is the focus of this book. Norms against denouncing are common, especially denouncing other group members.[31] Denunciations are seen as a betrayal of the community because they entail placing the interest of the self or the authorities over group loyalty. It is for this reason that colloquial terms for denouncers—snitch, tattletale, rat—often have negative connotations. People follow these norms because they fear sanctions within the community for violating them or because they have internalized the norm as a core personal value. In either case, the existence of such social norms can have a major impact on whether people denounce.[32]

The power of these norms can be seen among entertainment-industry workers in the United States during the late 1940s and early 1950s. Due to fears about communism, actors, writers, and directors from Hollywood—many at the height of their careers—were subpoenaed by the United States government to appear before the House Un-American Activities Committee (HUAC) and answer questions about their connections to the Communist Party. Those who refused to denounce others were blacklisted from the industry, their careers effectively over. Yet of the 110 people who were subpoenaed and forced to testify before HUAC, 52 sacrificed their careers and refused to incriminate others.[33] As actor Larry Parks explained to the committee,

> I would prefer not to mention names, if it is at all possible, of any-one. I don't think it is fair to people to do this. I have come to you at your request. I have come and willingly [*sic*] tell you about myself. I think that, if you would allow me, I would prefer not to be questioned about names . . . to force a man to do this is not American justice.[34]

He later pleaded, "Don't present me with the choice of either being in contempt of this Committee and going to jail or forcing me to really crawl through the mud to be an informer. For what purpose?"[35]

Such norms would appear to be in opposition to the interests of the authorities, as they privilege the interests of the community over the interests of the state. Local norms against denouncing hinder authorities from gaining information, and—as a consequence—information-gathering likely requires stronger authority-based incentives or institutional features more conducive to voluntary denunciations than would otherwise be necessary. Yet if countervailing pressures to denounce did not exist, there would be little inhibiting people from seeking the benefits available through denunciation. Somewhat paradoxically, the presence of community norms against denouncing helps to ensure that denunciations result in centralized social control rather than chaos. In this sense, not denouncing does not weaken the authorities, but instead supports them.

BEYOND REPRESSION

Although thus far this book has focused on repressive regimes, denunciations take place in all types of societies. In modern America, they take several different forms, four of the most prevalent being plea-bargaining, whistle-blowing, crime reporting, and denunciations associated with counterterrorism efforts.[36] Unlike denunciations commonly seen in repressive regimes, these are not generally allegations of improper speech, nor are many of the alleged crimes victimless. Denunciations in today's United States include allegations of the full range of criminal activity, from illegal drug use to tax fraud to plotting terrorist attacks. Despite this variation, these denunciations often follow the familiar dynamics of the coercion and volunteer models common throughout repressive regimes.

Plea-Bargaining

It is estimated that 90 to 95 percent of criminal cases in the United States never go to trial, but instead result in plea bargains where the defendant accepts some level of guilt or provides useful information in exchange for a lesser charge or a more lenient sentence.[37] A subset of plea bargains involve denunciations, where the defendant agrees to provide specific information about the illegal activities of others in exchange for benefits. Such "state's evidence" agreements allow the coercion model to pervade the criminal justice system. It is estimated that defendants provide incriminating information in an attempt to obtain benefits in as many as 68 percent of all cases,[38] and in federal cases defendants actually receive some benefit for their evidence in 10 to 20 percent of cases per year.[39]

State's evidence agreements have a long history in the United States, dating back to the seventeenth century, when they were known as "approvements." They were formally acknowledged by the United States Supreme Court in 1878, when the practice of granting immunity to offenders who provided evidence against their accomplices was codified in case law.[40]

These agreements are reached in various ways, contingent largely on when in the criminal justice process the potential defendant offers or is induced to cooperate. If negotiations begin during his or her first encounter with the police, an arrest may not be made and the crime never recorded. If the arrest has already occurred, certain aspects of the crime may be modified or omitted from official reports. If cooperation is obtained later in the criminal justice process, the defendant may be offered a lighter punishment or no punishment at all, often through a reduction in the severity of the charge. Prosecutors have almost complete discretion in charging decisions and charges can be easily dropped or altered. Prosecutors may also make favorable recommendations to the judge at sentencing.

If defendants do not cooperate, they lose access to these potential mitigators. Non-cooperators may also face additional negative consequences. Prosecutors have the freedom to charge defendants for more serious offenses, and the Supreme Court has ruled that the government can seek and impose harsher punishment in retaliation for an accused person's refusal to cooperate.[41] Although negative incentives are likely the most powerful, there can be positive incentives for cooperation as well. Federal agencies spend up to $100 million annually on direct financial assistance for cooperators,[42] and local police departments also have money available for such practices.

Given this institutional structure, defendants in the US criminal justice system are eager to provide the information that they believe the authorities want, regardless of whether it is true. The unreliability of cooperators has been emphasized repeatedly in both federal and state court cases. As one court declared, "It is difficult to imagine a greater motivation to lie than the inducement of a reduced sentence."[43] Many prosecutors have also noted the clear incentives offenders have to exaggerate or falsify information.[44] When prosecutors or investigators indicate or imply—sometimes unintentionally—that they are following a particular lead, the cooperator often affirms that individual's guilt, even if this requires modifying his or her story. Prosecutors refer to this as "This Is What They Want To Hear Time rather than This Is What Happened Time."[45] As Judge Stephen Trott stated,

> Criminals are likely to say and do almost anything to get what they want, especially when what they want is to get out of trouble with the law. This willingness to do anything includes not only truthfully spilling the beans on friends and relatives, but also lying, committing perjury, manufacturing evidence, soliciting others to corroborate their lies with more lies, and double-crossing anyone with whom they come into contact, including—and especially—the prosecutor.[46]

Even though it is well-known that they have an incentive to lie, it is often impossible to fully determine whether a specific cooperator is telling the truth. Even when certain aspects of a story can be corroborated, it is rare to be able to confirm every detail. For example, the fact that an alleged phone call took place may be verified, but it may not be possible to confirm the specific remarks reported by a cooperator.[47] As legal scholar Alexandra Natapoff put it, the problem is "not that criminal informants always lie. Rather, it can be extremely hard to tell when they do and when they don't."[48]

Studies of false murder convictions have found that up to 56 percent are the result of perjury by cooperators seeking plea bargains.[49] Yet there are few consequences for lying. Despite many lawyers believing that perjury among cooperators is widespread, fewer than 0.1 percent of arrests for federal offenses are for perjury.[50] Individuals have an incentive to tell the authorities whatever they think will provide personal benefit and they often have the means to get away with it.

This is not to say that plea-bargaining does not help to some extent in the identification of wrongdoing. As one court declared,

> our criminal justice system could not adequately function without information provided by informants. . . . Without informants, law enforcement authorities would be unable to penetrate and destroy organized crime syndicates, drug trafficking cartels, bank frauds, telephone solicitation scams, public corruption, terrorist gangs, money launderers, espionage rights, and the like.[51]

Plea-bargaining indeed facilitates the capturing of some number of criminals. Yet the way in which the system is structured often privileges the quantity of information over the quality of evidence. Identifying additional criminals is given more weight than fully prosecuting substantiated crimes. Instead, known criminals are given lesser sentences while the people who have been denounced may find themselves falsely convicted.[52]

Whistle-Blowing

Another common form of denunciation in modern America is whistle-blowing: the reporting of illegal or improper behavior that takes place within an organizational context. Whistle-blowers are "employees or former employees who report misconduct to persons who have the power to take action."[53] Whistle-blowing can occur internally, when an individual reports wrongdoing to someone within the organization, or externally, when he or she reports wrongdoing to someone outside of the organization, often a legal authority or regulatory official or the press. In some cases, a whistle-blower will first go to an internal source and, if he or she does not receive a satisfactory response, will then make an external complaint.

Because whistle-blowing occurs within organizations, it typically involves white-collar offenses, including tax fraud, securities fraud, procurement fraud, money-laundering, bribery, and the waste or abuse of expenditures. It also includes the reporting of nonfinancial crimes, including workplace harassment or abuse, racist or sexist work environments, violations of employment or environmental regulations, and falsifying data to regulators.

Unlike plea-bargaining, whistle-blowing can be either coercive or voluntary. Coercive whistle-blowing generally involves positive incentives. The False Claims Act, which was passed in 1987, allows whistle-blowers to receive up to 30 percent of any costs recovered from those who defraud the government. Over the first eight years of the law's existence, relevant whistle-blowing increased from 33 to 274 cases per year.[54] Voluntary whistle-blowing offers no tangible rewards, either from the government or other regulators.

Some whistle-blowing preserves anonymity. On the assumption that whistle-blowers face retaliation for their actions, the Sarbanes-Oxley Act of 2002 required that all public companies provide their employees with an anonymous means of reporting misdeeds.[55] Anonymity protects whistle-blowers from retaliation or ostracism within their organizational community. However, the extent to which they are actually at risk for retaliation is unclear.[56]

Although the popular press often depicts whistle-blowers as altruists, evidence does not support this. Whistle-blowers do not have stronger moral judgment than people who observe malfeasance and do not report it.[57] Indeed, the former may often be motivated by personal or social advantage, seeking to gain financial payments or to harm a particular colleague. As a 2008 book on the subject concludes, "If 'purely altruistic' means that there is absolutely no benefit to the actor, there would be virtually no whistle-blowing."[58] Some whistle-blowers appear to have mixed motives, with at least some of the motivation self-serving. As criminologist Terance Miethe reports based on interviews, "the respondent will usually say one thing ('It was the morally right thing to do') but later in the interview will invariably convey a different motivation ('The boss was a sniveling bastard so I nailed him')."[59]

Given the role self-interest plays in inducing whistle-blowers to come forward, it seems likely that they sometimes fabricate information in an attempt to gain personal or social benefits. Although it is difficult to say how often this occurs, the infrequency with which whistle-blowing reports result in useful information is suggestive. For example, the United States

General Accounting Office (GAO) established a whistle-blowing hotline in 1979 so that individuals could call in to report fraud, waste, and abuse in federal expenditures. Over the first decade of its existence, the GAO—which did not offer rewards—received over 94,000 calls regarding the private use of government property, fraud by benefits recipients, mismanagement by government employees, and work-hour abuses. Of these, approximately 10,000 (11 percent) were deemed worthy of investigation. Of the calls that were investigated, approximately 1,100 of the allegations were substantiated.[60] This means that only about 1 percent of these denunciations resulted in useful information. Unfortunately, the details and motivations of the other 99 percent are unknown.

This is not to say that the hotline was ineffective. Indeed, the GAO considered it a success, as they identified $20 million in misspent funds and a further $24 million in future savings.[61] As with many such institutions, the GAO authorities viewed their hotline as beneficial, despite the preponderance of unhelpful information.

Crime Reporting

The third major category of denunciations in the contemporary United States is crime reporting, where individuals report non-business-related offenses to the police or other law-enforcement officials. These include property crimes such as theft or vandalism and violent crimes such as assault or murder. According to criminologist Barbara Warner, a person's decision to report a crime "may be the most influential decision in the criminal justice system" because "those who report crime are the true 'gatekeepers.'"[62] This is because there is often "no feasible way to solve most crime except by securing the cooperation of the citizens to link a person to the crime."[63] Studies that have looked at the level of police mobilizations instigated by citizens find upward of 70, 80, and even 90 percent.[64]

Not all crime reports are denunciations. Many are made by victims, while other people notify the authorities of crimes without providing any indication of who committed them. However, many other reports *are* denunciations, which the police and community organizations facilitate in a variety of ways. Thousands of local Neighborhood Watch programs coordinate monitoring and the reporting of criminal activities within communities.[65] The Crime Stoppers program has hundreds of national and international chapters, which manage local tip hotlines where callers can report crimes anonymously and earn cash rewards. Both of these programs are often incorporated into "community policing" initiatives and are meant to involve community members in the active identification and reporting of criminal suspects.

Perhaps the most well-known example of a program aimed at facilitating crime reporting is the "See Something, Say Something" campaign, which seeks to elicit information about terrorist threats. Started by the New York Metropolitan Transportation Authority after the terrorist attacks of September 11, 2001, this program has since spread nationally under the aegis of the Department of Homeland Security. People who come forward and report suspicious behavior are guaranteed legal protection: the law states that "any person who, in good faith and based on objectively reasonable suspicion, makes, or causes to be made, a voluntary report of covered activity to an authorized official shall be immune from civil liability under Federal, State, and local law for such report."[66]

Despite the ubiquity of such programs, the majority of crimes go unreported. It has been estimated that in 2016, only 42 percent of violent crimes were reported, along with 36 percent of property crimes.[67] And many of the crimes that are reported go unsolved: clearance rates are less than 50 percent for violent crimes and below 20 percent for property crimes.[68] This is not because of a shortage of police resources: it is estimated that doubling or tripling the number of detectives would have virtually no effect.[69] Instead, the issue is that too few people provide the authorities with the local information needed to make an arrest and conviction.

It is possible that individuals do not report on others because they lack the authority-based incentives to do so. As one of the rare instances of a program that does offer monetary incentives for information, the Crime Stoppers tip hotline represents an interesting counterexample. Although Neighborhood Watch programs do not lead to an increase in reporting rates,[70] Crime Stoppers receives a large number of calls, likely due to the cash rewards it offers.[71] Supporting the idea that incentives drive crime reports, when the 2008 recession hit, the number of calls skyrocketed:

> Calls to the Southwest Florida Crime Stoppers hot line in the first quarter of this year were up 30 percent over last year. San Antonio had a 44 percent increase. Cities and towns from Detroit to Omaha to Beaufort County, N.C., all report increases of 25 percent or more in the first quarter, with tipsters telling operators they need the money for rent, light bills or baby formula.[72]

However, as would be expected in the coercion model, many of these self-interested tips are not particularly beneficial to the authorities. One study of Crime Stoppers found that only

1 percent of calls actually led to arrests; another study found little better at 1.9 percent.[73]

Indeed, convincing people to denounce others truthfully has proved enormously challenging for the criminal justice system and has led to a great deal of research exploring bystanders' reluctance to report witnessed crimes.[74] One study using staged bicycle thefts found that 93 percent of witnesses did not intervene and only 5 percent alerted the police.[75] A series of shoplifting experiments found that people are generally unwilling to report such crimes, with reporting rates as low as 2 percent.[76] These results, however, should be relatively unsurprising. In contexts without authority-based incentives and lacking enduring social relations it is little wonder that few people report. Even third parties who report real crimes to the authorities often have a preexisting family or friendship relation with the victim, giving them a strong motivation to desire harm for the perpetrator.[77]

Counterterrorism

Denunciations have been an important part of counterterrorism efforts ever since the terrorist attacks of September 11, 2001. In addition to domestic tip hotlines such as the "See Something, Say Something" campaign, denunciations have been used extensively to fight terrorism abroad, as American forces are in particular need of local information in foreign contexts. The most infamous method of eliciting denunciations is surely the use of "enhanced interrogation techniques," where suspected terrorists were questioned about their co-conspirators and future planned attacks. These techniques are extremely coercive in nature and involve stress positions, waterboarding, and various forms of deprivation.[78] Debates about their use generally take the form of morality versus expediency, where some people argue that the techniques are never morally justified and others that the end justifies the means. As has been seen in other instances of the coercion model, however, the expediency argument is dubious. In situations where individuals face intense coercive pressure, they often provide false information in the hope that this will cause it to stop.[79]

Although it is difficult to assess the effectiveness of such techniques due to the classified nature of the materials, Central Intelligence Agency reports do not contradict this viewpoint. The agency concluded at the end of the Cold War that such techniques were not particularly effective,[80] and admitted in a 2004 report, "Measuring the effectiveness of [enhanced interrogation techniques] is a more subjective process and not without some concern."[81] Don Dzagulones was an interrogator with the United States Army who witnessed and participated in torture in Vietnam. As he bluntly explained, the idea that such techniques lead to viable information is a myth:

> If [effective torture] happened, I am certainly not aware of it. Like prisoner X comes in, you beat the living snot out of him. He tells you about a Viet Cong ambush that is going to happen tomorrow, you relay this information to the infantry guys, and they counter-ambush and the good guys win and the bad guys lose, all because you tortured a prisoner. Never happened.[82]

The use of denunciation in counterterrorism efforts has other forms that go beyond interrogation. Tip hotlines have been widely used in Iraq and Afghanistan, where citizens are encouraged to report terrorist activity anonymously and voluntarily.[83] One hotline has received as many as 1,200 false calls for every five legitimate tips. Many of these false calls were intended to confuse and mislead the occupying forces and support the insurgency, a phenomenon that generally does not occur when a single authority has a monopoly on violence.[84] It appears that some of the legitimate tips did lead to valuable intelligence. These increased in response to insurgent violence against civilians and insurgent appropriation of civilian property, as individuals sought to punish the insurgents who had harmed them.[85]

Denunciations have been especially widely used—and have had especially adverse consequences—in the war in Afghanistan. After invading the country in 2001, US forces sought local allies to provide intelligence and encouraged them to denounce active terrorists. By April 2002, however, al-Qaida had fled the country and the Taliban had surrendered their weapons and retired to their homes. There were no more terrorists, yet the American forces were charged with an overriding mandate to defeat terrorism.[86] This led to a problem:

How do you fight a war without an adversary? Enter Gul Agha Sherzai—and men like him around the country. Eager to survive and prosper, he and his commanders followed the logic of the American presence to its obvious conclusion. They would create enemies where there were none, exploiting the perverse incentive mechanism that the Americans—without even realizing it—had put in place. Sherzai's enemies became America's enemies, his battles its battles. His personal feuds and jealousies were repackaged as "counterterrorism," his business interests as Washington's. And where rivalries did not do the trick, the prospect of further profits did. (One American leaflet dropped by plane in the area read: "Get Wealth and Power Beyond Your Dreams. Help Anti-Taliban Forces Rid Afghanistan of Murderers and Terrorists.")[87]

Because of the positive incentives set up by US authorities, local Afghans jockeyed for power by feigning support for the Americans while denouncing their enemies as terrorists.[88] The Americans considered these denunciations valid and relied on them even when their only supporting evidence was innocuous behavior such as the "use of a guest house" or the "possession of Casio watches."[89] This led to many pro-American Afghans being arrested, interrogated, or killed by unsuspecting US forces.[90]

Ultimately, this behavior undermined social control rather than bolstering it. By killing the wrong people, the Americans effectively created the terrorists they were trying to eradicate. Only those few Afghans who had gained their trust had the power to denounce, while the rest of the population remained powerless. For many people from tribes other than the rising power brokers, violent resistance or flight became the only tenable options.[91]

There are two key differences between the system of denunciation established in Afghanistan and those detailed in the previous chapters. First, the people who were denounced had little connection to actual terrorism, as Afghan denouncers were strategic and the Americans had no way of adequately investigating their claims. In the settings of the previous chapters, although many denunciations were false, there was some correlation (or perception of one) between actual misbehavior and the people punished. In Afghanistan, all that mattered was one's alignment with powerful figures. Second, only people trusted by the Americans were able to denounce. In the previous chapters, denunciations were egalitarian. Conditions in Afghanistan gave power to those locals who had the Americans' trust and impelled others to flee and revolt. Social control was not imposed, not because too many people denounced, but because a few local actors were able to monopolize denunciations for their own personal benefit.

SOCIAL CONTROL AND
RETRIBUTIVE JUSTICE

As the previous sections have shown, denunciations in modern America are in many ways similar to those in repressive regimes. This similarity arises from the common interests of authorities and denouncers in both types of settings: authorities desire to punish misbehavior and deter future wrongdoing, while individuals seek to gain benefits from the authorities or harm social rivals. On a deeper level, these similarities reveal a tension between backward-looking punishment and forward-looking deterrence that arises from the dynamics of the two models.

In many contexts, punishing past behavior and deterring future behavior are aligned. By punishing transgressions, both violators and outside observers are deterred from committing future crimes. Punishment begets generalized deterrence, so long as a sufficient percentage of perpetrators are apprehended.

The particular dynamics of denunciation in the coercion and volunteer models somewhat decouples this relationship. Under the two models, when witnesses do not have ulterior motives, most crimes are not reported; when they do have ulterior motives, many individuals are denounced falsely or for negligible behavior. Many serious crimes are at risk of going unsolved or undetected, and people who are denounced falsely are at risk of suffering unjust punishment.

Consider the contrast between two regimes—one focused on backward-looking punishment, the other on forward-looking deterrence.[92] In the first scenario, the regime would face challenges in properly identifying wrongdoers, as many perpetrators would not be denounced and many of those who were denounced would not be perpetrators. In order to disburse punishment as accurately as possible, the authorities would likely strive to minimize false denunciations. This could be accomplished by requiring thorough investigations to corroborate a denouncer's report before providing any authority-based rewards or harming the person denounced. The authorities might also punish false denouncers. Together, these institutional features would greatly curtail the number of denunciations made but increase their accuracy, allowing the authorities to err on the side of not punishing innocents. Ultimately, few individuals would be punished, but the accuracy among those punished would be high. This type of behavior, where wrongdoers are punished proportionally to their crimes and the innocent go unpunished, is commonly known as retributive justice.

In the second regime, the authorities would be dealing with similarly incomplete and inaccurate information, but would be more focused on deterrence than on punishment. However, to better deter criminals, it is to the authorities' benefit to punish more people. Some of those punished could even be innocent, so long as it is credible that they might have committed a crime. The presence of a denunciation can help to signal credibility to outside observers. By punishing a mix of guilty and innocent people who have all been denounced, authorities can give the impression that a high percentage of perpetrators are apprehended and punished. This serves to increase deterrence, as the likelihood of punishment for committing a crime appears high, even though its accuracy may be low. To accomplish this, the deterrent regime would likely encourage many denunciations, allowing anyone to make them and not implementing safeguards to prevent false or petty reports.[93] Such an approach is consistent with utilitarian theories of justice, which focus on the outcome of punishment rather than its accuracy.

The difference between these two regimes is not binary, but represents a continuum along which retrospective punishment and prospective deterrence are emphasized differentially. The more a society favors deterrence, the more it resembles the repressive regimes in the previous chapters. The more it favors accurate punishment, the more it resembles the ideals of liberal democracy.[94] As punishment and deterrence are both goals of democratic societies, this creates a tension in how to structure legal institutions. The current system of plea-bargaining has elements of deterrence: it seeks to identify a greater number of criminals at the expense of giving lighter punishments to people already in custody and at the risk of punishing some who have done no wrong. Counterterrorism efforts move even further along the continuum toward deterrence, and many innocent people (as in Afghanistan) have been harmed as a result. Yet focusing on accurate punishment and protecting the innocent can sometimes result in so few people being punished that social control is not enacted at all. In the absence of deterrence, criminal behavior becomes tacitly permitted.[95] By decoupling punishment from deterrence, the two models of denunciation lead to trade-offs with which all types of societies must grapple.

This discussion of punishment versus deterrence is predicated on the assumption that denunciations follow either the coercion or the volunteer model, leading to incomplete and unreliable information. Indeed, that is what all the settings examined thus far suggest. However, there may be certain rarer conditions under which denunciations are not purely self-interested. This would occur in a third model, which I call the prosocial model of denunciation.

THE PROSOCIAL MODEL

The case studies in the previous chapters suggest that people will inevitably provide denunciations out of self-interest. Yet individuals often behave in cooperative ways in their everyday lives, working together and providing one another with assistance. It stands to reason that under certain conditions people might denounce others not solely to benefit themselves but also in hopes of benefiting other members of the community. These would be instances of prosocial denunciation.[96]

Conceptually, prosocial behavior is distinct from altruism. In order for an act to be altruistic, it must have the ultimate goal of increasing another person's welfare.[97] Like ideological behavior, altruism is selfless in that the purpose of the behavior is external to the self.[98] Prosocial behavior, on the other hand, is a mix of self-interest and a desire to help others.[99] In other words, it occurs when self-interest and others-interest are aligned and action is motivated by a desire to benefit both.[100] It is not necessary for unselfish motives to predominate over selfish ones for a behavior to be prosocial, so long as both are present.[101]

In prosocial denunciation, a denouncer does not seek to be the sole beneficiary of his or her denunciatory act, but also intends to benefit others.[102] Such denunciations most commonly arise from fear of a perceived threat that endangers both the individual and the community. Repelling the threat becomes a way of helping the community to survive, along with the individual within it. When people feel threatened and the authorities are receptive and responsive to denunciations, prosocial denunciations are likely to become widespread.

Perceived threats can take many different forms; their key feature is that they represent generalized threats at the group level, not threats targeted at specific individuals.[103] These may be physical threats such as gang activity, crime, or unsafe health practices that endanger public health. They can also be less tangible, such as threats to community beliefs or values. In the case of intangible threats, prosocial denunciations can arise from concerns that immoral conduct is threatening the spiritual or moral purity of the individual and the community as a whole. Had villagers truly feared that the perpetuation of Jewish practices by conversos represented an ecclesiastical threat to their souls, the Spanish Inquisition could have taken this form. Instead, concern about conversos as a religious threat never coalesced in the general population.

In the prosocial model, denouncers are oriented toward people who are perceived as threatening the community in some way. Such threats are generally seen as coming from outsiders, either literal out-groups or community members whose behavior or social standing marks them as marginalized. Prosocial denouncers want those who represent the threat to be punished, not in order to win favor with the authorities or to harm a rival, but to stop the threat from endangering their way of life.

Another way to conceptualize the prosocial model is to consider the three sets of actors involved in denunciations: denouncers, the people denounced, and the authorities. Recall that the critical relationship in the coercion model is between the denouncer and the authorities, as denouncers seek primarily to satisfy the authorities' demands. The critical relationship in the volunteer model is between the denouncer and the person denounced, as denouncers seek to harm particular individuals within their community. The critical relationship in the prosocial model is between the person denounced and the authorities. In this model, the denouncer's primary concern is that the threat represented by offending individuals be neutralized. The denouncer does not seek direct benefits from the authorities and

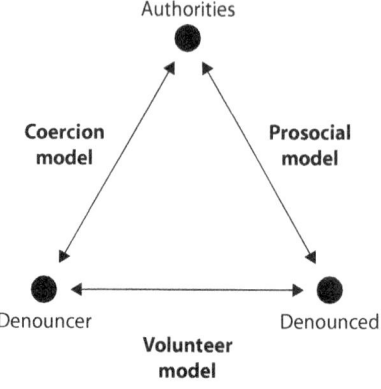

FIGURE 5.2 Three models of denunciation.

is not concerned with the specific identity of the person denounced vis-à-vis him- or herself. Rather, the denouncer perceives a threat and wants the authorities to remove it. The representation of the three models is depicted in figure 5.2, where each leg of the triangle indicates the key relationship for that model.

Of course, it is important to emphasize that the prosocial model (indeed, all three models) serves as an ideal type. Despite their distinctiveness in figure 5.2, no real-world scenario perfectly reflects any one of the three models. As we have seen, particular settings correspond more with one model than the other, but within any given setting individuals can have a variety of reasons for why they denounce, and even a single individual can have mixed motives. Yet in the aggregate, the tendencies of denouncers can help us understand a lot about the dynamics of denunciation within that setting.

Like incentives under the coercion model, the perceived threats that motivate denunciations in the prosocial model can vary in intensity. The stronger the perceived threat, the more likely denunciations of this type are to be widespread. At its extreme, this leads to a phenomenon known as moral panic.[104]

Moral panics involve a widespread and disproportionate reaction against a perceived communal threat that "is much like a fever: heightened emotion, fear, dread, hostility, and a strong feeling of righteousness."[105] Often this results in rapidly spreading denunciations and demands for excessive punishment.[106] Because of their intensity, moral panics are usually short in duration; either the threat is vanquished or, more commonly, the feared consequences fail to occur. The moral panic framework has been used to describe phenomena ranging from fear of communism in the 1950s to concern about mugging in the 1970s to worry about satanic child abuse in the 1980s.[107]

Moral panic—and the prosocial model more generally—can have a variety of origins. In some cases, the authorities conduct an intentional campaign to arouse fear and direct hostility toward a particular group. In others, a particular threat is promoted by the media or interest groups; in still others, it arises from the grassroots. Because of this heterogeneity and the emotional nature of the phenomenon, there is no particular institutional feature that gives rise to prosocial denunciations; the prosocial model is not as easy to instigate or maintain as the volunteer and coercion models. This is not to say, however, that institutions of social control do not play a role. If the authorities are not receptive to denunciations or do not punish those denounced, then denouncing is unlikely to occur even if the perceived threat remains.

Perhaps the most famous instance of the prosocial model taken to extremes is the Salem Witch Trials, which swept through the Massachusetts Bay Colony in 1692.[108] Early in that year, two young girls of Salem Village began having strange episodes in which they experienced "odd postures, foolish, ridiculous speeches, distempers, fits."[109] After repeated attempts to treat the girls, the local physician concluded that they had been bewitched. Under repeated questioning, the girls named three culprits: Sarah Good and Sarah Osburn, two women living at the margins of Salem society, and Tituba, the Indian slave of the minister. On February 29, 1692, four men of Salem Village formally denounced the three women.

The suspects were arrested and questioned in front of much of the village. Whereas Sarah Good and Sarah Osburn denied the charges, Tituba readily admitted that "the devil came to me and bid me serve him."[110] When asked who else hurt the children, she mentioned a larger conspiracy that included a tall man of Boston and two unknown women. She further described their desire to kill children. From this admission, fear spread throughout Salem and the neighboring villages and more and more people were denounced for witchcraft in a panicked attempt to stop the threat. By the time the trials ended less than a year later, more than one hundred and fifty people had been denounced and twenty people had been put to death.[111]

Although there were no real witches in the Massachusetts Bay Colony, many people were swept up in the misguided attempt to keep themselves and the community safe from the perceived threat. When individuals feel threatened, they become liable to see crimes where none exist. Because of this, the prosocial model can lead to the same flood of false and petty denunciations as the other two models, as individuals report their vaguest suspicions or interpret innocuous behavior as malfeasant. The greater the perceived threat, the greater the quantity and the lower the quality of denunciations. Correspondingly, the more that people denounce each other for imagined wrongdoings, the less safe everyone feels, as the threatening behavior appears to grow in scope.

Given these dynamics, the prosocial model leads to different predictions than the other two. First, we can expect denouncers in the prosocial model to denounce outsiders whom they find threatening. These will be largely out-group members who fit the in-group's stereotypical representation of the threat, whether old widows who look like witches or young teenagers who dress like gangsters. Under the prosocial model, therefore, we would expect more intergroup denouncing than is found in the other two models; it is the different and unfamiliar that generates the threat. Similarly, denouncers should tend to report people lower in status than themselves; this again would tend to single out outcasts and outsiders, who are not viewed as upstanding members of the community.[112] Also, whereas the coercion model predicts that denouncers will denounce multiple people and the volunteer model predicts that denouncers will be more selective, the prosocial model predicts that many people will denounce the same individual. Once a person is identified as a threat, fear may lead to a bandwagon effect, where that individual's suspected guilt is reinforced throughout the community and many people make identical denunciations.[113] Finally, in this model we can expect many unintentionally false denunciations when the perceived threat is strong.[114]

The prosocial model has two additional expectations, neither comparable to the predictions of the other models. The first is that denunciations will spread through networks of affiliation. When someone is labeled as threatening in a highly fearful environment, family members or others close to that person can become suspect themselves through association.[115] As a result, under the prosocial model, denunciations can be expected to follow chains of relationships. Second, the prosocial model is likely to transform into the coercion or volunteer model once the panic (which is usually short-lived) abates. Even after the panic has died away, as long as the authorities remain receptive to denunciations, individuals may begin to denounce in order to gain benefits from the authorities or to harm their neighbors. There is some evidence that such a shift may have occurred in Salem: although the initial denunciations within villages were against women who fit stereotypical descriptions of witches, denunciations ultimately tended to cross a preexisting political divide regarding whether to align the community with or distance it from the growing commercialism of the nearby port.[116]

In modern settings, prosocial denouncing should be observable in contexts where groups of people feel threatened or unsafe.[117] One possible example is the early years of the Crime Stoppers program. Although it now appears to follow the coercion model, the program was born in a very different social and political climate. In the 1970s, rising crime rates led many citizens to consider crime to be one of the worst problems in their communities.[118] Drugs and violence were seen as particularly dangerous threats to society, and from 1965 to the mid-1970s many Americans' fear of criminal victimization increased substantially.[119] Fifty-five percent of adults said they were uneasy walking the streets of their own neighborhoods.[120] As one report put it, "Crime and the fear of crime have, like a dark dye, permeated the fabric of American life."[121] Some people began referring to people unaffected by crime as the "not yet victimized," emphasizing its inevitability.[122]

It was in this atmosphere that the Crime Stoppers tip hotlines were created, first in Albuquerque, New Mexico, and then rapidly expanding to hundreds of local chapters around the country. Callers to the hotlines expressed an oppressive sense of threat that justified denouncing others in their own community. As one caller said, "There's too damned much crime. I'd turn in my own mother if she broke the law." Another declared, "Trying to get people who threaten society behind bars is not snitching! It is being responsible."[123] In the early days of the program, many people probably called Crime Stoppers out of a desire to live without fear and to increase their own and the community's safety. Without further investigation, however, it is impossible to know if this was indeed the case. Even if the calls were initially motivated by the perceived threat, it is unclear how long that sense of threat lasted. By the time of the financial crisis in 2008—and likely far sooner—individuals were responding primarily to authority-based incentives rather than acting out of fear.

Although the prosocial model produces denunciations that are intended to be beneficial to the community, it can lead to the same false and petty denunciations seen in the other two models. Furthermore, it can result in unwarranted persecution and discrimination against members of a feared group. Such discrimination is evident when members of minority groups are denounced by majority group members for innocuous behavior. Several incidents that took place while this book was being written highlight this phenomenon: a white employee at a Starbucks coffee shop called the police on two black men who were waiting for a friend;[124] a white woman reported a black graduate student who was taking a nap in the common area of their dormitory to the police;[125] and a different white woman called the police on four people emerging from an Airbnb rental—three of them black—because she suspected a burglary.[126] In all three cases, those reported were innocent, yet they either suffered arrest or were treated with suspicion by the police, simply because the callers perceived ordinary behavior as threatening.

These types of incidents encapsulate the way in which denunciations can lead to social control even when there is no wrongdoing and no explicit punishment. The power that members of high-status groups have to mobilize the police forces members of other groups to adjust their behavior to conform with majority preferences if they want to avoid hardship. Police officers' willingness to assume that such unfounded denunciations are legitimate reinforces inequalities between groups. The prosocial model can enhance social control, but often at the expense of certain people who are victimized based solely on their group membership.

THE END OF DENUNCIATIONS?

Denunciations allow central authorities to monitor and police behavior in local communities, and community complainants are the "prime movers of every known legal system."[127] Yet as surveillance technologies rapidly improve, the need for local information may be increasingly satisfied by machines rather than individuals. If these trends continue, will denouncers ultimately become obsolete?

The past decade has seen the rise of big data analytics, which policing organizations are now using to monitor the populations they serve. These techniques allow for a greater number of people to be surveilled across a larger number of dimensions than at any time in history.[128] The internet, in particular, allows for a "new surveillance," which has become ubiquitous and increasingly unavoidable.[129] Making a phone call, sending an email, using a credit card, and browsing the internet all leave digital traces that can be collected and analyzed. Because of these developments, surveillance has become "more specialized and technical, and, in many ways, more penetrating and intrusive" than ever before.[130]

If these trends continue, there may come a time when central authorities have the means of accessing extensive information about the behavior of local individuals without the need for participation from the populace. The distinction between public and private may blur as people are constantly observed, identified, and recorded. This wellspring of data could then be automatically processed, with software detecting illegal or deviant behavior and notifying the proper authorities. This would be policing without denouncers or informants, and it is limited only by a regime's technical capabilities and its willingness to implement such methods.[131]

The question here is not whether such developments are positive or negative, but whether this trend will herald the end of denunciations. There are two major reasons to doubt this. For one, any new surveillance technology, no matter how sophisticated, tends to be met with neutralization techniques that mask behavior from its detection. Many individuals want at least some aspects of their lives to be private, and criminals in particular have a strong incentive to maintain privacy in order to conduct illicit activities. This means that the improvement of surveillance technology alone is unlikely to be sufficient to make denunciations obsolete as a means of social control; there will always be those who seek to escape technology's reach or exploit gaps or flaws in the system.

Most importantly, however, is the fact that denunciations are about far more than the eliciting and reporting of information, and their impact goes beyond punishment and deterrence. As has been seen, denunciations have a variety of additional effects. These include the legitimation of authorities' right to resolve and adjudicate complaints, creating the impression of broad support for a regime through widespread participation, and the strengthening of political and social engagement, binding local citizens to centralized authorities. These added effects help to consolidate authorities' power and increase regime stability. Law enforcement without citizen participation, even if comprehensive, loses this illusion of generalized support and fails to strengthen bonds between local individuals and authorities. By excluding citizen involvement, authorities may become entirely disconnected from the communities they govern, which may ultimately be destabilizing. Even in a world of widespread and automated surveillance, denunciations augment social control in ways that pure surveillance cannot.

For these reasons, denunciations are likely to persist into the future regardless of technological improvements in state-sponsored surveillance. To the extent that authorities desire stability and control, denunciations will continue. This is true regardless of whether a government is authoritarian or democratic, new or established, weak or strong. Centralized governance inevitably seeks to maintain its authority, and individuals strive to better themselves socially and economically and to increase safety within their local communities. Understanding how these systems function in all their complexity is important because institutions favorable to the reporting of denunciations are likely to appear again and again. And many of us, for one reason or another, will participate.

NOTES

I. A THEORY OF DENUNCIATION

1. This quote is reported by Gellately (1990, 139). A similar phenomenon occurred in the Soviet Union in the late 1930s, where the tide of letters became so great that authorities began to rail against false denunciations (Fitzpatrick 1996).

2. Lucas 1996.

3. "Immediately, while he was still speaking, Judas, one of the twelve, arrived, and with him there was a crowd with swords and clubs, from the chief priests, the scribes, and the elders. Now the betrayer had given them a sign, saying, 'The one I will kiss is the man; arrest him and lead him away under guard.' So when he came, he went up to him at once and said, 'Rabbi!' and kissed him. Then they laid hands on him and arrested him" (Mark 14:43–46 [New Revised Standard Version]).

4. Information about denunciations in these settings can be found in the following sources: Nazi Germany (Diewald-Kerkmann 1995; Dörner 1998; Johnson 1999; Mann 1987; Ruckenbiel 2005), the Dominican Republic (Derby 2003), Italy (Canali 2004; Franzinelli 1999; Franzinelli 2001), Argentina (Ruggiero 1988), Guatemala (Manz 1988), Libya (Davis 1990), Romania (Ioanid 2008; Vatalescu 2004), Revolutionary France (Lucas 1996), the Republic of Venice (Amato 2014), Romanov Russia (Lapman 1982), Early Modern Spain (Beinart 1981; Antón 1984), the Soviet Union (Fitzpatrick 1996; Goldman 2011), China (Chen and Chen 1953; Courtois and Kramer 1999), and North Korea (Rigoulot

1999). This is not meant to be an exhaustive list of settings; rather, it is intended to illustrate the scope of regimes with widespread denunciations across time and place.

5. Lease 1996.

6. Schrecker 1998.

7. Tattling is evident in children as early as fourteen months (Dunn and Munn 1985), and becomes prevalent by the age of two. Among two-year-olds, tattling represents 87 percent of communications about siblings' behavior (den Bak and Ross 1996), and among three- and four-year-olds in a classroom setting, 93 percent of statements made to an authority figure about another student (Ingram and Bering 2010).

8. Goffman 2009; Comfort 2008.

9. Sykes 2007.

10. Fitzpatrick and Gellately 1997, 2.

11. Davenport 2007; Goldstein 1978.

12. An exception is Nazi Germany, about which there has been much scholarly debate regarding the role of ordinary Germans in Nazi terror (e.g., Browning 1993; Goldhagen 1996).

13. Parrondo 1985, 49.

14. For example, in the 1940s and 1950s the House Un-American Activities Committee encouraged denunciations for Communist behavior, even though being a Communist was not illegal in the United States.

15. This is not to say that Juanes del Vallejo was unharmed by Juan de Veteta's exclamation, but simply that harming him was not the primary intent.

16. Factors relating to the use of denouncers versus informants are addressed in the concluding chapter.

17. Innes 2003.

18. Black 1976.

19. Cohen 1985. It is important to specify *formal* social control as opposed to social control more generally. As Meier (1982, 35) noted, "No definition of the term [social control] is agreed upon by sociologists." It has been used to mean various things since its initial formulation, including social norms and socialization processes. Formal social control, which is sometimes referred to as governmental social control, clarifies the aspect of social control under investigation.

20. Foucault (1977, 27) explains that "there is no power relation without the correlative constitution of a field of knowledge, nor any knowledge that does not presuppose and constitute at the same time, power relations."

21. Note that social control is distinct from social order. Widespread denunciation may increase social control at the expense of social order. More likely, widespread denunciation erodes trust and damages social relationships, replacing community-based forms of order with order built on hierarchy and domination.

22. The ideal type is a conceptual tool developed and utilized by Weber (e.g., [1922] 1978).

23. Coser 1977.

24. Goldman 2011, 30. Communist China during the 1950s was a similarly incentivized environment, where not denouncing others could have adverse consequences (Strauss 2002).

25. Despite the occasional presence of positive incentives, I still refer to this model as the coercion model. The term "coercion" effectively captures the key dynamic—the authorities' attempts to directly shape the behavior of individuals through specific incentives.

26. It is for this reason that I group positive and negative incentives together within the same model, as both lead to the same effective orientation of the denouncer. Thus, I predict them to have the same effect on denouncer behavior, with the qualification that negative incentives tend to be perceived more strongly than positive ones and thus should have a greater impact (Kahneman and Tversky 1979).

27. Gellately 1996; Diewald-Kerkmann 1995.

28. Labianca and Brass 2006, 597.

29. Coser 1956; Labianca, Brass, and Gray 1998; Gersick, Dutton, and Bartunek 2000.

30. Geschiere 1997.

31. Black 1984; Harrigan and Yap 2017.

32. Thiranagama and Kelly 2011, 15.

33. Kalyvas 2006, 363.

34. Frank 1985.

35. The desire to gain relative to another and the desire to harm another are not necessarily coterminous. However, they are generally interconnected. Rivalries often give rise to negative ties, and disliking

someone often leads to a desire to gain at his or her expense. Although there are surely cases of denunciation where only one of these factors is evident—e.g., someone harms another person without regard to his or her own relative well-being or purely for instrumental gain and without malice—these are likely rarer than their joint occurrence.

36. Berkowitz and LePage 1967.

37. Sunstein and Thaler 2008.

38. It is useful to consider this model in relation to the perspective that a strong central authority *increases* the likelihood of cooperation within local communities, instead of diminishing it (Erikson and Parent 2007; Baldassari and Grossman 2011). Erikson and Parent (2007) argue that central authorities are limited in their information-gathering capabilities and therefore any local intervention is clumsy and unpredictable in nature, meaning that either party could be ultimately advantaged. This leads to local cooperation as parties attempt to avoid the uncertain involvement of the authorities because it poses a risk to both of them. What the volunteer model reveals is that by relaxing one of these conditions—the unpredictability of the authorities' judgment—the presence of a strong authority can instead facilitate the breakdown of local cooperation.

39. Note, however, that the two models are not mutually exclusive. Their theoretical separation does not preclude the possibility of people denouncing for social gain in real-world environments where authority-based incentives are offered. Although this may happen with some regularity in settings where incentives are mild, the stronger the incentives, the more the coercion model should reflect its ideal type. Especially when these incentives are negative, denouncers likely do not take the time or effort to consider how to obtain lesser social benefits. Fear for personal safety crowds out all other considerations.

40. Gramsci 1992.

41. Maier 2004; Borejsza and Ziemer 2006.

42. Unfortunately, it is extremely difficult to assess popular opinion within repressive regimes. See Corner (2009) for a detailed discussion of the associated issues.

43. Fitzpatrick and Gellately 1997, 10.
44. Glaeser 2011.
45. Miron and Brehm 2006.
46. Fitzpatrick (1996), for example, describes the prevalence of false denunciations in the Soviet Union.
47. Although denunciations motivated by security concerns are not prevalent in repressive regimes, the final chapter addresses particular conditions under which they may be widespread.
48. Nagel and Olzak 1982; Eder et al. 2002.
49. Petersen 2002.
50. This is not to argue that intergroup conflict is irrelevant. Intergroup dynamics do interact with the coercion and volunteer models in important ways, without serving as the primary motivation for denouncing. These are addressed in chapters 2 and 4, in the discussion of the Spanish Inquisition and Nazi Germany.
51. Kuran 1997.
52. Centola, Willer, and Macy 2005.
53. This is not meant to promote either form of repression, but simply to understand their dynamics.
54. Johnson 1997; Gellately 1990; Ayçoberry 2000.
55. Gellately 1997. Of course, there are additional reasons why the Soviet Union would maintain a larger police force than the Nazis. However, to the extent that both are considered to have been effective at maintaining social control, this is a suggestive comparison.
56. Mallmann and Paul 1994; Delarue 1964.
57. When positive incentives are offered, however, they may be grateful.
58. More specifically, five of the six dimensions predict contrasting patterns, while the sixth expects a similar pattern in both models.
59. Labianca, Brass, and Gray 1998; Gersick, Dutton, and Bartunek 2000.
60. Leskovec, Huttenlocher, and Kleinberg (2010) find that the number of incoming negative ties is not a good predictor of future negative ties. In other words, negative ties do not tend to cluster around particular individuals, indicating that negative relationships are indeed idiosyncratic.
61. Burt 2000.
62. Simmel 1904, 514.

63. Gould 2003. For example, the directive "Give me that" said to a subordinate is likely perceived as an understandable and inoffensive request. However, that same phrase said to a person of similar status is a much more ambiguous statement; it may be interpreted as an acceptable request or as an unwelcome attempt to show dominance. Regardless of the speaker's intent, such a statement is more likely to lead to anger and conflict in the latter context than in the former.

64. It might seem plausible that there should be a seventh expectation, that reciprocal denunciations should occur more frequently in the volunteer model than in the coercion model. This would be the case if enmity is generally reciprocal in nature. However, there are reasons to believe that negative ties are *not* highly reciprocal. As Labianca (2014) argues, "We might expect that the base rate is much lower for reciprocity to occur in negative ties than in positive ties. Individuals might act to hide their negative ties as much as possible from their targets because negative ties violate typical norms" (245). Empirical studies tend to support Labianca's contention (Szell and Thurner 2010); not only do people hide their negative ties, but they also avoid the people with whom they have them (Harrigan and Yap 2017). Reciprocity rates are significantly lower for negative ties than they are for positive ties and private enemies far outnumber public ones. Similarly, Eisenkraft, Elfenbein and Kopelman (2017) have shown that, whereas people easily identify their friends, they have difficulty identifying those who feel competitive toward them. These are also reasons why preemptive denouncing is generally not an option.

65. Specifically I use within-case variation, which is the primary source of causal inference within comparative historical analysis (Lange 2012; Mahoney and Rueschemeyer 2003). By comparing subgroups within cases that reflect either an incentivized or a voluntary environment, it is possible to assess the effect of an institutional change on motivations to denounce. The disaggregation and testing of the same theoretical constructs across disparate cases then provides greater generalized support for the mechanisms being studied (Smelser 2013; Rueschemeyer 2003).

66. Chapters 2 and 3, along with parts of the theory described in chapter 1, are adapted and expanded from Bergemann (2017).

2. THE SPANISH INQUISITION

1. This estimate is based on a catalog of approximately one hundred thousand trial summaries from 1540 to 1700, which covers less than half of the full time period of the Inquisition (Contreras and Henningsen 1986). This also excludes the earliest decades, when the Inquisition was most active.

2. Unfortunately, almost all of the records that survive are trial summaries, so little is known about those who were accused but did not necessarily stand trial. The records analyzed in this chapter are a rare exception.

3. Rawlings 2006. For example, in Toledo an estimated eight thousand cases were brought before the Inquisition from 1481 to 1530 (Dedieu 1992).

4. This is not to say that the marriage was not without its tensions. As an anonymous manuscript reported in 1476, "When the Queen heard of [Ferdinand's] coming, she became very agitated, and could not bear not to ride out herself, together with some horsemen, and she ordered them to stick their lances in those [of Ferdinand's] cavalry" (Edwards 2014, 15).

5. As Henry Lea explained, "It is difficult to exaggerate the disorder pervading the Castilian kingdoms, when the Spanish monarchy found its origin in the union of Isabella of Castile and Ferdinand of Aragon" (Lea 1906, vol. 1, 1).

6. To be more precise, the Muslims were expelled from Castile in 1502, but they were not expelled from Aragon until 1526.

7. The Inquisition had no jurisdiction over Jews or other non-Christians. Inquisitors could only judge and punish people who had been baptized as Christians and were suspected of betraying the faith.

8. Ferdinand continued to use the Inquisition as a means of centralizing control in Aragon. Local officials regularly called on the inquisitors to subordinate themselves to the city elites when establishing a new office. Not only did Ferdinand not permit this, but local elites were eventually required to declare an oath of fealty to the Inquisition, rather than vice versa.

9. Haliczer 1973.

10. Netanyahu 2001. MacKay (1972) emphasized the anti-converso riots in 1473 as indicative of widespread hostility toward this population (see also Rawlings 2006).

11. Beinart 1981, 21.

12. According to Fuentes (2006), visits in Granada were less frequent. He found that inquisitors in the sixteenth century typically spent only four months of the year on visitations. In many years, they did not go on visitations at all. Contreras (1982) reported a similar finding for Galicia. The frequency of visits seems to have varied by the tribunal and the year; they also generally decreased over time.

13. Homza 2006, 63.

14. In some cases, such as Ciudad Real, the Edict of Grace was extended to sixty days.

15. I use the pronoun "he" to refer to denouncers and those denounced in this and subsequent chapters, as the majority of denouncers and those denounced were male.

16. García Cárcel 1976; Haliczer 1990; Lea 1906, vol. 2; Kamen 1999.

17. To put this in terms of game theory, the former period involved two choices: confessing (with denouncing), which entailed a moderately bad outcome with complete certainty; and not confessing, which entailed a very bad outcome with probability p, and no negative consequences otherwise $(1 - p)$. Under the volunteer model, the game vis-à-vis the authorities shifted such that both denouncing and not denouncing entailed a very bad outcome with probability q and no negative consequences otherwise $(1 - q)$. Of course, there were other potential costs and benefits associated with denouncing; this is simply meant to illustrate the difference between the two periods in this context. There was also no first-mover advantage in either case, as people who were denounced could still denounce others.

18. Haliczer 1990.

19. The rules of torture were specific. Only two types of torture were prevalent in the early years of the Inquisition: what we now call waterboarding and being suspended by the wrists, sometimes with weights attached to the feet. These conformed with a prohibition against the shedding of blood. If a defendant confessed during torture, he was required to ratify the confession the following day in order for it to be

considered legitimate. The frequency with which torture was applied, however, may have been rare (Kamen 1999).

20. Beinart (1981) argued that the defense lawyers of Ciudad Real generally did their best for their clients; Haliczer (1990) observed often perfunctory defenses in Valencia due to allegiance to the Church. Lea (1906, vol. 3) noted that in the inquisitorial instructions of 1484, there was a clause requiring advocates to betray their clients if they discovered them to be guilty.

21. Imprisonment tended to be in the individual's own house or that of a relative. Inquisitors' prisons were used primarily for holding people who had not yet completed their trials, not the penanced or reconciled. Exile usually barred a defendant from his home village, the tribunal village, Madrid, and potentially a few other villages. Terms of exile generally lasted for a few years.

22. Lea 1906, vol. 3.

23. Bleeders performed bloodletting on patients, an act believed to cure illness and disease.

24. Homza 2006.

25. Homza 2006, 16. "Bachiller" signified a basic university education.

26. Lea (1906) recounted a failed plot to physically resist the imposition of the Inquisition in Seville, as did Kamen (2014b). Roth (2002), however, concluded that these stories were unsubstantiated.

27. Homza 2006, 11.

28. Kamen 1999, 179.

29. The perception of illegitimacy may have been compounded by the fact that there was no historical precedent for doubting the sincerity of the conversos in their faith. As Kamen noted, "When the great controversies broke out in Toledo, half a century after the 1391 riots, not a single Christian writer doubted that the New Christians were for the most part orthodox in belief and intention" (1999, 36).

30. Vassberg 1996; Haliczer 1990.

31. It may seem that there is an obvious answer to this question: that pre-existing animosity led Old Christians to denounce conversos, regardless of the legitimacy of the Inquisition. However, during the Inquisition's first several decades, it was primarily conversos denouncing other conversos. This may have been because Old Christians did not interact

with conversos very much; it is also possible that the supposed animosity between the two groups has been exaggerated. This point is addressed in more detail later in the chapter.

32. Homza 2006, 65.

33. Kamen 1999.

34. García Cárcel 1976.

35. Lea 1906, vol. 2.

36. Beinart 1981.

37. Dedieu 1992.

38. Parrondo 1985, 126.

39. Edwards 1988, 14.

40. Parrondo 1985, 173.

41. Rawlings 2006, 117.

42. Flynn (1995) states that the Inquisition's zeal in prosecuting blasphemous statements was due to a philosophical perspective that exclamations indicated the true sentiment of the soul. However, this did not seem to be a popularly held opinion, at least among those making the exclamations.

43. The doubts and opinions of which conversos were commonly accused were often not unique to this population. This must have made the expansion of the Inquisition's purview to all Christians in 1525 an especially smooth transition.

44. Beinart 1981.

45. Homza 2006, 28.

46. Beinart 1981, 95.

47. Braunstein 1936, 55; García Cárcel 1976.

48. Although dissatisfaction with the Inquisition continued, this generally resulted in calls for procedural reforms and the prevention of abuses rather than protests against the validity of the Inquisition itself (Kamen 2014b).

49. This protection was fundamentally different from that offered by the Edict of Grace. As will become clear, denouncers were protected from any hardship that could arise from the act of denouncing, as opposed to being protected from the denunciations of others.

50. Of course, there were surely some denouncers in the earlier period who recognized that they could both gain protection from the authorities and harm particular neighbors. However, the stronger the negative

incentives, the less likely individuals are to consider this latter possibility, as their fear keeps them focused on the immediate danger to themselves. In other words, self-preservation takes priority over the lesser benefits that accrue from harming particular others.

51. This is not a purely theoretical argument; although this and the previous section focus on the institutional environment, the next section demonstrates that patterns of denunciations did indeed shift in predicted ways.

52. Melammed 2002. It turns out that both women managed to identify the majority of their accusers: Isabel correctly named five out of six and María five out of five. However, their accuracy rates were 5 percent and 9 percent, respectively. This gives every indication that they had no idea who had accused them and were simply naming everyone who came to mind. Unfortunately for them, the witnesses called in to verify the enmity of the correctly identified accusers claimed to have little or no memory of the purported slights. Both Isabel and María were found guilty and were burned at the stake.

53. Lea 1906, vol. 3, 65.

54. Beinart 1981, 130.

55. This is also in accordance with modern studies showing that negative ties are often not reciprocated (Harrigan and Yap 2017); in other words, people may not have a good sense of who dislikes them because individuals often "lump it" when they have grievances and avoid conflict (Black 1984). This make secrecy particularly valuable, as it greatly reduces the ability of those denounced to guess the identities of their accusers.

56. The fact that so few defendants were exonerated further supports the contention that those denounced did not know the identities of their denouncers. Otherwise, they would presumably have been more successful at securing acquittals.

57. Haliczer 1973, 67.

58. Lea 1906, vol. 2.

59. Kamen 1999; Beinart 1981. Lea (1906, vol. 2) mentioned being able to find only one instance of a perjurer being burnt.

60. Parrondo 1985, 144.

61. Ibid., 99.

62. Haliczer 1990.

63. Ibid. Lea (1906, vol. 3), however, asserted that cases tended to be addressed quickly in the earliest years of the Inquisition.
64. Kamen 1999. It was only in the revised instructions of 1561 that supporting dependents out of the sequestrations was permitted.
65. Lea 1906, vol. 3, 115.
66. These records were transcribed and published in their original fifteenth-century Spanish by Carlos Carrete Parrondo (1985).
67. The associated *Book of Confessions*, along with records of the trials that ensued, no longer exist.
68. Antón 1984.
69. Edwards 1988, 24.
70. Antón 1984.
71. Parrondo 1985, 52.
72. Ibid., 166.
73. Edwards 1988, 8; Parrondo 1985, 149.
74. Parrondo 1985, 20.
75. Ibid., 19.
76. Ibid., 52.
77. Ibid., 64.
78. Edwards 1988, 9; Parrondo 1985, 146.
79. Parrondo 1985, 36.
80. Ibid., 71.
81. Ibid., 79. Although this exclamation is clearly not Jewish in nature, it may have some relation to Averroism, which involved the denial of religion, the afterlife, and the immortal soul, and which had some influence on Jewish thinking during this time period (Netanyahu 2001).
82. Edwards 1988, 15; Parrondo 1985, 176.
83. Beinart 1981; Gitlitz 2002; Escudero 1998.
84. Kamen 1999; Edwards 1997.
85. Roth 2002; Netanyahu 2001; Rawlings 2006.
86. Haliczer 1990; Kamen 2014b.
87. Haliczer 1990; Kamen 1999. Braunstein (1936) also noted that almost all trials in Majorca from 1488 to 1536 were against conversos.
88. Antón 1984; Edwards 1988; Parrondo 1985.
89. Beinart 1981; Haliczer 1990.
90. Beinart 1981.

91. This quote comes from Kamen 1999, 42.
92. Edwards 1988.
93. The inquisitors made threats against Jews to help uncover conversos, but it is unclear how seriously these were taken.
94. The chi-square test of independence determines whether there is a significant difference between sets of categorical variables. For example, it estimates the probability that differences between the prevalence of Jewish crimes in the early period compared to the later period are due to random chance. Due to the small cell counts for several of the comparisons in the tables, I verified those results using Fisher's exact test and the results were the same.
95. This change cannot be attributed to the fact that villagers were running out of Judaizers to denounce. Recall that denunciations spanned approximately one hundred villages, meaning there was a large population who could be denounced. Furthermore, as will be discussed later in the chapter, the Inquisition was interested in denunciations against both the living and the dead, which further expanded the population of potential heretics.
96. Parrondo 1985, 30.
97. Distance is measured as the crow flies.
98. This last category—relatives—is rare and occurred in only nine of the cases.
99. Parrondo 1985, 145.
100. Ibid., 48.
101. For 17 percent of denunciations in the early period and 20 percent in the later period, there are no textual clues indicating the closeness of the relationship.
102. Blockmans and Janse 1999; Crawford 2014; O'Day 2000.
103. Parrondo 1985, 95.
104. Ibid., 96.
105. Ibid., 129.
106. Ibid., 130.
107. Ibid., 108.
108. Roth 2002; Netanyahu 2001; Kamen 1999; Lea 1906, vol. 1.
109. Quote reported by Roth 2002, 215.
110. Parrondo 1985, 31.

111. Furthermore, animosity by the living toward the dead should fade with time, as negative ties tend to decay without regular interaction.
112. This may also have allowed villagers to appear cooperative while questioning the legitimacy of the institution; denouncing dead individuals may have been a means of appeasing the authorities while protecting the living.
113. Kamen 2014a, 19.
114. Kamen 2014b, 233.
115. Beinart 1981, 168. However, it is unlikely that such affirmations did much to reduce the number of opportunistic denunciations.

3. ROMANOV RUSSIA

1. Russia was also referred to as Muscovy during this time period.
2. Dunning 2010.
3. Platonov 1970.
4. Crummey 1987, 231.
5. Stone 2006.
6. So important was Filaret in these early years that historian John Keep (1960) declared him to be the second most significant ruler of Russia in the seventeenth century—and more highly ranked than his son—despite the fact that Filaret was never technically the tsar.
7. Shubin 2009, 217. Another historian voiced a similar sentiment: that "the society suffered a complete political, social, institutional and moral collapse . . . at the lowest depths, the tsars' government had virtually ceased to function, society was in chaos, foreign invaders and native brigands stalked the land, and desperate men and women fed on one another—figuratively and sometimes literally" (Crummey 1987, 205).
8. Kleimola 1972; Hellie 1997; Lapman 1982.
9. There were two types of voevoda in Muscovy: town governors and military field commanders (Brown 2012). This chapter refers to the former type.
10. An exception was when the voevoda himself was denounced for treasonous behavior. In such cases, he recused himself from the investigation.

11. Note that the institutional conditions in Muscovy were not nearly as favorable for denouncers as they were in Spain during the Spanish Inquisition. The reasons why individuals nevertheless denounced will be addressed later in the chapter.

12. In contrast to the previous chapter, when a denounced Russian was held in jail, his property was not confiscated and his family was not put in any danger. However, it is somewhat difficult to establish whether defendants paid for their own imprisonment, although there is some evidence that prisoners had to obtain their own food (Keep 1956). In 1658, the authorities decreed that the state would pay the costs of custody for those awaiting trial in Word and Deed cases, but it is unclear whether defendants paid for themselves before that (Kollmann 2012).

13. This technique appears to have fallen out of favor toward the end of the 1500s (Kollmann 2004).

14. There is some debate as to which individuals within the central government handled Word and Deed cases. Tel'berg (1911) asserted that the tsar was directly involved in their judgment. More likely, the top officials at the Service Chancellery were the main adjudicators of such cases, with occasional input from nobles (Rustemeyer 2006; Lapman 1982).

15. A sentence of exile did not banish an individual from Russia, but instead assigned him to forced labor in Siberia or another area.

16. Lapman 1982, 202. Furthermore, only in 1649 was retribution for the non-reporting of crimes codified into law. Prior to 1649, no such laws were in place (Kleimola 1972).

17. In a database of one hundred thousand payments made by authorities, there are only four records of payments for reporting a Sovereign's Word or Deed. In all four cases, the payments were nominal amounts and occurred after the period of observation (Hellie 1997). Of the 453 denunciations examined in this chapter, in only one is a reward mentioned.

18. Maksimov 1869; Novombergskii 1911; Lapman 1982; Hellie 1997.

19. I refer to this category as "in custody" for ease of description, even though those being arrested were technically in the process of being taken into custody when they declared knowledge of a Word or Deed.

20. This does not mean that both types of incentives necessarily have equal power to affect behavior. The risk of loss tends to have more of an

impact on behavior than equivalent gains, so negative incentives likely serve as more powerful drivers of behavior (Kahneman and Tversky 1979).

21. Kollmann 2012, 82.

22. Hellie 1997, 14.

23. Hellie 1997; Rustemeyer 2006.

24. Rustemeyer (2006) estimated ten thousand to twelve thousand cases of Word and Deed in the eighteenth century, but declared that it is impossible to estimate the number of cases in the seventeenth century. Although this makes a direct comparison impossible, the fact that there are known to have been hundreds of thousands of denunciations in Spain during the Inquisition indicates that denunciations were likely much more prevalent in the latter setting.

25. Kollmann 2012.

26. Nancy Kollmann noted, however, that "in political crime cases . . . the investigative process was kept as secret as possible" (2012, 122). Even if this is true, it is clear that secrecy was never emphasized to the same extent as it was in the Spanish Inquisition.

27. Rustemeyer 2006.

28. It is unclear how many of the people denounced received a custody arrangement versus imprisonment.

29. Lapman 1982, 110.

30. Olearius 1967, 183.

31. Levesque 1800, vol. 4, 100.

32. Le Clerc 1783, vol. 3, 79.

33. Novombergskii 1911.

34. Lapman 1982.

35. Ibid.

36. More specifically, 47 percent of denunciations in this sample are from the 1640s, while only 32 percent of the other 404 cases came from that decade. Although 32 percent is still a large proportion of all denunciations, it suggests a gentler increase than that seen in figure 3.2.

37. The category of churchpeople includes monks, abbots, priests, archpriests, deacons, church scribes, and monastic workers.

38. Kivelson 1988, 8.

39. Some of the remaining individuals not included in table 3.1 can be roughly grouped together as local administrative personnel, as they

were elected or appointed to governmental positions, but their status is unclear.

40. Hellie 1971.

41. These social categories were not proportionally represented according to their population. Although peasants made up 14 percent of denouncers and 15 percent of those denounced, they were about 80 percent of all Russians during this time period (Hellie 2006; Vodarskii 1977).

42. Others who have looked at Russian denunciations have categorized them somewhat differently. Tel'berg (1911) identified four categories: treason, revolt, and threats to injure the tsar's physical health; insulting remarks addressed to the tsar; unauthorized deliberations on state affairs; and slips of the tongue and missed elements in the tsar's full title. Rustemeyer (2006) viewed three categories as most prevalent in her examination of Word and Deed cases through the eighteenth century: denunciations for riots, for verbal crimes, and for border flight. The categories used here follow Lapman (1982).

43. Lapman 1982, 163.

44. Ibid., 119.

45. Ibid., 165.

46. Ibid., 169.

47. Ibid., 166.

48. Ibid., 164.

49. Ibid., 168. Although punishments against denouncers appear to have been rare, here is an example where the denouncer was punished for his behavior.

50. Ibid., 176.

51. Ibid., 175.

52. Ibid., 171.

53. Ibid., 172.

54. Ibid., 173.

55. There is some debate among historians about denunciations as signifiers of generalized beliefs about the Sovereign. Pipes (1974) and Hellie (1977) state that ordinary citizens viewed the tsar as God and that denunciations reflect this. Others view the way that individuals discussed the sovereign as based on convention, not actual belief (Keenan 1986). Denunciations have also been described as reflecting the belief that the

tsar's power was universal but not unlimited (Lukin 2000). Rather than engage with this debate, I focus on denouncer motivation and the interpersonal dynamics between denouncers and those denounced.

56. For example, a person could be beaten with the knout, have his tongue cut off, and then be sentenced to exile in Siberia (Hellie 1997).

57. Due to the small cell counts for several of the comparisons in the tables, I verified those results using Fisher's exact test and the results were the same.

58. Lapman 1982, 107.

59. Ibid., 114.

60. Of the denunciations found to be false, 76 percent involved the denouncer admitting to the fabrication. The other 24 percent were concluded to be false by the authorities without a confession. Of the denunciations deemed to be true, 53 percent involved an admission of guilt by the person denounced, while 47 percent did not include a direct confession.

61. Rustemeyer (2006) asserted that denouncing arose out of loyalty, due to citizens' acceptance of the sacredness of the tsar's honor. The prevalence of intentionally false denunciations, however, belies this.

62. This is the same reason why those in custody reported economic crimes; both behaviors are manifestations of the same strategy.

63. Lapman 1982, 33.

64. Ibid., 34.

65. Ibid., 59.

66. Ibid., 40.

67. Ibid., 109.

68. Ibid., 169.

69. Ibid., 167.

70. Ibid., 183.

71. Ibid., 105.

72. Denunciations made sooner were not more likely to be true than those made later. Emotional intensity likely spurred people to fabricate denunciations shortly after a fight if they did not have something more truthful to denounce.

73. Lapman 1982, 112.

74. This accords well with experimental findings that negative emotion is the proximate mechanism leading to more costly punishment (Fehr and

Gächter 2002; Seip, Van Dijk and Rotteveel 2014). In other words, individuals are willing to accept harm to themselves in order to punish someone who has angered them.

75. This is despite the fact that there is no evidence that the Sovereign's Word and Deed ever revealed a single real threat to the tsar (Hellie 1997). Nevertheless, the existence of the institution and the fact that it was used to report wrongdoing helped the authorities to enact social control and dissuade Muscovites from betraying the sovereign.

76. 1649 Ulozhenie vol. 2, 17 (Hellie 1998).

77. 1649 Ulozhenie vol. 2, 14 (Hellie 1998).

78. Rustemeyer 2006.

79. Lapman 1982, 219.

80. Only twenty-one of the denunciations examined in this chapter involved people related or formerly related by contract, such as masters and serfs or bondsmen. Thirteen of them note that the relationship was already damaged. Contractual relationships did not generally lead to denunciations unless there was already a preexisting negative tie.

4. NAZI GERMANY

1. Mallmann and Paul 1994; Delarue 1964.

2. Gellately 1990; Johnson 1997; Ayçoberry 2000. Some specific estimates are: 291 Gestapo officers in the Düsseldorf region of 4,000,000 inhabitants (Gellately 1990); 15 in Krefeld, and 75 in Cologne, which worked out to about one officer for every 10,000 residents (Johnson 1999); and one for every 25,000 residents of Prussia in 1935 and one for every 10,500 residents in Saxony in 1936 (Mallmann 1997).

3. Estimates are highly inexact and range from 1 to 2 percent of the population (Johnson 1999) to 5 to 10 percent (Gieseke 2014). With a population of approximately 79,000,000 in 1939, this suggests anywhere from 790,000 to 7,900,000 denunciations.

4. Evans 2004.

5. Peukert 1987. In particular, Gellately (2001a) pointed to concerns about women working and a falling birthrate.

6. Broszat 1981.

7. Evans 2004, 264.

8. Broszat 1981.
9. Benz 2006.
10. Peukert 1987.
11. Bergerson 2004. Volksgemeinschaft is a complex and multifaceted social concept. It contains many criteria: "ethnic origin as the ultimate point of reference; an appeal to inner experience; tension between utopian expectations and the radical willingness to fulfill them; racist separation; unconditional trust in the *Führer*; and a deadly violence that was directed internally as well as externally" (Steber and Gotto 2014, 2).
12. Connelly 1996; Tormey 1995.
13. Reuband (2001) has noted that the interrelationships between the Gestapo and the various other organizations that received denunciations remains unclear. Although many denunciations were passed on to the Gestapo, the circumstances under which this did not occur are not well understood. In cases where denunciations were not passed on, the recipient organization generally attempted to resolve matters itself.
14. Browder 1996.
15. For an example of such a form, see Mann 1987, 69.
16. By contrast, the regular courts often used a panel of laypeople and judges to decide cases. By 1939, this practice was discontinued and local courts mimicked the three-judge model.
17. Müller 1991, 147.
18. Johnson 1999.
19. Stephenson 2013. The term "ordinary Germans" refers to people who were not part of any marginalized group in this particular context.
20. Johnson 1999.
21. Gellately 1996; Diewald-Kerkmann 1995; Mallmann and Paul 1994.
22. Johnson 1999, 284.
23. This is not to say that the authorities did not also receive a large number of denunciations regarding marginalized groups, but rather that they generated a greater percentage of the leads themselves. If anything, the authorities became hyper-responsive to denunciations that might lead them to Communist or Jewish transgressors (Gellately 2001b).
24. Diewald-Kerkmann 1995.

25. Bergerson 2004. Similarly, a Mrs. Müller attempted to gain help from the authorities in securing a new apartment in 1940. In justifying her request, she indicated that she had birthed five children for the Reich and that her husband had been in the army for half a year (Connelly 1996). Such criteria, along with membership in Nazi groups, typically led to successful requests (Mann 1987). As Ruckenbiel (2005) noted, what was most important was being active in the Nazi Party, giving charity to the Nazi cause, and helping with the war effort.

26. Joshi 2003, 106. Although in this particular example a signed letter was more effective than an anonymous one, in general this was not the case.

27. The Gestapo's investigation found that Miss Wollenberg was racially "Aryan," but had been orphaned at the age of two. Her aunt—who was married to a Jewish man—assumed Miss Wollenberg's guardianship (Joshi 2003).

28. Gellately 1990, 154.

29. Ibid., 153. Of course, this credulity was not taken to extremes; although the Gestapo took every denunciation seriously, they still investigated each charge before deciding whether it merited punishment or a trial.

30. Ibid., 155.

31. Gellately 1990.

32. Ayçoberry 2000.

33. Gellately 1996, 943.

34. Johnson 1997. In a more complete study with 3,175 respondents, Johnson (2011) found similar results. Among non-Jewish Germans, he found that 46 percent had listened to illegal broadcasts, 32 percent told illegal anti-Nazi jokes, 14 percent criticized Hitler, and 19 percent criticized the Nazis.

35. The courts were at first horrified by this, but there was little they could do. Eventually, a compromise was reached in which only a "standard club" was used in interrogation beatings (Müller 1991).

36. Ibid., 142.

37. Gellately 1997, 202.

38. Mann 1987; Dörner 2001.

39. Johnson 1999, 345.

40. Müller 1991.

41. Dörner 1995.
42. Mallmann and Paul 1994.
43. Gellately 1990.
44. Johnson 1999.
45. Both of these sources also omit denunciations that were sent to party organizations or newspapers and were not forwarded to the Gestapo.
46. Mann 1987; Joshi 2003; Ruckenbiel 2005; Gellately 1990; Gellately 2001a; Diewald-Kerkmann 1995; Johnson 1999.
47. Mann 1987; Diewald-Kerkmann 1995; Johnson 1999; Gellately 1990; Gellately 2001a; Joshi 2003; Ruckenbiel 2005.
48. Mann 1987. For the remaining denunciations, it is unclear how the information first came to the Gestapo's attention.
49. Ruckenbiel 2005. As in the case of the denunciations discussed by Mann above, it is unclear how the information in the remaining cases first came to the Gestapo's attention.
50. Mann 1987; Ruckenbiel 2005; Diewald-Kerkmann 1995; Gellately 1996.
51. Ruckenbiel 2005.
52. Johnson 1999; Diewald-Kerkmann 1995; Dörner 1995; Ruckenbiel 2005. For the particular crime of listening to illegal radio broadcasts, however, Gellately (1996) found in his sample that eighty-six denouncers were male and seventy-seven were female.
53. Johnson 1999; Ruckenbiel 2005.
54. Although denouncers included a wide range of people, Johnson (1999, 368) described the typical denouncer as "male, middle aged, middle class." Unfortunately, scholars do not tend to present characteristics of those denounced. What is possible to say is that they tended to come from the same social status as their denouncers (Hüttenberger 1981; Gellately 1996).
55. Mann 1987.
56. Joshi 2003.
57. Mann 1987; Johnson 1999.
58. Gellately 1990, 181.
59. Owings 1993. Unlike the other examples in this chapter, this one does not come from Gestapo case files or court documents, but rather from the denounced individual's own recounted experience. Why the staff

members denounced Maria when Jane was the one who listened to the illegal broadcasts is unclear.

60. Müller 1991, 147.

61. For example, 28 percent of those denounced in Düsseldorf, Geldern, and Kleve had their cases dismissed, while 26 percent received a warning. The rest suffered harsher consequences, with 22 percent imprisoned and 14 percent placed in protective custody, 2 percent put to death and 2 percent sent to concentration camps. For the remaining 6 percent, the outcome is unknown (Ruckenbiel 2005).

62. Johnson 1999. Note that these particular numbers refer to all Gestapo files, not just those initiated by denunciations. However, it is likely that a similar discrepancy exists in the latter files.

63. Gellately (1996), however, cautioned that many people may have had mixed motives.

64. In his study of Special Court trials, Hüttenberger (1981) similarly concluded that most denunciations were personal in nature, arising from local conflicts. However, he did not provide the specific percentages for this result.

65. Johnson (1999) included a further category listed as "Other." As he did not explain what this label indicates, I include it in the "Unknown" category. This amounted to 4 percent of denunciations in Krefeld and 15 percent in Cologne.

66. Diewald-Kerkmann (1995). Others scholars group personally motivated denunciations somewhat differently, but these are generally decomposable into two broad categories: economic rivalries and personal conflicts (Johnson 1999; Mann 1987; Ruckenbiel 2005). Johnson (1999) found that about half of personally motivated denunciations were over economic matters and the other half on non-economic conflicts between neighbors or lovers. Mann (1987) found that 60 percent originated from arguments (including those in the workplace), while 16 percent were due to economic motives or competition; he did not specify the origins of the remaining 24 percent. Ruckenbiel (2005) found that 84 percent of personally motivated denunciations were based on conflicts or disputes, 11 percent involved workplace or economic motives, and 5 percent were for other reasons.

67. Joshi 2003, 102.

68. Gellately 1990, 147.
69. Mallmann 1997, 32.
70. Joshi 2003, 108.
71. Ibid., 121.
72. Gellately 1990, 152.
73. Johnson 1999; Joshi 2003; Ruckenbiel 2005.
74. Ruckenbiel 2005; Gellately 1996; Hüttenberger 1981. Stephenson (2013) and Diewald-Kerkmann (1995) both assert that the practice of subordinates denouncing their superiors was more common than is generally recognized, but such denunciations still appear to have been less prevalent than denouncing someone of the same status.
75. By contrast, Gordon (1984) argued that most of the 452 Düsseldorf files she examined regarding racial crimes were true reports. She based this solely on the fact that those who were found guilty had similar demographic characteristics to those who were not, and concluded that this indicated that everyone was likely guilty. However, this argument is not convincing; many of the alleged crimes—both punished and unpunished—could equally well have been false. Alternatively, demographic similarity may be unrelated to the truthfulness of denunciations.
76. Gellately 1990, 169.
77. Mallmann 1997.
78. Gellately 1988, 681.
79. Gellately 1990, 143.
80. Gellately 1990.
81. Ibid., 152.
82. Gellately 1988, 680.
83. Gellately 1990. Ruckenbiel (2005) mentioned two laws passed in 1933 and 1934 detailing punishments for false denunciations; in a further example of official ambivalence, these laws do not appear to have been enforced.
84. Perhaps the gentlest chastisement came from a speech given by Joseph Goebbels, the Reich Minister of Propaganda, to Nazi Party officials on November 5, 1943:

> There is no one in Germany today, I think I can claim, who embraces the enemy's slogans. That every now and then someone complains, grouses, gripes—well, I do that sometimes too. One should not take

too much offense at that. I once wrote in an article: "Scolding is the bowel movement of the soul," and that's the way it is. Somehow man has to get rid of his inner displeasure. One should not take too much offense at that or take it too tragically (Dörner 2001, 66).

Goebbels declared that Germans were generally decent people; there was no need to denounce minor grumblings of displeasure.

85. Gellately 1990.
86. Johnson 1999.
87. Gellately 2001a.
88. Ruckenbiel 2005.
89. Mallmann 1997.
90. Mann 1987, 300.
91. Kohlhaas 1995.
92. Mallmann 1997.
93. This is not to say that many people did not support the Nazis (Johnson 1999). However, this support was more reasoned than fanatic; although people may have supported certain parts of the Nazi agenda, they did not necessarily agree with others.
94. Benz 2006.
95. Gellately 1990; Ayçoberry 2000.
96. Connelly 1996, 82.
97. Ayçoberry (2000) and Gellately (1990) suggest that members of the Hitler Youth may have become militarized rather than ideologized. Peukert (2001) states that the movement became increasingly less successful over time, while Johnson (1999) expresses surprise that not many of the denunciations he examined came from members of the Hitler Youth.
98. Mann 1987. For an alternative viewpoint, Browder (1996) cautioned against reading too much into comparisons such as those presented in table 4.3. He claimed that reports from party or state agencies screened out useless information and the lack of screening on denunciations gives them an inflated representation. However, it remains undeniable that a great deal of the Gestapo's police work was dedicated to investigating denunciations. Without this, it is unlikely that the agency would have gained a reputation of being all-seeing and all-knowing.
99. Arendt 1973.

100. Gellately 1997, 221.

101. For an alternative view, see Johnson (1999), who argued that many residents of Nazi Germany were not afraid of being arrested during the Nazi years. However, perceptions of the Nazis' omnipresence may have nevertheless affected Germans' behavior, even if some individuals did not regularly experience fear.

102. This quote was voiced by Interior Minister Bechler of the Soviet-occupied territory (Vogt 2000, 191).

103. Ibid., 195.

104. Dack 2016, 153.

105. Vogt 2000, 191.

106. Dack 2016, 154.

107. Ibid., 154.

108. Mallmann 1997.

109. Sangster 2016, 406.

110. For an example from Poland, in 1948 Jan Burda was charged with having collaborated with the Nazis during their occupation. The witnesses for the prosecution

> questioned [Burda's] takeover of a formerly Jewish property and the subsequent establishment of a restaurant . . . something that amounted to two separate concessions granted by the occcupation authorities. Although Burda explained his good luck as a result of an unforeseen tragedy—his hand had been amputated as a result of injuries sustained in [an] attack and had rendered him incapable of farming his land—these witnesses were skeptical of any preferential treatment bestowed by the occupation authorities—much less two acts of favoritism—and took this as proof of Burda's collaboration with the Nazis. . . . Even the fact that Burda was later arrested and imprisoned by the Germans for the illegal production of vodka did little to alleviate the suspicions of some of his fellow townsmen. (McClintock 2015, 115).

Burda was not without his defenders, but he was found guilty by two jurors who had been chosen for their "political reliability." The ruling was based on the obviously fabricated testimony of one witness, along with two other accounts that were later proven to have been motivated by personal conflict.

5. DENUNCIATIONS: PRESENT AND FUTURE

1. Fitzpatrick 1996, 107.
2. Kuran 1997. In the words of Beetham (2013, 18),

> Action expressive of consent, even if undertaken purely out of self-interest, will . . . create a normative commitment on the part of those engaging in them . . . such actions have a publicly symbolic or declaratory force, in that they constitute an express acknowledgement on the part of the subordinate of the position of the powerful, which the latter are able to use as confirmation of their legitimacy to third parties not involved in the relationship, or those who have not taken part in any expressions of consent.

3. Centola, Willer, and Macy 2005.
4. Social life indeed contracts to few close relationships in highly repressive regimes (Völker and Flap 2001).
5. This discussion is not meant to endorse repression, but to explain the dynamics and implications of the two models. As will be seen shortly, instances of both models also exist in modern democracies.
6. Gellately 1996. There are surely additional reasons why the Soviet Union maintained a larger per capita police force than the Nazis. However, to the extent that both are considered to have been effective at maintaining social control, this is a suggestive comparison.
7. Even in the Spanish Inquisition, where the same inquisitors were present under both edicts, individuals were more willing to travel to voluntarily denounce under the Edict of Faith, reducing the effort required of each inquisitor.
8. This implicit conflict applies specifically to settings where incentives are negative. When incentives are positive, there is no perception of implicit conflict.
9. The system here has some similarity to how the Catholic Church was able to regulate the marriages and divorces of European royalty

(Ermakoff 1997). In this setting, the church imposed normative demands on what constituted a legitimate marriage. Their success hinged on the aristocrats' acceptance of this system because it provided an avenue for strategic gain vis-à-vis other aristocrats. Similar to repression under the volunteer model, the ultimate consequence of individual strategic action was to increase institutional legitimacy and impose new behavioral constraints.

10. Weber (1922) 1978.

11. By this definition of legitimacy, it is possible for rulers to be legitimate generally while being illegitimate in regard to specific laws or edicts. Although many of Ferdinand and Isabella's acts were likely seen as legitimate, for many people the Spanish Inquisition was not.

12. Over time, it is likely that the Inquisition gradually became more accepted as a part of life and its legitimacy increased. Perhaps this explains in part why the Edict of Grace was replaced by the Edict of Faith approximately fifteen years later.

13. As Beetham (2013) has argued, when legitimacy is absent, "power does not necessarily collapse, or obedience cease, since it can continue to be kept in place by incentives and sanctions. However, coercion has to be much more extensive and omnipresent, and that is costly to maintain" (28).

14. These are intended as general tendencies; regimes can also use denouncers and informants simultaneously.

15. Crummey 1987, 231.

16. Urgency is often associated with a lack of legitimacy, but this is not always the case. Although authorities lacking legitimacy tend to want urgently to strengthen social control, legitimate authorities may have a similar desire due to paranoia or concern about a particular subset of the population.

17. These did not tend to be groups of an inherently subversive nature, but people in social environments such as churches, schools, or workplaces.

18. Gellately 1996.

19. This is not to say there were no denunciations in East Germany. In the early years of the regime, some people did denounce spontaneously (Bruce 2010).

20. East German officials certainly thought so: the Stasi regarded spontaneous denouncers with suspicion and considered them to be possible enemy agents (Gellately 1996).

21. Ash 1997.

22. This discussion assumes that internal threats to the regime are relatively disorganized and diffuse (as they were in East Germany). When this is not the case, informants may be particularly useful. For example, extracting information about criminal enterprises or resistance movements may require having people embedded and actively monitoring the group. The discussion in this section is not meant to preclude the possibility of regimes using both denouncers and informants; in some instances they can complement each other.

23. Kahneman and Tversky 1979.

24. This does not mean that informing will necessarily be more prevalent than denouncing in settings with low urgency, but rather that the relative frequency of informants is likely to increase.

25. An additional form of social control is random violence, which does not require citizen participation at all. However, this is much more common in civil wars and insurgencies than in repressive regimes where the authorities maintain a monopoly on violence (Kalyvas 2004; Kalyvas 2006; Lyall 2009). Even so, violence that is truly random is a poor form of social control; it may indeed terrify a population, but it does not deter unwanted behavior effectively. As long as members of the population perceive the violence to be random, working against the regime is just as risky as working for it.

    Instead, indiscriminate violence is most effective to the extent to which the "randomly" targeted victims are not chosen completely at random (Herreros 2006). Rather, they need to have some relation to the people actually committing deviant acts in order for there to be a deterrent effect. In order to effectively control and deter unwanted behavior, the authorities generally need local information, which requires citizen participation. Those punished must appear to be credible offenders, whether through actual evidence or fabricated confessions. As indiscriminate violence becomes more effective, it becomes less indiscriminate and begins to look more like one of the aforementioned models.

26. Homza 2006, 6.

27. Roth 2002, 226. Many similarly fled from Ciudad Real in anticipation of the Inquisition and from Barcelona, as well (Beinart 1981; Kamen 2014b).
28. Goldman 2011.
29. Ibid., 125.
30. As sociologist Georg Simmel explains ([1900] 2004, 178), "without the general trust that people have in each other, society itself would disintegrate."
31. Sykes 2007; Whitman and Davis 2007; Asbury 2011; Akerstrom 1991. Akerstrom describes a snitch as "someone who is a member of the group . . . When he disclaims membership, he is no longer a snitch" (p. 105; see also Van Vugt and Hart 2004).
32. Whitman and Davis 2007.
33. Ceplair and Englund 1983.
34. Vaughn 1972, 131.
35. Navasky 2003, ix.
36. These four types are not meant to be exhaustive. Other forms of denouncing exist in contemporary America, including snitching by prisoners and tattling by children. I focus on these four specifically because they are all methods of social control used by centralized authorities, and they are all relatively common in modern life.
37. Grossman and Katz 1983; Natapoff 2009; Weinstein 1999.
38. Maxfield and Kramer 1998.
39. United States Sentencing Commission; Weinstein 1999.
40. *United States v. Ford* 1878. The ruling stated:

> Prosecutors . . . should explain to the accomplice that he is not obliged to criminate himself, and inform him just what he may reasonably expect in case he acts in good faith, and testifies fully and fairly as to his own acts in the case, and those of his associates. When he fulfills those conditions he is equitably entitled to a pardon, and the prosecutor, and the court if need be, when fully informed of the facts, will join in such a recommendation (Hughes 1992).

41. Natapoff 2009.
42. Curriden 1995.

43. *United States v. Cervantes-Pacheco* 1987.
44. Yaroshefsky 1999.
45. Ibid., 955.
46. Trott 1996, 1383.
47. As Yaroshefsky (1999, 921) explained, "Accomplice testimony is often the most damaging evidence against a defendant because the cooperator has first-hand knowledge of the pattern of criminal activity. Consequently, a cooperator can manipulate the details of the events without arousing much, if any, suspicion and still be believable to a jury."
48. Natapoff 2009, 72.
49. Gross and O'Brien 2008. Other researchers have found that 46 percent (Warden 2004), 43 percent (Gross et al. 2005), and 21 percent (Dwyer, Neufeld, and Scheck 2000) of their samples of false capital convictions were influenced by perjury.
50. Motivans 2017. Perjury does not even merit its own category in the Department of Justice statistics; it is instead combined with contempt and intimidation.
51. *United States v. Bernal-Obeso* 1993.
52. Although plea-bargaining infuses the criminal justice system, the current structure is not inevitable. In the early 1800s, prosecutors began bargaining with those accused of murder and liquor law violations over what they would be charged with. It was only toward the end of the nineteenth century that judges began to endorse the concept of plea-bargaining and began working with prosecutors to allow reduced sentences. From this point onward, the practice spread to encompass all types of crimes (Fisher 2003).
53. Miethe 1999, 11.
54. Miceli, Near, and Dworkin 2008.
55. Lipman 2011.
56. Although some famous cases of whistle-blowing involve retaliation, findings on whistle-blowers in general are mixed. Some studies report that the majority of these people face negative consequences (Rothschild and Miethe 1999), while others state that retaliation is rare (Near and Miceli 1996). Retaliation also appears to vary by industry (Pershing 2003).
57. Mesmer-Magnus and Viswesvaran 2005.

58. Miceli, Near, and Dworkin 2008, 37. Dozier and Miceli (1985) made similar remarks.
59. Miethe 1999, 14.
60. Flesher and Buttross 1992.
61. Ibid.
62. Warner 1992, 72. Liska (1992) similarly described crime reporting as a "critical component in activating the criminal justice system" (21).
63. Reiss 1971, 105.
64. Black and Reiss 1970; Reiss 1971; Lundman 1980.
65. Garofalo and McLeod 1989.
66. 6 U.S. Code § 1104.
67. Morgan and Kena 2016. Violent crimes include rape, sexual assault, robbery, aggravated assault, and simple assault. Property crimes include household burglary, motor vehicle theft, and property theft.
68. FBI: Uniform Crime Reporting, 2016.
69. Eck et al. 1987.
70. Rosenbaum 1988.
71. Crime Stoppers USA does not provide information on the number of calls received, but they do report having cleared over one million cases by 2018.
72. Dewan and Goodman 2008.
73. Gresham, Stockdale, and Bartholomew 2003; Challinger 2004.
74. This research started largely with the discovery of the "bystander effect," in which a greater number of witnesses to a crime reduces the likelihood of any of them reporting it (Darley and Latané 1968).
75. Van Dijk 1983.
76. There is considerable variation in results across studies. In addition, some studies take their baseline percentages (which are the ones reported here) from an extremely small control condition. Researchers have found that bystanders report apparent criminal activity at the following rates: 2 percent (Bickman 1976); 7.5 percent (Dertke, Penner, and Ulrich 1974); 28 percent (Gelfand et al. 1973); and 41 percent (Bickman and Rosenbaum 1977). The high percentage in the last study is likely due to its often-unrealistic scenario, where each subject was required to interact with an authority figure immediately after observing wrongdoing while being observed by others the subject knew had seen him or her observe the misconduct.

77. Bottomly and Coleman 1980.
78. As defined by the UN Convention Against Torture, these techniques constitute torture: "Any act by which severe pain or suffering, whether physical or mental, is intentionally inflicted on a person for such purposes as obtaining from him or a third person information or a confession" (quoted in Blakeley 2011, 547).
79. Bell 2008.
80. Blakeley 2011.
81. CIA Inspector General 2004, 85.
82. Conroy 2000, 113. Similarly, much of the information provided by detainees at the Guantanamo Bay Detention Camp appears to have been false (Deutschmann 2016; Lasseter and Rosenberg 2011).
83. Shaver and Shapiro 2016; Wright and Zakharov 2017; Wright et. al. 2017.
84. A recent exception is a hotline for US Immigration and Customs Enforcement, which was flooded with calls falsely reporting space aliens as a means of protest against deportation activities (Criss 2017).
85. Wright and Zakharov 2017; Wright et. al. 2017; Kalyvas 2006.
86. Gopal 2014.
87. Ibid., 109. The United States paid between $5,000 and $25,000 for each "terrorist" handed in (Khan 2008).
88. Similarly self-serving dynamics can be seen in Brook's (2005) investigation of Chinese cooperation with Japanese occupation forces during World War II. He concludes, "If occupation creates collaboration from below, collaboration demands compromise from above" (23).
89. Denbeaux, Denbeaux, Gratz, and Gregorek 2011.
90. Gopal 2014.
91. These dynamics were in stark contrast with the northern part of the country:

> In the northern province of Balkh . . . two warlords—Rashid Dostum and Muhammad Atta—jockeyed for control, leading to multiple small-scale skirmishes. The possibility of open warfare seemed all too real, but things never came to a head. Instead, United Nations negotiators were able to preserve the peace, as Atta accepted a governorship and Dostum a post in Kabul. I asked Eckart Schiewek, then a political advisor with the UN mission to

Afghanistan, why the outcome was so different, why the southern pattern of killings had never taken hold. "There were no American troops," he replied, pointing out that almost the entire US military presence was concentrated in the Pashtun south and east near the Pakistani border. "You couldn't call on soldiers to settle your feuds" (Gopal 2014, 130).

It was only in the American-occupied south, where US forces relied on denunciations, that there was a strong resurgence of the Taliban.

92. In this discussion, crimes are given as defined by legal institutions.

93. Recall the reputation of the Gestapo: "omniscient, omnipotent and omnipresent" (Mallmann and Paul 1994).

94. Retributive justice is not the only type of justice associated with punishment that occurs in modern democracies. Restorative justice, where the focus is on the needs of the victim and offenders, also occurs. The modern United States—the focus of this section—generally emphasizes retributive justice over restorative justice. The tenets of retributive justice, especially that innocents should not be punished, generally resonate with conceptions of liberal democracy (Ware 1992).

95. This is apparent in the #MeToo movement, which protests sexual harassment and assault. Authorities have historically treated claims of this type with skepticism, and confirmatory evidence can be difficult to obtain. This skepticism discourages victims from coming forward and often leads to accused harassers going unpunished. Yet by allowing such behavior to go unpunished, sexual harassment and assault become tacitly permitted. This is exactly the absence of social control.

96. Similar to the other two models, this is intended as an ideal type. Substantial heterogeneity can occur within any actual context.

97. Batson 2014.

98. This is not to say that individuals cannot benefit personally from altruism, but that such benefits are not a factor in motivating the behavior (MacIntyre 1967). Nor is this to argue that altruistic denouncing cannot exist. All three models are meant to explain general tendencies, not to explain every individual denunciation.

99. Dozier and Miceli 1985; Staub 1978.

100. Such behavior has also been referred to as "enlightened self-interest," where what benefits the group also benefits the individual (Batson and Powell 2003). This is distinct from collectivism, which posits "Not me or thee but we" (Dawes, van de Kragt, and Orbell 1988).

101. Staub 1978. Altruism is sometimes seen as a subset of prosocial behavior. As Batson and Powell (2003) explained, "Prosocial behavior covers the broad range of actions intended to benefit one or more people other than oneself—behaviors such as helping, comforting, sharing, and cooperating. The word altruism has at times been used to refer to a subset of these behaviors—for example, self-sacrificial helping or helping in the absence of obvious, external rewards" (463).

102. Although denouncing in the volunteer and coercion models does ultimately benefit the authorities, this is not generally its intent.

103. This is the case even if particular individuals are ultimately harmed. For example, a spree of robberies or an active serial killer endangers the entire community, as everyone is at risk of being targeted.

104. The initial formulation of moral panic appeared in Stanley Cohen's *Folk Devils and Moral Panics* (1972). Cohen observed the hysterical and disproportionate response of British residents to the Mods and the Rockers, two youth-based cultural groups. After one minor episode during a holiday in which several storefronts were damaged, British citizens panicked about these relatively harmless groups, and the media began publishing articles about how to deal with this "massive" new threat.

105. Goode and Ben-Yehuda 2010, 35.

106. As typically defined, moral panics do not require denunciations to be considered moral panics, as the identification and eradication of suspected deviant behavior may be accomplished by other means. Denunciations frequently play an important role, however.

107. Pontikes, Negro, and Rao 2010; Hall et al. 1978; Nathan and Snedeker 1995.

108. Erikson 1966.

109. Boyer and Nissenbaum 1974, 2.

110. Rosenthal 2009, 128.

111. This was all without any particular encouragement from the central authorities, though the local magistrates became caught up in the threat and altered legal institutions in ways that unwittingly facilitated the panic's spread.

112. Garland 2008; deYoung 2011. Some theorists have argued, however, that contemporary moral panics constitute a new type composed of horizontal relationships between fragmented groups trying to sway public opinion (McRobbie and Thornton 1995).

113. When this occurs, the individuals denounced become symbolic of the group or category that represents the perceived threat (Jensen 2007).

114. If the authorities also subscribe to the fear, then they may become increasingly desirous of denunciations and increasingly quick to punish. Thus, authorities under threat may behave similarly to the repressive authorities seen in the previous chapters.

115. This is typically referred to as stigma by association (Goffman 1963).

116. Boyer and Nissenbaum 1974.

117. Some refer to these as "pessimized" conditions. Pessimized conditions exist when an environment is seen as troubling or intolerable, and where corrective action is needed (Pfuhl 1992).

118. National Advisory Commission on Criminal Justice Standards and Goals 1973; Rosenbaum 1988.

119. Skogan and Maxfield 1980.

120. Harris 1975.

121. Figgie 1980, 8.

122. Moore and Trojanowicz 1988, 1.

123. Pfuhl 1992, 523.

124. Stevens 2018. The men were subsequently released without being charged.

125. Caron 2018.

126. Victor 2018.

127. Black 1970, 747.

128. Brayne 2017.

129. Marx (2016) defined the new surveillance as the "scrutiny of individuals, groups, and contexts using technical means to extract or create information" (20).

130. Marx 1988, 2.
131. China has already developed a social credit score for its citizens, where surveillance cameras and digital software aggregate a range of behaviors—including purchasing decisions, leisure activities, driving behavior, and online activities—to create individual scores that determine access to a variety of services (Ma 2018).

REFERENCES

Akerstrom, Malin. 1991. *Betrayal and Betrayers: The Sociology of Treachery.* New Brunswick, NJ: Transaction Publishers.

Amato, Laura. 2014. "The Obscure Party: Anonymous Denunciations in the Republic of Venice." *Acta Histriae* 22, no. 1: 145–56.

Antón, José Maria Monsalvo. 1984. "Herejía conversa y contestación religiosa a fines de la Edad Media: Las denuncias a la Inquisición en el obispado de Osma." *Studia historica: Historia medieval* 2: 109–38.

Arendt, Hannah. 1973. *The Origins of Totalitarianism.* New York: Houghton Mifflin Harcourt.

Asbury, Bret D. 2011. "Anti-Snitching Norms and Community Loyalty." *Oregon Law Review* 89, no. 4: 1257–311

Ash, Timothy Garton. 1997. *The File: A Personal History.* New York: Vintage.

Ayçoberry, Pierre. 2000. *The Social History of the Third Reich, 1933–1945.* New York: New Press.

Baldassarri, Delia, and Guy Grossman. 2011. "Centralized Sanctioning and Legitimate Authority Promote Cooperation in Humans." *Proceedings of the National Academy of Sciences* 108, no. 27: 11023–27.

Batson, C. Daniel. 2014. *The Altruism Question: Toward a Social-Psychological Answer.* New York: Psychology Press.

Batson, C. Daniel, and Adam A. Powell. 2003. "Altruism and Prosocial Behavior." In *Handbook of Psychology*, edited by Irving B. Weiner. New York: Wiley.

Beetham, David. 2013. *The Legitimation of Power*. Basingstoke, UK: Macmillan.

Beinart, Haim. 1981. *Conversos on Trial: The Inquisition in Ciudad Real*. Translated by Yael Guiladi. Jerusalem: Hebrew University.

Bell, Jeannine. 2008. "Behind This Mortal Bone: The (In)Effectiveness of Torture." *Indiana Law Journal* 83: 339–61.

Benz, Wolfgang. 2006. *A Concise History of the Third Reich*. Berkeley: University of California Press.

Bergemann, Patrick. 2017. "Denunciation and Social Control." *American Sociological Review* 82, no. 2: 384–406.

Bergerson, Andrew Stuart. 2004. *Ordinary Germans in Extraordinary Times: The Nazi Revolution in Hildesheim*. Bloomington: Indiana University Press.

Berkowitz, Leonard, and Anthony LePage. 1967. "Weapons as Aggression-Eliciting Stimuli." *Journal of Personality and Social Psychology* 7, no. 2: 202.

Bickman, Leonard. 1976. "Attitude Toward an Authority and the Reporting of a Crime." *Sociometry* 39, no. 1: 76–82.

Bickman, Leonard, and Dennis P. Rosenbaum. 1977. "Crime Reporting as a Function of Bystander Encouragement, Surveillance, and Credibility." *Journal of Personality and Social Psychology* 35, no. 8: 577–86.

Black, Donald J. 1970. "Production of Crime Rates." *American Sociological Review* 35, no. 4: 733–48.

——. 1976. *The Behavior of Law*. Bingley, UK: Emerald Group.

——, ed. 1984. *Toward a General Theory of Social Control: Selected Problems*. Orlando: Academic Press.

Black, Donald J., and Albert J. Reiss Jr. 1970. "Police Control of Juveniles." *American Sociological Review* 35, no. 1: 63–77.

Blakeley, Ruth. 2011. "Dirty Hands, Clean Conscience? The CIA Inspector General's Investigation of 'Enhanced Interrogation Techniques' in the War on Terror and the Torture Debate." *Journal of Human Rights* 10, no. 4: 544–61.

Blockmans, Willem Pieter, and Antheun Janse. 1999. *Showing Status: Representation of Social Positions in the Late Middle Ages*. Vol. 2. Turnhout: Brepols.

Borejsza, Jerzy W., and Klaus Ziemer, eds. 2006. *Totalitarian and Authoritarian Regimes in Europe: Legacies and Lessons from the Twentieth Century*. New York: Berghahn Books.

Bottomley, A. K., and C. A. Coleman. 1980. "Police Effectiveness and the Public: The Limitations of Official Crime Rates." In *The Effectiveness of Policing*, edited by J. M. Hough and R. V. G. Clarke, 70–97. Farnborough, UK: Gower.

Boyer, Paul, and Stephen Nissenbaum. 1974. *Salem Possessed: The Social Origins of Witchcraft*. Cambridge, MA: Harvard University Press.

Braunstein, Baruch. 1936. *The Chuetas of Majorca: Conversos and the Inquisition of Majorca*. New York: Ktav.

Brayne, Sarah. 2017. "Big Data Surveillance: The Case of Policing." *American Sociological Review* 82, no. 5: 977–1008.

Brook, Timothy. 2005. *Collaboration: Japanese Agents and Local Elites in Wartime China*. Cambridge, MA: Harvard University Press.

Broszat, Martin. 1981. *The Hitler State: The Foundation and Development of the Internal Structure of the Third Reich*. London: Longman.

Browder, George C. 1996. *Hitler's Enforcers: The Gestapo and the SS Security Service in the Nazi Revolution*. Oxford: Oxford University Press.

Brown, Peter B. 2012. "Command and Control in the Russian Army." In *Warfare in Eastern Europe, 1500–1800*, edited by Brian L. Davies, 249–314. Leiden: Brill.

Browning, Christopher R. 1993. *Ordinary Men: Reserve Police Battalion 101 and the Final Solution in Poland*. New York: Harper.

Bruce, Gary. 2010. "Participatory Repression? Reflections on Popular Involvement with the Stasi." *Deutschland Archiv* 43: 1088–91.

Burt, Ronald S. 2000. "Decay Functions." *Social Networks* 22, no. 1: 1–28.

Canali, Mauro. 2004. *Le spie del regime*. Bologna: Il Mulino.

Caron, Christina. 2018. "A Black Yale Student Was Napping, and a White Student Called the Police." *New York Times*, May 9.

Centola, Damon, Robb Willer, and Michael Macy. 2005. "The Emperor's Dilemma: A Computational Model of Self-Enforcing Norms." *American Journal of Sociology* 110, no. 4: 1009–40.

Ceplair, Larry, and Steven Englund. 1983. *The Inquisition in Hollywood: Politics in the Film Community, 1930–1960*. Berkeley: University of California Press.

Challinger, Dennis. 2004. *Crime Stoppers Victoria: An Evaluation*. Canberra: Australian Institute of Criminology.

Chen, Theodore Hsi-En, and Wen-Hui C. Chen. 1953. "The 'Three-Anti' and 'Five-Anti' Movements in Communist China." *Pacific Affairs* 26, no. 1: 3–23.

CIA Inspector General. 2004. "Special Review: Counterterrorism Detention and Interrogation Activities." Central Intelligence Agency, May 7.

Cohen, Stanley. 1972. *Folk Devils and Moral Panics: The Creation of the Mods and Rockers*. London: MacGibbon and Kee.

——. 1985. *Visions of Social Control: Crime, Punishment, and Classification*. Cambridge: Polity Press.

Comfort, Megan. 2008. *Doing Time Together: Love and Family in the Shadow of the Prison*. Chicago: University of Chicago Press.

Connelly, John. 1996. "The Uses of Volksgemeinschaft: Letters to the NSDAP Kreisleitung Eisenach, 1939–1940." *Journal of Modern History* 68, no. 4, 899–930.

Conroy, John. 2000. *Unspeakable Acts, Ordinary People: The Dynamics of Torture*. Berkeley: University of California Press.

Contreras, Jaime. 1982. *El Santo oficio de la inquisición en Galicia 1560-1700: Poder, sociedad y cultura*. Madrid: Akal.

Contreras, Jaime, and Gustav Henningsen. 1986. "Forty-Four Thousand Cases of the Spanish Inquisition (1540–1700): Analysis of a Historical Data Bank." In *The Inquisition in Early Modern Europe: Studies on Sources and Methods*, edited by Gustav Henningsen and John Tedechi, 100–29. Dekalb: Northern Illinois University Press.

Corner, Paul. 2009. *Popular Opinion in Totalitarian Regimes: Fascism, Nazism, Communism*. Oxford: Oxford University Press.

Coser, Lewis. 1956. *The Functions of Social Conflict*. New York: Free Press.

—— 1977. *The Sociology of Max Weber*. New York: Vintage.

Courtois, Stéphane, and Mark Kramer, eds. 1999. *The Black Book of Communism: Crimes, Terror, Repression*. Cambridge, MA: Harvard University Press.

Crawford, Michael. 2014. *The Fight for Status and Privilege in Late Medieval and Early Modern Castile, 1465–1598*. Philadelphia: Pennsylvania State University Press.

Criss, Doug. 2017. "Top-Level Trolling Overloads ICE's Undocumented Immigrant Hotline with Calls about Space Aliens." CNN, April 28.

Crummey, Robert O. 1987. *The Formation of Muscovy, 1304–1613*. New York: Longman.

Curriden, Mark. 1995. "The Informant Trap: Secret Threat to Justice." *National Law Journal*, February 27.

Dack, Mikkel. 2016. "Retreating into Trauma: The *Fragebogen*, Denazification, and Victimhood in Postwar Germany." In *Traumatic Memories of the Second World War and After*, edited by Peter Lees and Jason Crouthamel, 143–70. Cham: Palgrave Macmillan.

Darley, John M., and Bibb Latané. 1968. "Bystander Intervention in Emergencies: Diffusion of Responsibility." *Journal of Personality and Social Psychology* 8, no. 4: 377–83.

Davenport, Christopher. 2007. "State Repression and Political Order." *Annual Review of Political Science* 10: 1–23.

Davis, Brian Lee, 1990. *Qaddafi, Terrorism, and the Origins of the U.S. Attack on Libya*. New York: ABC-CLIO.

Dawes, Robyn M., Alphons J. C. van de Kragt, and John M. Orbell. 1988. "Not Me or Thee but We: The Importance of Group Identity in Eliciting Cooperation in Dilemma Situations: Experimental Manipulations." *Acta Psychologica* 68, no. 1: 83–97.

Dedieu, Jean-Pierre. 1992. *L'administration de la foi: L'Inquisition de Tolède, XVIe–XVIIIe siècle*. Madrid: Casa de Velázquez.

Delarue, Jacques. 1964. *The Gestapo: A History of Horror*. New York: Morrow.

den Bak, Irene M., and Hildy S. Ross. 1996. "I'm Telling! The Content, Context, and Consequences of Children's Tattling on Their Siblings." *Social Development* 5, no. 3: 292–309.

Denbeaux, Mark, Joshua Denbeaux, David Gratz, and John Gregorek. 2011. "Report on Guantánamo Detainees: A Profile of 517 Detainees Through Analysis of Department of Defense Data." *Seton Hall Law Review* 41: 1211.

Derby, Lauren, 2003. "In the Shadow of the State: The Politics of Denunciation and Panegyric During the Trujillo Regime in the Dominican Republic, 1940–1958." *Hispanic American Historical Review* 83, no. 2: 295–344.

Dertke, Max C., Louis A. Penner, and Kathleen Ulrich. 1974. "Observer's Reporting of Shoplifting as a Function of Thief's Race and Sex." *Journal of Social Psychology* 94, no. 2: 213–21.

Deutschmann, Emanuel. 2016. "Between Collaboration and Disobedience: The Behavior of the Guantánamo Detainees and Its Consequences." *Journal of Conflict Resolution* 60, no. 3: 555–82.

Dewan, Shaila, and Brenda Goodman. 2008. "As Prices Rise, Crime Tipsters Work Overtime." *New York Times*, May 18.

deYoung, Mary. 2011. "Folk Devils Reconsidered." In *Moral Panic and the Politics of Anxiety*, edited by Sean Hier, 118–33. London: Routledge.

Diewald-Kerkmann, Gisela. 1995. *Politische Denunziation im NS-Regime oder die kleine Macht der "Volksgenossen."* Bonn: Verlag J. H. W. Dietz Nachfolger.

Dörner, Bernward. 1995. "Heimtücke: Zur Praxis der Geheimen Staatspolizei bei der Verfolgung von Verstößen gegen das Heimtücke-Gesetz." In *Die Gestapo: Mythos und Realität*, edited by Gerhard Paul and Klaus-Michael Mallmann, 325–42. Darmstadt: Primus.

——. 1998. *Heimtücke: Das Gesetz als Waffe. Kontrolle, Abschreckung und Verfolgung in Deutschland 1933–1945.* Paderborn: Schöningh.

——. 2001. "NS-Herrschaft und Denunziation: Anmerkungen zu Defiziten in der Denunziationsforschung." *Historical Social Research* 26, no. 2/3: 55–69.

Dozier, Janelle Brinker, and Marcia P. Miceli. 1985. "Potential Predictors of Whistle-Blowing: A Prosocial Behavior Perspective." *Academy of Management Review* 10, no. 4: 823–36.

Dunn, Judy, and Penny Munn. 1985. "Becoming a Family Member: Family Conflict and the Development of Social Understanding in the Second Year." *Child Development* 56, no. 2: 480–92.

Dunning, Chester S. L. 2010. *Russia's First Civil War: The Time of Troubles and the Founding of the Romanov Dynasty*. University Park: Pennsylvania State University Press.

Dwyer, Jim, Peter J. Neufeld, and Barry Scheck. 2000. *Actual Innocence: Five Days to Execution and Other Dispatches from the Wrongly Convicted*. New York: Doubleday.

Eck, J. E., and W. Spelman, with D. Hill, D. W. Stephens, J. R. Stedman, and G. R. Murphy. 1987. *Problem Solving: Problem-Oriented Policing in Newport News*. Washington, DC: Police Executive Research Forum.

Eder, Klaus, Bernd Giesen, Oliver Schmidtke, and Damian Tambini. 2002. *Collective Identities in Action: A Sociological Approach to Ethnicity*. Aldershot, UK: Ashgate.

Edwards, John. 1988. "Religious Faith and Doubt in Late Medieval Spain: Soria circa 1450–1500." *Past & Present* 120: 3–25.

——. 1997. "Was the Spanish Inquisition Truthful?" *Jewish Quarterly Review* 87, nos. 3–4: 351–66.

——. 2014. *Ferdinand and Isabella*. London: Routledge.

Eisenkraft, Noah, Hillary Anger Elfenbein, and Shirli Kopelman. 2017. "We Know Who Likes Us, but Not Who Competes Against Us: Dyadic Meta-Accuracy Among Work Colleagues." *Psychological Science* 28, no. 2: 233–41.

Erikson, Emily, and Joseph Parent. 2007. "Central Authority and Order." *Sociological Theory* 25, no. 3: 245–67.

Erikson, Kai. 1966. *Wayward Puritans: A Study in the Sociology of Deviance*. New York: John Wiley.

Ermakoff, Ivan. 1997. "Prelates and Princes: Aristocratic Marriages, Canon Law Prohibitions, and Shifts in Norms and Patterns of Domination in the Central Middle Ages." *American Sociological Review* 62, no. 3: 405–22.

Escudero, José Antonio. 1998. "Netanyahu y los orígenes de la Inquisición española." *Revista de la Inquisición* 7: 9–36.

Evans, Richard J. 2004. *The Coming of the Third Reich*. New York: Penguin.

Federal Bureau of Investigation. 2016. "Crime in the United States." https://ucr.fbi.gov/crime-in-the-u.s/2016/crime-in-the-u.s.-2016.

Fehr, Ernst, and Simon Gächter. 2002. "Altruistic Punishment in Humans." *Nature* 415, no. 6868: 137.

Figgie, Harry E. 1980. *The Figgie Report on Fear of Crime: America Afraid*. Willoughby, OH: Research & Forecasts.

Fisher, George. 2003. *Plea Bargaining's Triumph: A History of Plea Bargaining in America*. Stanford, CA: Stanford University Press.

Fitzpatrick, Sheila. 1996. "Signals from Below: Soviet Letters of Denunciation of the 1930s." *Journal of Modern History* 68, no. 4: 831–66.

Fitzpatrick, Sheila, and Robert Gellately, eds. 1997. *Accusatory Practices: Denunciation in Modern European History, 1789–1989*. Chicago: University of Chicago Press.

Flesher, Dale L., and Thomas E. Buttross. 1992. "Whistle-Blowing Hotlines." *Internal Auditor* 49, no. 4: 54–59.

Flynn, Maureen. 1995. "Blasphemy and the Play of Anger in Sixteenth-Century Spain." *Past & Present* 149: 29–56.

Foucault, Michel. 1977. *Discipline and Punish: The Birth of the Prison*. New York: Vintage.

Frank, Robert H. 1985. *Choosing the Right Pond: Human Behavior and the Quest for Status*. New York: Oxford University Press.

Franzinelli, Mimmo. 1999. *I tentacoli dell'Ovra: Agenti, collaboratori e vittimi della polizia politica fascista.* Turin: Bollati Boringhieri.

——. 2001. *Delatori: Spie e confidenti: L'arma segreta del regime fascista.* Cles: Oscar Mondadori.

Fuentes, José María García. 2006. *Visitas de la Inquisición al Reino de Granada.* Granada: Universidad de Granada.

García Cárcel, Ricardo. 1976. *Orígenes de la Inquisición española: El Tribunal de Valencia, 1478–1530.* Barcelona: Ediciones Peninsula.

Garland, David. 2008. "On the Concept of Moral Panic." *Crime, Media, Culture* 4, no. 1: 9–30.

Garofalo, James, and Maureen McLeod. 1989. "The Structure and Operations of Neighborhood Watch Programs in the United States." *Crime & Delinquency* 35, no. 3: 326–44.

Gelfand, Donna M., Donald P. Hartmann, Patrice Walder, and Brent Page. 1973. "Who Reports Shoplifters? A Field-Experimental Study." *Journal of Personality and Social Psychology* 25, no. 2: 276.

Gellately, Robert. 1988. "The Gestapo and German Society: Political Denunciation in the Gestapo Case Files." *Journal of Modern History* 60, no. 4: 654–94.

——. 1990. *The Gestapo and German Society: Enforcing Racial Policy, 1933–1945.* New York: Oxford University Press.

——. 1996. "Denunciations in Twentieth-Century Germany: Aspects of Self-Policing in the Third Reich and the German Democratic Republic." *Journal of Modern History* 68: 931–67.

——. 1997. "Denunciations and Nazi Germany: New Insights and Methodological Problems." *Historical Social Research* 22: 228–39.

——. 2001a. *Backing Hitler: Consent and Coercion in Nazi Germany.* Oxford: Oxford University Press.

——. 2001b. "Denunciation as a Subject of Historical Research." *Historical Social Research* 26, nos. 2–3: 16–29.

Gersick, Connie, Jane E. Dutton, and Jean M. Bartunek. 2000. "Learning from Academia: The Importance of Relationships in Professional Life." *Academy of Management Journal* 43, no. 6: 1026–44.

Geschiere, Peter. 1997. *The Modernity of Witchcraft: Politics and the Occult in Postcolonial Africa.* Charlottesville: University Press of Virginia.

Gieseke, Jens. 2014. *The History of the Stasi: East Germany's Secret Police, 1945–1990.* New York: Berghahn.

Gitlitz, David Martin. 2002. *Secrecy and Deceit: The Religion of the Crypto-Jews*. Albuquerque: University of New Mexico Press.

Glaeser, Andreas. 2011. *Political Epistemics: The Secret Police, the Opposition, and the End of East German Socialism*. Chicago: University of Chicago Press.

Goffman, Alice. 2009. "On the Run: Wanted Men in a Philadelphia Ghetto." *American Sociological Review* 74, no. 3: 339–57.

Goffman, Erving. 1963. *Stigma: Notes on the Management of Spoiled Identity*. Englewood Cliffs, NJ: Prentice-Hall.

Goldhagen, Daniel J. 1996. *Hitler's Willing Executioners: Ordinary Germans and the Holocaust*. New York: Alfred A. Knopf.

Goldman, Wendy. 2011. *Inventing the Enemy: Denunciation and Terror in Stalin's Russia*. Cambridge: Cambridge University Press.

Goldstein, Robert Justin. 1978. *Political Repression in Modern America from 1870 to the Present*. Boston: G. K. Hall.

Goode, Erich, and Nachman Ben-Yehuda. 2010. *Moral Panics: The Social Construction of Deviance*. New York: John Wiley.

Gopal, Anand. 2014. *No Good Men Among the Living: America, the Taliban, and the War Through Afghan Eyes*. New York: Metropolitan Books.

Gordon, Sarah Ann. 1984. *Hitler, Germans, and the "Jewish Question."* Princeton, NJ: Princeton University Press.

Gould, Roger. 2003. *Collision of Wills: How Ambiguity About Social Rank Breeds Conflict*. Chicago: University of Chicago Press.

Gramsci, Antonio. 1992. *Prison Notebooks*. Edited by Joseph Buttigieg. New York: Columbia University Press.

Gresham, Peter J., Janet Stockdale, and Ivon Bartholomew. 2003. *Evaluating the Impact of Crimestoppers*. Home Office Online Report 22/03. London: Home Office.

Gross, Samuel R., et al. 2005. "Exonerations in the United States 1989 Through 2003." *Journal of Criminal Law and Criminology* 95, no. 2: 523–60.

Gross, Samuel R., and Barbara O'Brien. 2008. "Frequency and Predictors of False Conviction: Why We Know So Little, and New Data on Capital Cases." *Journal of Empirical Legal Studies* 5, no. 4: 927–62.

Grossman, Gene M., and Michael L. Katz. 1983. "Plea Bargaining and Social Welfare." *American Economic Review* 73, no. 4: 749–57.

Haliczer, Stephen. 1973. "The Castilian Urban Patriciate and the Jewish Expulsions of 1480–92." *American Historical Review* 78, no. 1: 35–58.

——. 1990. *Inquisition and Society in the Kingdom of Valencia, 1478–1834.* Berkeley: University of California Press.

Hall, Stuart, Chas Critcher, Tony Jefferson, John Clarke, and Brian Roberts. 1978. *Policing the Crisis: Mugging, the State, and Law and Order.* London: Macmillan.

Harrigan, Nicholas, and Janice Yap. 2017. "Avoidance in Negative Ties: Inhibiting Closure, Reciprocity, and Homophily." *Social Networks* 48: 126–41.

Harris, Louis. 1975. "Crime Rates: Personal Uneasiness in Neighborhoods." *Chicago Tribune*, June 6.

Hellie, Richard. 1971. *Enserfment and Military Change in Muscovy.* Chicago: University of Chicago Press.

——. 1977. "The Structure of Modern Russian History: Toward a Dynamic Model." *Russian History* 4, no. 1: 1–22.

——, ed. and trans. 1988. *The Muscovite Law Code (Ulozhenie) of 1649.* 2 vols. Irvine, CA: Charles Schlacks Jr.

——. 1997. "The Origins of Denunciation in Muscovy." *Russian History* 24, no. 1–2: 11–26.

——. 2006. "The Peasantry." In *The Cambridge History of Russia*, vol. 1, *From Early Rus' to 1689*, edited by Maureen Perrie, 708–10. Cambridge: Cambridge University Press.

Herreros, Francisco. 2006. "'The Full Weight of the State': The Logic of Random State-Sanctioned Violence." *Journal of Peace Research* 43, no. 6: 671–89.

Homza, Lu Ann, ed. 2006. *The Spanish Inquisition, 1478–1614: An Anthology of Sources.* Indianapolis: Hackett.

Hughes, Graham. 1992. "Agreements for Cooperation in Criminal Cases." *Vanderbilt Law Review* 45: 1.

Hüttenberger, Peter. 1981. "Heimtückefälle vor dem Sondergericht München 1933–1939." In *Bayern in der NS-Zeit*, vol. 4, edited by Martin Broszat, 435–526. Munich: Oldenbourg.

Ingram, Gordon P. D., and Jesse M. Bering. 2010. "Children's Tattling: The Reporting of Everyday Norm Violations in Preschool Settings." *Child Development* 81, no. 3: 945–57.

Innes, Martin. 2003. *Understanding Social Control: Deviance, Crime, and Social Order.* Maidenhead, UK: McGraw-Hill.

Ioanid, Radu, 2008. *The Holocaust in Romania: The Destruction of Jews and Gypsies Under the Antonescu Regime, 1940–1944*. Chicago: Ivan R. Dee.

Jensen, Gary F. 2007. *The Path of the Devil: Early Modern Witch Hunts*. Lanham, MD: Rowman & Littlefield.

Johnson, Eric A. 1997. "Gender, Race and the Gestapo." *Historical Social Research/Historische Sozialforschung* 22, no. 3–4: 240–53.

——. 1999. *Nazi Terror: The Gestapo, Jews, and Ordinary Germans*. New York: Basic Books.

——. 2011. "Criminal Justice, Coercion and Consent in 'Totalitarian' Society: The Case of National Socialist Germany." *British Journal of Criminology* 51, no. 3: 599–615.

Joshi, Vandana. 2003. *Gender and Power in the Third Reich: Female Denouncers and the Gestapo (1933–45)*. London: Palgrave Macmillan.

Kahneman, Daniel, and Amos Tversky. 1979. "Prospect Theory: An Analysis of Decision Under Risk." *Econometrica: Journal of the Econometric Society* 47, no. 2: 263–92.

Kalyvas, Stathis N. 2004. "The Paradox of Terrorism in Civil War." *Journal of Ethics* 8, no. 1: 97–138.

——. 2006. *The Logic of Violence in Civil War*. Cambridge: Cambridge University Press.

Kamen, Henry. 1999. *The Spanish Inquisition: A Historical Revision*. New Haven, CT: Yale University Press.

——. 2014a. *Spain, 1469–1714: A Society of Conflict*. 4th ed. London: Routledge.

——. 2014b. *The Spanish Inquisition: A Historical Revision*. 4th ed. New Haven, CT: Yale University Press.

Keenan, Edward L. 1986. "Muscovite Political Folkways." *Russian Review* 45, no. 2: 115–81.

Keep, J. L. H. 1956. "Bandits and the Law in Muscovy." *Slavonic and East European Review* 35, no. 84: 201–22.

——. 1960. "The Régime of Filaret, 1619–1633." *Slavonic and East European Review* 38, no. 91: 334–60.

Khan, Rukhsana Mahvish. 2008. *My Guantanamo Diary: The Detainees and the Stories They Told Me*. New York: Public Affairs.

Khodarkovsky, Michael. 2002. *Russia's Steppe Frontier: The Making of a Colonial Empire, 1500–1800*. Bloomington: Indiana University Press.

Kivelson, Valerie. 1988. "Community and State: The Political Culture of 17th Century Muscovy and the Provincial Gentry of the Vladimir-Suzdal Region." Dissertation, Stanford University.

Kleimola, Ann, 1972. "The Duty to Denounce in Muscovite Russia." *Slavic Review* 31, no. 4: 759–79.

Kohlhaas, Elisabeth. 1995. *Die Mitarbeiter der regionalen Staatspolizeistellen: Quantitative und qualitative Befunde zur Personalausstattung der Gestapo.* In *Die Gestapo: Mythos und Realität*, edited by Gerhard Paul and Klaus-Michael Mallmann, 219–35. Darmstadt: Primus.

Kollmann, Nancy. 2004. "Society, Identity and Modernity in Seventeenth Century Russia." In *Modernizing Muscovy: Reform and Social Change in Seventeenth-Century Russia*, edited by Jarmo Kotilaine and Marshall Poe, 417–32. London: Routledge.

——. 2012. *Crime and Punishment in Early Modern Russia.* Cambridge: Cambridge University Press.

Kuran, Timur. 1997. *Private Truths, Public Lies: The Social Consequences of Preference Falsification.* Cambridge, MA: Harvard University Press.

Labianca, Giuseppe. 2014. "Negative Ties in Organizational Networks." *Research in the Sociology of Organizations* 40: 239–59.

Labianca, Giuseppe, and Daniel J. Brass. 2006. "Exploring the Social Ledger: Negative Relationships and Negative Asymmetry." *Academy of Management Review* 31, no. 3: 596–614.

Labianca, Giuseppe, Daniel Brass, and Barbara Gray. 1998. "Social Networks and Perceptions of Intergroup Conflict: The Role of Negative Relationships and Third Parties." *Academy of Management Journal* 41, no. 1: 55–67.

Lange, Matthew. 2012. *Comparative-Historical Methods.* Los Angeles: Sage.

Lapman, Mark Charles. 1982. "Political Denunciations in Muscovy, 1600 to 1649: The Sovereign's Word and Deed." Dissertation, Harvard University.

Lasseter, Tom, and Carol Rosenberg. 2011. "Guantanamo Prisoner Threat Assessments Shaped by a Few, Often-Questionable Informants: Analysis." McClatchy-Tribune News Service, April 23.

Lea, Henry C. 1906. *A History of the Inquisition of Spain.* 4 vols. New York: Macmillan.

Lease, Gary. 1996. "Denunciation as a Tool of Ecclesiastical Control: The Case of Roman Catholic Modernism." *Journal of Modern History* 68, no. 4: 819–30.

Le Clerc, M [Nicolas-Gabriel]. 1783. *Histoire Physique, Morale, Civile et Politique de la Russie Ancienne*. 6 vols. Paris: Froullé.

Leskovec, Jure, Daniel Huttenlocher, and Jon Kleinberg. 2010. "Predicting Positive and Negative Links in Online Social Networks." *Proceedings of the 19th International Conference on World Wide Web*. New York: ACM.

Levesque, Pierre-Charles. 1800. *Histoire de Russie*. Vol. 4. Hamburg: P. F. Fauche.

Lipman, Frederick D. 2011. *Whistleblowers: Incentives, Disincentives, and Protection Strategies*. Hoboken, NJ: John Wiley.

Liska, Allen E., ed. 1992. *Social Threat and Social Control*. Albany: State University of New York Press.

Lucas, Colin. 1996. "The Theory and Practice of Denunciation in the French Revolution." *Journal of Modern History* 68, no. 4: 768–85.

Lukin, Alexander. 2000. *Political Culture of the Russian "Democrats."* Oxford: Oxford University Press.

Lundman, Richard J. 1980. *Police and Policing: An Introduction*. New York: Holt, Rinehart and Winston.

Lyall, Jason. 2009. "Does Indiscriminate Violence Incite Insurgent Attacks? Evidence from Chechnya." *Journal of Conflict Resolution* 53, no. 3: 331–62.

Ma, Alexandra. 2018. "China Has Started Ranking Citizens with a Creepy 'Social Credit' System." *Business Insider*, April 8.

MacIntyre, A. 1967. "Egoism and Altruism." In *The Encyclopedia of Philosophy*, Vol. 2, edited by Paul Edwards, 462–66. New York: Macmillan.

MacKay, Angus. 1972. "Popular Movements and Pogroms in Fifteenth-Century Castile." *Past & Present* 55, no. 1: 33–67.

Mahoney, James, and Dietrich Rueschemeyer. 2003. *Comparative Historical Analysis in the Social Sciences*. Cambridge: Cambridge University Press.

Maier, Hans, ed. 2004. *Totalitarianism and Political Religions*. Translated by Jodi Bruhn. New York: Routledge.

Maksimov, S. V. 1869. "Gosudarstvennye prestuphiki." *Otechestvennye zapiski* 186, no. 10: 229–72.

Mallmann, Klaus-Michael. 1997. "Social Penetration and Police Action: Collaboration Structures in the Repertory of Gestapo Activities." *International Review of Social History* 42: 25–44.

Mallmann, Klaus-Michael, and Gerhard Paul. 1994. "Omniscient, Omnipotent, Omnipresent? Gestapo, Society and Resistance." In *Nazism and*

German Society, 1933–1945, edited by David F. Crew, 166–96. London: Routledge.

Mann, Reinhard. 1987. *Protest und Kontrolle im Dritten Reich: Nationalsozialistische Herrschaft im Alltag einer rheinischen Grossstadt.* Frankfurt: Campus Verlag.

Manz, Beatriz. 1988. *Refugees of a Hidden War: The Aftermath of Counterinsurgency in Guatemala.* Albany: State University of New York Press.

Marx, Gary. 1988. *Undercover: Police Surveillance in America.* Berkeley: University of California Press.

——. 2016. *Windows into the Soul: Surveillance and Society in an Age of High Technology.* Chicago: University of Chicago Press.

Maxfield, Linda Drazga, and John H. Kramer. 1998. "Substantial Assistance: An Empirical Yardstick Gauging Equity in Current Federal Policy and Practice." *Federal Sentencing Reporter* 11, no. 1: 6–17.

McClintock, Louisa Marie. 2015. "Projects of Punishment in Postwar Poland: War Criminals, Collaborators, Traitors, and the (Re)Construction of the Nation." Dissertation, University of Chicago.

McRobbie, Angela, and Sarah L. Thornton. 1995. "Rethinking 'Moral Panic' for Multi-Mediated Social Worlds." *British Journal of Sociology* 46, no. 4: 559–74.

Meier, Robert. 1982. "Perspectives on the Concept of Social Control." *Annual Review of Sociology* 8: 35–55.

Melammed, Renée Levine. 2002. *Heretics or Daughters of Israel? The Crypto-Jewish Women of Castile.* New York: Oxford University Press.

Mesmer-Magnus, Jessica R., and Chockalingam Viswesvaran. 2005. "Whistleblowing in Organizations: An Examination of Correlates of Whistleblowing Intentions, Actions, and Retaliation." *Journal of Business Ethics* 62, no. 3: 277–97.

Metzger, Bruce M., and Roland E. Murphy, eds., 1991. *The New Oxford Annotated Bible with the Apocryphal/Deuterocanonical Books: New Revised Standard Version.* New York: Oxford University Press.

Miceli, Marcia P., Janet Pollex Near, and Terry M. Dworkin. 2008. *Whistle-Blowing in Organizations.* Hove, UK: Psychology Press.

Miethe, Terance D. 1999. *Whistleblowing at Work: Tough Choices In Exposing Fraud, Waste, and Abuse on the Job.* Boulder, CO: Westview Press.

Miron, Anca M., and Jack W. Brehm. 2006. "Reactance Theory, 40 Years Later." *Zeitschrift für Sozialpsychologie* 37, no. 1: 9–18.

Moore, Mark Harrison, and Robert C. Trojanowicz. 1988. *Policing and the Fear of Crime*. Perspectives on Policing, 3. Washington, DC: US Department of Justice, National Institute of Justice.

Morgan, Rachel E., and Grace Kena. 2016. *Criminal Victimization, 2016*. Bureau of Justice Statistics. https://www.bjs.gov/index.cfm?ty=pbdetail& iid=6166.

Motivans, Mark. 2017. *Federal Justice Statistics, 2014—Statistical Tables*. Washington, DC: Bureau of Justice Statistics.

Muir, R. 1911. *New School Atlas of Modern History: A Series of 48 Plates, Containing 120 Coloured Maps & Diagrams, with an Introduction Illustrated by 29 Maps and Plans in Black and White*. New York: Henry Holt.

Müller, Ingo. 1991. *Hitler's Justice: The Courts of the Third Reich*. Cambridge, MA: Harvard University Press.

Nagel, Joane, and Susan Olzak. 1982. "Ethnic Mobilization in New and Old States: An Extension of the Competition Model." *Social Problems* 30, no. 2: 127–43.

Natapoff, Alexandra. 2009. *Snitching: Criminal Informants and the Erosion of American Justice*. New York: New York University Press.

Nathan, Debbie, and Michael Snedeker. 1995. *Satan's Silence: Ritual Abuse and the Making of a Modern American Witch Hunt*. New York: Basic Books.

National Advisory Commission on Criminal Justice Standards and Goals. 1973. *Courts: Report of the National Advisory Commission on Criminal Justice Standards and Goals*. https://www.ncjrs.gov/App/publications /Abstract.aspx?id=10859.

Navasky, Victor S. 2003. *Naming Names*. New York: Hill and Wang.

Near, Janet P., and Marcia P. Miceli. 1996. "Whistle-Blowing: Myth and Reality." *Journal of Management* 22, no. 3: 507–26.

Netanyahu, Benzion. 2001. *The Origins of the Inquisition in Fifteenth Century Spain*. New York: New York Review Books.

Novombergskii, Nikolai Iakovlevich. 1911. *Slovo i delo gosudarevy*. Moscow: A. J. Snegirevoj.

O'Day, Rosemary. 2000. *The Professions in Early Modern England, 1450–1800: Servants of the Commonweal*. Harlow, UK: Pearson Education.

Olearius, Adam. 1967. *The Travels of Olearius in Seventeenth-Century Russia*. Translated and edited by Samuel H. Baron. Stanford, CA: Stanford University Press.

Owings, Alison. 1993. *Frauen: German Women Recall the Third Reich*. Rutgers, NJ: Rutgers University Press.

Parrondo, Carlos Carrete. 1985. *Fontes Iudaeorum Regni Castellae: El Tribunal de la Inquisición en el Obispado de Soria (1486–1502)*. Volume 2. Salamanca: Universidad Pontificia de Salamanca.

Pershing, Jana L. 2003. "To Snitch or Not to Snitch? Applying the Concept of Neutralization Techniques to the Enforcement of Occupational Misconduct." *Sociological Perspectives* 46, no. 2: 149–78.

Petersen, Roger, 2002. *Understanding Ethnic Violence: Fear, Hatred, and Resentment in Twentieth-Century Eastern Europe*. Cambridge: Cambridge University Press.

Peukert, Detlev. 1987. *Inside Nazi Germany: Conformity, Opposition, and Racism in Everyday Life*. New Haven, CT: Yale University Press.

——. 2001. "Youth in the Third Reich." In *Life in the Third Reich*, edited by Richard Bessel, 25–40. Oxford: Oxford University Press.

Pfuhl, Erdwin H. Jr. 1992. "Crimestoppers: The Legitimation of Snitching." *Justice Quarterly* 9, no. 3: 505–28.

Pipes, Richard. 1974. *Russia Under the Old Regime*. New York: Charles Scribner's Sons.

Platonov, Sergeï Fedorovich. 1970. *The Time of Troubles: A Historical Study of the Internal Crises and Social Struggle in Sixteenth- and Seventeenth-Century Muscovy*. Lawrence: University Press of Kansas.

Pontikes, Elizabeth, Giacomo Negro, and Hayagreeva Rao. 2010. "Stained Red: A Study of Stigma by Association to Blacklisted Artists During the 'Red Scare' in Hollywood, 1945 to 1960." *American Sociological Review* 75, no. 3: 456–78.

Rawlings, Helen E. 2006. *The Spanish Inquisition*. Malden, MA: Blackwell.

Reiss, Albert J. 1971. *The Police and the Public*. New Haven, CT: Yale University Press.

Reuband, Karl-Heinz. 2001. "Denunziation im Dritten Reich: die Bedeutung von Systemunterstützung und Gelegenheitsstrukturen." *Historical Social Research/Historische Sozialforschung* 26, no. 2–3: 219–34.

Rigoulot, Pierre. 1999. "Crimes, Terror, and Secrecy in North Korea." In *The Black Book of Communism: Crimes, Terror, Repression*, edited by Stéphane Courtois and Mark Kramer, 548–64. Cambridge, MA: Harvard University Press.

Rosenbaum, Dennis P. 1988. "Community Crime Prevention: A Review and Synthesis of the Literature." *Justice Quarterly* 5, no. 3: 323–95.

Rosenthal, Bernard. 2009. *Records of the Salem Witch-Hunt*. Cambridge: Cambridge University Press.

Roth, Norman. 2002. *Conversos, Inquisition, and the Expulsion of the Jews from Spain*. Madison: University of Wisconsin Press.

Rothschild, Joyce, and Terance D. Miethe. 1999. "Whistle-Blower Disclosures and Management Retaliation: The Battle to Control Information About Organization Corruption." *Work and Occupations* 26, no. 1: 107–28.

Ruckenbiel, Jan. 2005. "Soziale Kontrolle im NS-Regime: Protest, Denunziation und Verfolgung; zur Praxis alltäglicher Unterdrückung im Wechselspiel von Bevölkerung und Gestapo." Dissertation, Siegen University.

Rueschemeyer, Dietrich. 2003. "Can One or a Few Cases Yield Theoretical Gains?" In Mahoney and Rueschemeyer, *Comparative Historical Analysis in the Social Sciences*, 305–36.

Ruggiero, Kristen, 1988. *And Here the World Ends: The Life of an Argentine Village*. Stanford, CA: Stanford University Press.

Rustemeyer, Angela. 2006. *Dissens und Ehre: Majestätsverbrechen in Russland (1600–1800)*. Wiesbaden: Otto Harrassowitz.

Sangster, Andrew. 2016. *The Agony of France*. Newcastle-upon-Tyne: Cambridge Scholars Publishing.

Schrecker, Ellen. 1998. *Many Are the Crimes: McCarthyism in America*. Princeton, NJ: Princeton University Press.

Seip, Elise C., Wilco W. Van Dijk, and Mark Rotteveel. 2014. "Anger Motivates Costly Punishment of Unfair Behavior." *Motivation and Emotion* 38, no. 4: 578–88.

Shaver, Andrew, and Jacob Shapiro. 2016. "The Effect of Civilian Casualties on Wartime Informing: Evidence from the Iraq War." Households in Conflict Network Working Paper 210. https://scholar.princeton.edu/sites/default/files/ashaver/files/shaver_shapiro_civcas_informing.pdf.

Shubin, Daniel H. 2009. *Tsars and Imposters: Russia's Time of Troubles*. New York: Algora.

Simmel, Georg. (1900) 2004. *The Philosophy of Money*. London: Routledge.

——. 1904. "The Sociology of Conflict. I." *American Journal of Sociology* 9, no. 4: 490–525.

6 U.S. Code § 1104: Immunity for Reports of Suspected Terrorist Activity or Suspicious Behavior and Response. https://www.law.cornell.edu /uscode/text/6/1104. 2011.

Skogan, Wesley G., and Michael G. Maxfield. 1980. *Coping with Crime: Victimization, Fear, and Reactions to Crime in Three American Cities.* Evanston, IL: Reactions to Crime Project, Center for Urban Affairs, Northwestern University.

Smelser, Neil J. 2013. *Comparative Methods in the Social Sciences.* New Orleans: Quid Pro.

Staub, Ervin. 1978. "Predicting Prosocial Behavior: A Model for Specifying the Nature of Personality-Situation Interaction." In *Perspectives in Interactional Psychology*, edited by Lawrence A. Pervin and Michael Lewis, 87–110. Boston: Springer.

Steber, Martina, and Bernhard Gotto, eds. 2014. *Visions of Community in Nazi Germany: Social Engineering and Private Lives.* Oxford: Oxford University Press.

Stephenson, Jill. 2013. *Women in Nazi Society.* London: Routledge.

Stevens, Matt. 2018. "Starbucks C.E.O. Apologizes After Arrests of 2 Black Men." *New York Times*, April 15.

Stone, David R. 2006. *A Military History of Russia: From Ivan the Terrible to the War in Chechnya.* Westport, CT: Greenwood.

Strauss, Julia C. 2002. "Paternalist Terror: The Campaign to Suppress Counterrevolutionaries and Regime Consolidation in the People's Republic of China, 1950–1953." *Comparative Studies in Society and History* 44, no. 1: 80–105.

Sunstein, Cass, and Richard Thaler. 2008. *Nudge: Improving Decisions about Health, Wealth, and Happiness.* New Haven, CT: Yale University Press.

Sykes, Gresham M. 2007. *The Society of Captives: A Study of a Maximum Security Prison.* Princeton, NJ: Princeton University Press.

Szell, Michael, and Stefan Thurner. 2010. "Measuring Social Dynamics in a Massive Multiplayer Online Game." *Social Networks* 32, no. 4: 313–29.

Tel'berg, G. G. 1911. "Izvet v gosudarevom dele." *Iuruducheskiia zapiski izd: Demidovskim iuridicheskim litseem* 4, no. 4: 670–721.

Thiranagama, Sharika, and Tobias Kelly, eds. 2011. *Traitors: Suspicion, Intimacy, and the Ethics of State-Building*. Philadelphia: University of Pennsylvania Press.

Tormey, Simon. 1995. *Making Sense of Tyranny: Interpretations of Totalitarianism*. Manchester, UK: Manchester University Press.

Trott, Stephen S. 1996. "Words of Warning for Prosecutors Using Criminals as Witnesses." *Hastings Law Journal* 47: 1381–432.

United States Sentencing Commission. 2006–2018. "Quarterly Sentencing Updates." https://www.ussc.gov/research/data-reports/quarter/quarterly -sentencing-updates.

United States v. Bernal-Obeso. 1993. 989 F.2d 331, 335 (9th Cir.).

United States v. Cervantes-Pacheco. 1987. 828 F2d 310 (5th Cir.).

United States v. Ford. 1878. 99 U.S. 594, 599.

van Dijk, Jan. 1983. *Bystanders Intervention in a Crime*. United States Department of Justice.

Van Vugt, Mark, and Claire M. Hart. 2004. "Social Identity as Social Glue: The Origins of Group Loyalty." *Journal of Personality and Social Psychology* 86, no. 4: 585.

Vassberg, David E. 1996. *The Village and the Outside World in Golden Age Castile: Mobility and Migration in Everyday Rural Life*. Cambridge: Cambridge University Press.

Vatulescu, Cristina. 2004. "Arresting Biographies: The Secret Police File in the Soviet Union and Romania." *Comparative Literature* 56, no. 3: 243–61.

Vaughn, Robert. 1972. *Only Victims: A Study of Show Business Blacklisting*. New York: G. P. Putnam's Sons.

Victor, Daniel. 2018. "A Woman Said She Saw Burglars. They Were Just Black Airbnb Guests." *New York Times*, May 8.

Vodarskii, Iasoslav Evgen'evich. 1977. *Naselenie Rossii v kontse XVII nachale XVIII veka*. Moscow: Nauka.

Vogt, Timothy R. 2000. *Denazification in Soviet-Occupied Germany: Brandenburg, 1945-1948*. Cambridge, MA: Harvard University Press.

Völker, Beate, and Henk Flap. 2001. "Weak Ties as a Liability: The Case of East Germany." *Rationality and Society* 13, no. 4: 397–428.

Warden, Rob. 2004. *The Snitch System: How Snitch Testimony Sent Randy Steidl and Other Innocent Americans to Death Row*. Chicago: Northwestern University School of Law, Center on Wrongful Convictions.

Ware, Alan. 1992. "Liberal Democracy: One Form or Many?" *Political Studies* 40: 130–45.

Warner, Barbara D. 1992. "The Reporting of Crime: A Missing Link in Conflict Theory." In Liska, *Social Threat and Social Control*, 71–87.

Weber, Max. (1922) 1978. *Economy and Society: An Outline of Interpretive Sociology*, edited by Guenter Roth, translated by Claus Wittich. Berkeley: University of California Press.

Weinstein, Ian. 1999. "Regulating the Market for Snitches." *Buffalo Law Review* 47: 563–644.

Whitman, Julie L., and Robert C. Davis. 2007. *Snitches Get Stitches: Youth, Gangs, and Witness Intimidation in Massachusetts*. Washington, DC: National Center for Victims of Crime.

Wright, Austin L., Luke N. Condra, Jacob N. Shapiro, and Andrew C. Shaver. 2017. "Civilian Abuse and Wartime Informing." Pearson Institute Discussion Paper 42. https://thepearsoninstitute.org/sites/default/files/2017-07/07272017%20Wright_WartimeInforming.pdf.

Wright, Austin L., and Alexei V. Zakharov. 2017. "Insurgent Predation And Wartime Informing." Working Paper. https://sites.tufts.edu/neudc2017/files/2017/10/537_PAPER_WRIGHT.pdf.

Yaroshefsky, Ellen. 1999. "Cooperation with Federal Prosecutors: Experiences of Truth Telling and Embellishment." *Fordham Law Review* 68: 917.

INDEX

Page references in italics refer to illustrations and their captions.